400

Rush Hour Recipes:

*Recipes, Tips, and Wisdom
for Every Day of the Year*

Brook Noel with Wendy Louise

*Keep on cooking
Brook*

ISBN: 1891400673
LCCN: 2004110036

Interior comic-like illustrations: Johnny Caldwell
Cover design: Saul Fineman, Fineman Communications
Interior design: Brook Noel

Manufactured in the United States of America
10 9 8 7 6 5 4 3 2

Acknowledgements

At this time The Rush Hour Column would like to thank all of our readers and submitters who have made our column and cookbook what they are today. Listed alphabetically by first name, our contributing cookbook-chefs for this volume are:

Annelle Mundt, Longview Texas
Audra LeNormand, Liberty Texas
Barbara, the Island of Nevis
Beth Sullivan, DeWitt Virginia
Betty Tillman, Chicago Illinois
Brenda West, Ohio
Caleb F., Wisconsin
Captain Jack, St. Thomas
Carolyn Miller, Fort Atkinson Wisconsin
Cathie Rosemann, Dallas /Fort Worth area
Carla McGrath and her mother Lorraine, Sheboygan Wisconsin
Charlotte Porter, our Nanny from Texas
Darlene Ashe, Ontario Canada
Darlene Feiereisen, Anaheim California
Don and Mary Perry
Donna Wood, Manitowish Waters Wisconsin
JoAnn Morell, Hot Springs Village Arkansas
Joan Egan, Milwaukee Wisconsin
Joyce Gearhart, Mount Wolf Pennsylvania
Josie Lynn Belmont, Woodbine Georgia
Judy B., Iowa
Judy Brown and her mother Bobbie, Midland Michigan
Judy Ring, Cocoa Florida
Julie Gullings, Moorhead Minnesota
Julie West, Windsor New Jersey
June Kirzan, Fox Point Wisconsin
Kay Edwards, Pompano Beach Florida
Karl Mueller, Milwaukee Wisconsin
Kim Meiloch, Milwaukee Wisconsin
Kita and Tina Schuele, Sabinal Texas
Kristy Clayman, Wauwatosa Wisconsin
Lacy Basinger, Grenada Mississippi
Laura Dunbar, Maumee Ohio
Linda Safranek, Omaha Nebraska

Loretta Poxleitner, Cottonwood Idaho
Lori Fairchild, Woodruff Wisconsin
Lucile F., Minneapolis Minnesota
MaryAnn Koopmann, Belgium Wisconsin
Marilyn Brinkley, San Diego California
Marilyn Stonecipher, Bloomington Indiana
Marsha L.P., Wisconsin
Mary W., Auburn Michigan
Michael Gulan, Saukville Wisconsin
Pat Pohl, Milwaukee Wisconsin
Patricia Kuhn, Fresno California
Patty Morell, Minneapolis Minnesota
Roberta Epstein, Las Vegas Nevada
Samantha S. and J.Andrew, Fredonia, Wisconsin
Sara Pattow, Port Washington Wisconsin
Sindi in Virginia
Vickie Eastham, Casselberry Florida
Vicki Lanzendorf, Madison Wisconsin
Victoria Beckham, Fort Worth Texas
Vicki Prochnow, Brown Deer Wisconsin
Wendy Louise, Fox Point Wisconsin

Thank you all for your wonderful additions to this volume, our first book of shared "rush hour cooking." We are already at work, selecting more recipes from our readers for next year and a second volume.

And a special thanks to Audrey for her encouragement and belief in the Rush Hour Cook series.

Contents

For a listing of recipes by main igredient, please see the index at the back of this book.

Foreword

Each year, from breakfast on January 1st to the last snack set out on December 31st a common dilemma arises amongst most households … the cook-in-charge asks what do I serve today? (followed by a daunting what about tomorrow, the next day, and the next?) until 52 weeks have been met and the family has been fed and satisfied (hopefully) for another year. Thus enters The Rush Hour Cook and her daily column, filled with a year's worth of wit and wisdom, tips and recipes, both culinary and creative—from her own kitchen, as well as the kitchens of her readers. Everyday thousands of household cooks sign-in to enjoy Brook Noel's internet column (www.rushhourcook.com) to enlighten cooks and brighten kitchens and households all over the world).

It is upon Brook's column, her own recipes, and her readers that this book is based. Within these pages you will find a year's worth of Rush Hour Information to help you serve up a varied, hearty, and satisfying menu for your family. Along with her almost effortless recipes and creative tips, the Rush Hour Cook serves up many ideas and suggestions for family wellness, purpose, growth, and commitment. Her Words of Wisdom, Weekly Challenges, and Thoughts for the Day offer verbal recipes to ponder and enlighten many a reader. Kid-Friendly Recipes and Kids-in-the-Kitchen Projects are also featured to include all ages—making kitchen activities an inclusive family affair in the Rush Hour Household.

Over 50 of our Rush Readers have been selected to blend their talents with ours, in presenting this first year's volume of family-favorite, budget-friendly, easy-to-read and easy-to-cook recipes—a year's compendium of the Rush Hour Cook's Daily Column. Written with common ingredients and realistic budgets in mind, this book offers-up a "delicious combination" of suggestions for food, thought, and family. From "home-spun" to gourmet, beginner to expert, for both young and old, there is something to be found for every palate and every taste bud.

So get yourself a cup of tea, open to today's date, and join the Rush Hour Cook for a wealth of information and ideas to keep your kitchen (and ours) humming all year long…

Wendy Louise, Contributing Editor

THE BIRTH OF
THE RUSH HOUR COOK

This all started very innocently. I am the owner of a successful, independent publishing company, and while talking to a trusted friend and colleague, I realized there was a need for quick dinner solutions with simplistic ingredients and surreal taste. After talking to many home cooks, I discovered people wanted simple, tasty, user-friendly recipes. They didn't want a huge cookbook where they might fix two or three dishes, but a reliable collection of Rush-Hour style recipes. It didn't take me long to decide that Champion Press would start just such a series.

What wasn't so clear was who would author this new, indispensable guide. Champion has a slew of successful cookbook authors. While trying to decide which writer to assign to the project, a friend of mine suggested that I author the series. Keep in mind that this same friend, when in college, witnessed my attempt to microwave a non-microwaveable pizza, and said nothing when I forgot to remove the plastic wrap. Needles to say, my lack of domesticity has long been evident. (I can't iron anything without creating more wrinkles than I started with; although I think this has to do more with my being left-handed than my actual skill level.) I do not sort laundry by colors, fabrics or labels. And, more than once, I have been spotted purchasing finger Jell-O™ pre-made at the deli. So I asked her, "Why on earth should I write a cookbook series?"

"Well," she said simply. "Think about it... you are the absolute Queen of Incapable Cooking." (I tried not to glare at her as I listened to this rationale.) She continued, "In order for you to find 1 recipe—you will have to cook 10-20—at least! You will have to taste-test more than probably any other cook on the planet! Plus, if you can cook something quickly—and have it taste good…well…then…it's fool proof!" she rambled excitedly.

"Huh," I replied.

While I wasn't thrilled with this exchange, I had to admit that her reasoning had merit. Earlier in the week, I had watched my daughter excitedly announce to fellow grocery shoppers that it "must be a holiday!"

When another shopper stated that she wasn't aware of any holidays, Sammy quickly explained, "My mom is cooking from a real-live recipe... not a box! It must be a holiday! She has never done that before." I smiled meekly, holding up my canister of marjoram in defense. The other woman snickered and cast a condescending stare.

Later that night, I brought the subject up to my husband and mother while I was busy wrapping leftovers in the kitchen. "Mom—did you buy this plastic wrap at the dollar store?" I asked while fighting with the plastic and its supposedly quick-cut-tooth-grabber on the box edge.

"Yes—why?" she asked from the table.

"It doesn't really work so well," I grumbled while yanking yet another yard in attempt to secure my dish. It took about 18 yards and two sailor knots to secure the plastic to the bowl. My husband was entering the kitchen just as I secured the last knot.

"Need some help, honey?"

"I'm fine; it's just the wrap." Of course, he then proceeded to wrap three more dishes with metric precision that didn't waste a millimeter of the dreaded plastic.

"Anyway," I said, returning to the table. "What would you guys think of me writing a cookbook?" My husband made this familiar noise that he makes when he thinks someone is telling a joke, but isn't sure. My mother tried to look engrossed by the television—even though it wasn't turned on. "Well?" I urged.

"Is something wrong with the television?" my mother asked.

"It's not turned on," I said simply.

"I better look into that," Andy said as he rose. Without so much as a backward glance, they both left the table.

In that moment, The Rush Hour Cook™ was born.

It hasn't been an easy road, but I'll admit I had ulterior motives for writing this series. I am energetic and frequently work out through the martial arts and running. While my physical endurance is strong, my diet appalls most people (and it actually appalls me as well.) I can live for a week on nothing more than soft pretzels and Twizzlers™. This is not something that makes me proud. My life is a zoo of insanity that allows very little time for cooking let alone making frequent trips to the grocery store. But as an Editor and Publisher, I frequently read about health issues, preservative dangers and other influences our diet has on our body. I wanted to see if I would actually feel better if I found my vitamins in food, instead of the buy-one-get-one-free sale at GNC. I also wanted to minimize my risk of future health ailments. After all, cook or no cook, I am a mom— and I want to be around many, many years to enjoy my beautiful child and family. I hope that throughout this process I can pass on some healthful knowledge and good habits along the way.

My last motive for authoring this series is to recreate the family dinner in my home. It's not uncommon for me to work 12 to 14 hour days. The thought of cooking at the end of an exhausting workday is about as intriguing as joining the

Polar Bear Club and jumping into frigid-degree water. Yet, without that meal to bond us as a family each night, we all too often go our separate ways. My daughter will grab a snack here or there, I will eat while reading something from my briefcase and my husband will grab a bite on his way home from the office or just eat an extra-large lunch. Our few precious hours at home together, become invaded by diversions. But I noticed when I did cook (those two or three times a year) or when my mother would come over and cook, we would all sit around the table and talk and enjoy and share.

I truly think that one of the biggest problems facing the American family today is the loss of the family dinner hour. Think about it—decades ago we shared two, if not three, meals together daily. These were basically mini-family-meetings, nourishing both body and soul. Now, statistics show we are fortunate to sit down together twice a week—to share a meal, much less linger over it!

In the end, I accepted my friend's challenge to write a cookbook series. I tried a lot of recipes, variations and methods. More food saw the garbage disposal than the pages of this book. But you will find within these pages the best-of-the-best recipes. Each recipe has been carefully tested for taste and time-saving ability. In addition, I created the Five Rules of Rush Hour Recipes and posted them on my cupboard. Besides for a few worthwhile rule-breakers, recipes that made it into this book had to meet the guidelines of "Rush Hour Recipes" found on the following page.

THE FIVE RULES OF RUSH HOUR RECIPES

1. All ingredients should be able to be pronounced accurately through the phonetic use of the English Language.

2. Each ingredient can be located in the market without engaging in a full scale scavenger hunt.

3. No list of ingredients shall be longer than the instructions.

4. Each recipe has to be durable enough to survive me, the Queen-of-Incapable–Cooking, and elicit a compliment at meal's end.

5. My finicky child will eat it—or some portion of it. I've learned not to be too picky on this one. Often I separate out part of the meal during preparation and customize it to her taste.

I dedicated myself to making this series one that you will cherish, love and refer to again and again. It has accomplished my aforementioned goals for a return to the family dinner hour and easy, healthy eating. It is my hope that this book and the Rush Hour series will help you reclaim the dinner hour in your home as well.

THE RUSH HOUR GUIDE TO HEALTHY EATING

As you move through this book you'll see that the menus feature both meat and meatless dishes. I subscribe to the belief that we can survive without shoveling loads of red meat and starches into our system. That's not to say I'm a carbo addict—but I am not a protein pusher either. I have had a long and turbulent relationship with food. I'll spare you the gory details but trust me when I say finding a healthy eating plan that is also fulfilling has not been easy.

I have tried diets where I have consumed protein by the pound and likewise I've tried diets where I consumed pounds of pasta. I've read studies where both plans offered many benefits—and likewise I've read studies which state both plans will surely erode the body. I've read that I should drink gallons of water, only to grab another magazine that tells me it will mess up my electrolytes. I've tried diets where I ate by food group, time, and moon cycle. And I've tried diets where I've dealt meal cards; counted calories and leg lifts; measured points, inches, heart rates, circumferences and diameters. They've all lead me back to the same place. "Garbage in, garbage out. Unbalanced in, unbalanced out."

I'm happy to report that I am now a size 4 (don't hate me, it didn't come easily). That's not due to a naturally friendly metabolism, genes or luck. Quite the contrary, for 15 years I battled daily with the scale and for 10 years had an active and consuming eating disorder. My weight topped at 204 when I entered the hospital to deliver my first child. I figured my child would weigh at least 90 pounds. Imagine my surprise when I left a day later with an 8 pound baby girl—and only 15 pounds lighter. From there, I spent seven years testing the spectrum of tricks and diet devices. I tried mail order, phone order, ab rollers—you name it, I owned it. I bring this up only because so many women battle with their weight and, of course, we are also facing unprecedented weight problems with our children. It took me so many years of unhealthy behavior to realize how important health is and to find a way to truly live a healthy life. For those who are interested, I want to share the keys to my success and perhaps they can open the door to yours.

Hop over the hoopla, fads and miracle cures. Ignore the magazines that tell you how to lose seven pounds by Thursday yet advertise 10 ways to make a sinful chocolate cake on the opposite page. Let it all go. You don't need to try to live up to some standard set by the latest fashion or diet guru. At the end of the day, the person you account to is you.

Satisfy your soul... not your scale. You are the one who needs to be satisfied. When we struggle with our weight and diet, it's often our soul that needs nourishing just as much as our body. What are you missing within yourself? Make a list and a plan of action for replenishing your self and your soul, as well as your body.

Start with a healthy attitude before your healthy diet. So many times we enter diets or new eating plans at a point where we are frustrated or disgusted with ourselves. No wonder we can't "stick to the plan." How can we expect to meet our goals when our attitudes are negative or depressed. Before beginning a healthy program, begin with a healthy and positive attitude.

Gather some teammates. You have probably heard the saying that "It takes a village to raise a child." Consider yourself at the child stage of a health program. Just as you wouldn't leave a child alone in new territory, don't sentence yourself to struggle in silence. Find a support network to share your success. Support was vital for me in turning over a new leaf. It's important to have at least three people in your support network. (If you have only two, it's very easy for it to fizzle.) I did e-mail support with two other gals who sought a healthy life. When we had our tough times, we could find strength in each other and the knowledge that we weren't alone.

Set realistic goals. Another vital part of my success was due to a Personal Wellness Coach. I used Carrie Myers Smith, President of WomeninWellness.Com as a guide and sounding board. In our first session, I wanted goals like... workout seven days a week, eat five healthy dinners, etc. Carrie combated my obsessive personality and offered baby steps instead. We started with very obtainable goals. Exercise twice the first week. Eat two healthy dinners. All in all I had about five simple goals. By focusing only on those goals, I became successful. As my confidence grew, I could build on those goals.

Try an "at least" mentality. Many times I had tried to makeover my life in a day or with a New Year's resolution. I wanted to wake up and magically engage in healthy behavior. What a recipe for failure. I remember how brutal I was to myself when my plans crumbled as I passed a Danish. When I started the Women in Wellness program, I developed what I refer to as an "at least mentality". Two of my goals for the first week were to exercise twice and eat two healthy dinners. I decided that no matter what happened over the course of the week, I would "at least" complete those two challenges. Furthermore, I would be pleased, no matter what happened, as long as I completed the two challenges. If I ate ice cream nonstop in between, I would still be nice to myself. I would be pleased that I had met the two simple goals and would add additional goals each week.

By doing this, I didn't have to give up and throw the baby out with the bathwater. Instead, I could increase my number of healthy behaviors over a period of time. As my healthy behaviors increased, there became less and less time for my destructive patterns. Eventually, the destructive patterns went away all on their own. The coolest part was, it didn't hurt! I didn't have any cravings. I didn't forbid anything. I simply focused on little healthy steps, two healthy steps at a time.

Erase excuses and energize your exercise. I don't love exercising, in fact, for most of my life I've detested it. I've tried step aerobics, Pilates, home workouts, group classes and many other scenarios, only to feel like participating was torture. When I finally realized it was a necessity to a healthy lifestyle I said, "Okay—then let's make it something good." I began to look for a program that matched my personality. I am competitive and like to measure my results. I found that running was a great source of exercise for me. Although I had never run more than a mile in my life and was sure I would hate it; I discovered I was wrong. I could compete in 5K's, 10K's or half-marathons and measure my progress and time. I could constantly push and improve to "beat my best." Granted, I'm not a great runner and I often walk/jog instead of run. My times are lousy by most people's standards—but I don't care. It's never been about "beating the world", it's about pushing me to be the "best me" I can be.

When I first started I couldn't walk 3 miles, let alone run them. Imagine when 4 months later I ran 13 miles. What a feeling! Sure, I was probably one of the last ones to finish—but that didn't matter—what did matter, was that I finished. When I relocated to the Midwest, running wasn't as pleasant in sub-zero temperatures. For the first time in my life, I enrolled in a martial arts class. Again, I could measure my progress by moving through the belt system. I've been involved in the martial arts for a year and just received my brown belt. I feel strong and comfortable in my body. The martial arts have become a lifeline for releasing stress and staying fit.

While stationary bicycling and step aerobics left me longing for a beach in Maui, I've finally found a program that matches what I need from exercise. So get creative and explore the options around you. I am convinced that there are enough exercises on this planet—from racquetball to spinning to tennis to aquatics to hiking—everyone can find something that matches their personality—it's just a matter of looking. Enough excuses.

JANUARY 1

For our family, New Year's Day traditionally includes a delectable brunch for family and friends. Here are some suggestions for a healthy and varied menu with which to greet the New Year. Remember to keep it easy and healthy (see notes on the use of flax seed, following the smoothie recipe). I've chosen this menu for today's brunch because of the ease of preparation and its variety for all ages and tastes.

The Rush Hour Cook's
Menu for a New Year's Day Brunch

o Smoothies (made to order)
o Sara's French Toast Casserole
o Cheese and Egg Scramble

Served with:
Assorted fruit juices (served in pretty crystal pitchers)
Assorted breakfast meats (sausages and bacon, precooked and held in warm oven)
Fresh fruit platter (bananas, grapes, tangerines, apples, kiwi, garnished with thawed frozen blueberries)
Yogurt
Cold cereals and milk (the small, fun individual boxes)
Coffee and/or espresso

The Rush Hour Cook's Morning Smoothie
1 to 2 servings

INGREDIENTS
1 cup frozen berries of your choice
½ of a peeled banana, frozen
½ cup plain, non-fat yogurt
½ cup orange juice
1 to 2 tablespoons ground flax seed* (optional)
1 scoop vanilla-flavored whey protein powder* (optional)
1 tablespoon organic greens* (optional)

*The asterisked ingredients can be purchased at health food stores or at a center like GNC® and are considered optional, according to your taste. I highly recommend the flax seed because of its health benefits. Recent studies have suggested that flax seed quite possibly lowers the risk of heart disease, diabetes, cholesterol, blood clots, some cancers, and also minimizes menopausal symptoms. Ground flax seed is an extremely good source for Omega-3 and soluble fiber.

For your New Year Smoothie, mix the first five ingredients together in a blender to desired consistency and taste. You may add more frozen banana or more yogurt or throw in a kiwi or additional berries to arrive at your desired flavor and consistency. Be creative. Serve in a chilled glass.

The last time I served this widely was at the Taste of Home show in Milwaukee. I did a cooking demo and this was all the rage! I received e-mails for months asking for extra copies of this recipe. My favorite berries are the frozen combo bags that have blackberries, raspberries, and blueberries.

RUSH HOUR HEALTH TIP
The Benefits of Flax Seed

This year, try incorporating flax seed into your regular diet with these simple ideas. Flax seed has a mild taste, much like ground nuts. (Note: you can purchase flax seed at natural health-food stores or at GNC® Centers.)

SUGGESTED USES:
1) Stir 1 teaspoon or 1 tablespoon of flax seed into a container of yogurt.
2) Sprinkle flax seed generously over a salad for extra "crunch."
3) Use flax seed as a partial substitute for recipes that call for breadcrumbs.
4) Add a few tablespoons when frying a pan of fresh vegetables.
5) Sprinkle flax seed over hot or cold cereals.

Sara's Fancy French Toast Casserole

6 to 8 servings

INGREDIENTS
1 cup brown sugar
½ cup butter, melted
3 teaspoons cinnamon, divided
3 to 4 tart apples, peeled, cored, and sliced into ¼-inch thick wedges
½ cup Craisins ® (dried cranberries) (or you could substitute raisins)
1 loaf French or Italian bread, cut into 1-inch thick slices
6 large eggs, lightly beaten
1½ cups milk
A dash of vanilla extract

Combine the brown sugar, melted butter, and 1 teaspoon of the cinnamon in bottom of a 13 X 9-inch baking dish. Slice in the apples and sprinkle on the Craisins ® (or raisins) and mix all until well coated. Spread evenly in the bottom of the casserole dish. Arrange the 1-inch thick bread slices to form a complete layer over the top of the apple mixture. Mix the eggs, milk, and remaining 2 teaspoons of cinnamon until well blended and pour over the bread, soaking the bread thoroughly. Cover with cooking foil and let the assembled casserole "set" for at least 4 hours (or overnight) in the refrigerator. Bake covered in a pre-heated 375-degree oven for 40 to 45 minutes. Uncover and bake 5 minutes more to gently crisp the top. Remove from oven and let stand a few minutes before serving. Serve warm.

RUSH HOUR OPTIONS
You may serve the casserole "as is" or you can offer the additions of whipped cream, heavy cream, sour cream, flax seed, crème fraiche, or vanilla (or cinnamon) ice cream!

Cheese and Egg Scramble

Scramble your eggs till fluffy but still moist (do not over cook) and transfer to a buttered casserole dish. Sprinkle the top with shredded Cheddar cheese and a little parsley. Hold to keep warm in a 200-degree oven, (along with the pre-cooked breakfast sausages and bacon from the menu). The cheese will melt over the top of the eggs and everything will be warm when you are ready to serve your entire menu.

JANUARY 2
Baked Potato Bonanza Bar

For a simple meal build a "potato bonanza." Baked potatoes are often thought of as an accompaniment but they can also make a wonderful main meal! Just add some veggies and some protein and serve with a "Bonanza Bar" of toppings. Let each person "dress" his or her potato according to their tastes.

INGREDIENTS (for Potato)
1 large baking potato per person
Vegetable oil

Preheat oven to 400 degrees. Scrub large, firm baking potatoes and blot dry with paper towels. Rub oil on the skins to avoid cracking. Pierce potatoes twice with a fork. For soft skinned potatoes, wrap in aluminum foil. For crispier skins do not use foil. Bake for 1 hour, or until soft when gently squeezed. (To microwave 2 potatoes at a time, prick with fork and cook 10 to 12 minutes or until soft to the touch. Do not try to do more than 2 potatoes at a time in the microwave.) Break open your baked potato, fluff the insides a bit and start putting on the toppings! Be creative...as you can see the list of choices is endless!

INGREDIENTS (for Bonanza Bar)
Bacon Bits ® (or crumbled cooked bacon)
Green onions, chopped (include the green tops)
Chives
Sour Cream or yogurt
Broccoli florets, steamed
Cheddar cheese, shredded
Leftover ham, roast beef, chicken or turkey, cubed or shredded
Cooked ground turkey (leaner than beef)
Any cheese (grated fresh Parmesan is wonderful and blue cheese
  crumbles are excellent)
Canned or sautéed mushrooms
Onions, diced (Spanish onion is fun because of its brilliant color)
Cooked ground beef (or taco style ground beef for a Tex-Mex flavor)
Leftover chili or taco meat
Warmed cheese sauce
Melted butter
Warmed gravy
Freshly cracked black pepper
Lemon or lime wedges (yes, freshly squeezed lemon or lime juice, instead

of butter for a fresh and light taste!)
Sour cream and caviar for the sophisticated palate or holiday guests
And let's not ignore pizza sauce and anchovies!

Weekly Challenge
CHOOSING PRIORITIES

With our New Year just beginning, what better time to think about what is most dear to us and what we hope to accomplish in the twelve months that are ahead. Take a moment after today's festivities to reflect on your priorities. Write down your three top priorities and paste them on an index card on your refrigerator. Each evening as you make your dinner preparations, glance at your goals. Try to take a step forward, no matter how small, each day. Other family members may also enjoy this activity.

Another wonderful idea is to make a reflecting mirror to hang at a child's level. Have each child decorate the frame of their "I Love Myself Mirror" with hearts and stars and bright colors. Every time they look in their mirror they will see how "beautiful" they are ... as the mirror reflects their spiritual beauty and positive qualities. This is a real self-confidence builder for small children.

PRIORITY POST-IT NOTES

In our Change Your Life Challenge Program we practice 3 POWER TO-DO's each day. The concept is to choose three things that you will do TODAY that move you toward your priorities and goals in life. Each day create such a Post-It and display it in a prominent location. To learn more about The Change Your Life Challenge: A 70 Day Life Makeover Program for Women, log onto www.changeyourlifechallenge.com

---

Worth the Click

With a new year here, why not start a free online diary? Take a moment to plan your year and record your priorities. My favorite free online diary site is www.diaryland.com

---

JANUARY 3

Joan's "Chicken in a Pot"
6 to 8 servings

INGREDIENTS
1 (3 pound) chicken, left whole
2 carrots, sliced
2 onions, sliced
2 celery stalks, with leaves, cut into 1-inch pieces
2 teaspoons salt
½ teaspoon black pepper
½ to 1 teaspoon crushed basil
½ cup water, chicken broth or white wine

Put vegetables in bottom of slow cooker. Salt and pepper the chicken and put on top of the vegetables. Pour in the ½ cup liquid and sprinkle with basil. Cover with lid and cook on low setting 7 to 10 hours (or 3 to 4 hours on high setting, adding another ½ cup liquid). Carefully remove chicken from the crockery-style pot using a spatula and place on serving platter Strain remaining cooking juices and make gravy.

JANUARY 4
Easy-Style Homemade Pot Roast of Beef
6 to 8 servings

INGREDIENTS
2 to 3 pounds round steak, trimmed of fat and cut into cubes
3 to 4 tablespoons brown sugar
2 teaspoons salt
3 tablespoons Worcestershire sauce
1 tablespoon vinegar
¼ teaspoon each: dill, chives, parsley, sweet basil, dry mustard
1 cup water
1 tablespoon grape jelly
2 tablespoons cornstarch, dissolved in ½ cup water

Place cubed meat in slow-cooker crockery pot. Mix the rest of ingredients together, stirring well and pour over meat. Stir again well to coat all. Cover with lid and cook on low setting for 5 to 7 hours, or until meat is very tender. Serve the meat and sauce on rolls. (Can shred the meat if desired.)

RUSH HOUR TIP
Using dark brown sugar in your recipes adds depth and a nice caramelizing flavor to sauces and glazes.

Where's the Beef?
http://beefitswhatsfordinner.com/

Thanks to the National Beef Council that is an easy question to answer. Log on to this web site and you'll find a free downloadable cookbook and many recipes and resources. My favorite feature? The downloadable wallet card that lists 19 cuts of beef and their nutritional information.

You'll find that card at:
http://beefitswhatsfordinner.com/nutrition/pdf/
LeanCutsWalletGuide.PDF

JANUARY 5
Super-Fast Salmon
6 servings

INGREDIENTS
1 teaspoon dried, dill weed, crumbled
2 ½ tablespoons Dijon mustard
1 tablespoon honey
6 salmon fillets
Vegetable oil spray (optional)

Preheat broiler to 450 degrees. Whisk dill weed, mustard, and honey together in a small bowl. Brush mixture over the flesh side of washed and dried salmon. Put fish skin side down on a sprayed baking sheet. Broil about 6 inches from heat for 5 to 7 minutes (depending on size of fillets) or until sides of fish flake with a fork.

A Thought for Today
FORGIVENESS

"Forgiveness doesn't make the other person right, it makes you free" ~Susie Omartian, author of *Praying God's Will for Your Life*

Holding on to our past grudges and hurts, hurts us the most! What or which people do you need to forgive from last year to make room for growth this coming year? Practice the art of forgiveness by making a phone call, writing a letter, or reaching out to someone you need to forgive. And I might add it is okay to forgive yourself too…sometimes we can be our own worst critic or enemy, and we need to take a step back in order to forgive ourselves so we can take a step forward.

JANUARY 6
Sanity-Saving Slow Cooker Chicken
4 to 6 servings

Simple, warming, and uncomplicated this recipe provides a nutritious and healthy dinner for your family. Do not over salt or over spice this recipe. Let the subtleties of the vegetables and simple ingredients stand on their own.

INGREDIENTS
1 chicken, skinned, patted dry and cut into fryer size pieces
1 medium size onion, cut into 1-inch cubes
1 (10.75 ounce) can of chicken broth
Vegetables to include: carrots, celery, and scrubbed potatoes, cut into
   uniform chunks (see tip)

Place onion in bottom of slow-cooker pot. Add skinless chicken pieces and arrange vegetables around all. Pour on broth. Cover and cook on low setting for at least 6 hours, or until everything is tender and juices from chicken run clear.

RUSH HOUR TIPS
To facilitate the even-cooking of vegetables in a slow cooker, cut them all approximately the same size so they cook at the same rate.

Did You Know? (Uesless Chicken Trivia)

Colonel Sanders (the founder of Kentucky Fried Chicken) was the second most recognized public figure in the world in 1979.

The chicken capital of the world is Gainesville, Georgia. There, it is illegal to eat chicken with a fork!

JANUARY 7

Simple Sour Cream Pasta
A KID FRIENDLY RECIPE
4 main servings, 6 to 8 side servings

INGREDIENTS
1 pound penne, cooked* according to package directions, drained and
  set aside
16 ounces low-fat sour cream
1 cup Parmesan cheese, divided

Preheat oven to 325 degrees. Mix sour cream with ½ cup of Parmesan cheese
and toss with the cooked pasta. Pour the mixture into a 9X13-inch baking dish
coated with cooking spray. Spread casserole out evenly and top with the remaining ½ cup Parmesan cheese. Bake for 30 minutes, or until warmed through
and casserole is bubbly.

This pasta recipe can be served as the main dish for a light supper along with
warmed bread and a nice salad (such as Bibb lettuce with a delicate vinaigrette)—
or it can make a great side dish with grilled meats or baked chicken

RUSH HOUR TIPS
*When pre-cooking pasta to be used in a baked casserole, or the like, be sure to cook
the pasta only until al dente (just firm, not mushy) being careful not to overcook. You
can stop the cooking by rinsing the pasta in cold water and setting aside until ready
to use. It is better to slightly undercook the pasta and let it finish cooking during the
final stages of the dish for which it is being prepared.*

*When boiling pasta my mother pours a little cooking oil onto the top of the boiling
water before she puts in her pasta. This method coats the pasta and helps keep it
from sticking together while being drained and set aside.*

*When setting cooked pasta aside toss it with an extra sprinkling of olive oil (or veg-
etable cooking oil) to keep it from sticking and clumping
together before you combine it into the rest of the dish.
Or you can use a small amount of melted butter.*

JANUARY 8
10 Minute Sukiyaki Stir-Fry
4 servings

Here is a quick and delicious stir-fry that takes only a few minutes of prep work and 10 minutes to cook! Have all your ingredients prepped in advance, because once you heat up the pan cooking goes very fast. This recipe tastes wonderful, fresh, and healthy.

Minute #0 - Get a large skillet (a wok isn't necessary, but is nice if you have one) medium hot and add 3 tablespoons of canola oil.

Minute #1 - Add 1 large onion, sliced into rings, and start sautéing.

Minute #2 - Add a package of sliced, fresh mushrooms to the pan and continue sautéing.

Minute #3 - Add 1 pound of lean beef, that has been thinly sliced into strips (see tip that follows recipe) and cook for 2 minutes.

Minute #5 - Add ½ pound of fresh spinach leaves (that have been cleaned, dried and de-veined)

Minute #6 - Add 3 (5-inch) stalks of celery that have been thinly sliced into julienne strips (see note below).

Minute #7 - Add in 4 green onions that have been cut into julienne* (including tops)

Minute #8 - Add 4 tablespoons of soy sauce and 2 tablespoons sugar

Minutes #9 and #10 - Add 1 can of beef broth and simmer for 2 minutes.

At the end of Minute #10 — Done!

Toss all to mix well and serve with white rice or cellophane noodles (very thin, transparent oriental noodles that take about 2 minutes to cook) on the side. Pass a garnish of crunchy Chinese noodles and additional soy sauce on the side, at time of serving.

RUSH HOUR WISDOM

The term julienne means to cut into very thin horizontal strips, about the size of matchsticks.

RUSH HOUR TIP

When slicing uncooked meat for stir-fry try putting the beef, pork, or chicken-breast meat into the freezer for 10 to 15 minutes before slicing. The starting-to-freeze-meat will make handling easier and slicing more uniform.

Weekly Challenge

LET'S GET PHYSICAL

Physical fitness is such a key to our well-being and mental outlook on life. When we feel fit and vital our minds also feel balanced and alert. The beginning of a new year is a great time to start a renewal program for the new you. So I am going to suggest that this Week's Challenge be a year-long challenge for you to devise a healthy and sensible eating plan for you and your family. Making even the smallest changes (cutting back on sugar or candy, minimizing salt, or even just cutting down on those second helpings or the snacks between meals) can all be ways to modify your eating. Replace a can of pop a day with a bottled water. Resist the urge to "super size" your meal when you go through the drive through. When you go to a movie, breeze right by the refreshment counter. Go to watch the movie, not munch your way through the movie! Or maybe your change will be as simple as replacing one heavy-meat-meal-night a week with a lighter salad or vegetarian-style dinner. Small changes can yield big rewards by the end of the year!

JANUARY 9
Homemade Potato Chips
A KIDS IN THE KITCHEN RECIPE

In our Daily Rush Hour Group (stop by at www.rushhourcook.com) we have one day a week, which is a "Kids in the Kitchen Day." Today we are going to make Homemade Potato Chips. (An adult will have to do the slicing but a child can do the rest.) This is a nice alternative to fried foods from the drive-thru lane!

INGREDIENTS
1 tablespoon of vegetable oil
A plastic bag
1 baking potato, sliced paper thin (by an adult)
A microwave safe dinner plate, coated with vegetable oil or cooking spray
½ teaspoon salt, or to taste

While your mom or dad slices the potato very, very thin (using a sharp knife or a slicing device called a Mandolin) you can put 1 tablespoon of vegetable oil into a plastic bag. Then put in the potato slices and shake the bag well to coat all the slices. Arrange the slices in a single layer on the microwave-safe plate (you will have to do several batches). Cook the first batch in the microwave for about 3 to 5 minutes (see tip), or until just lightly browned. The chips must be lightly browned in order to become crisp. Then repeat, until all chips are cooked. Toss them with salt (see tip) to taste and they are ready to eat!

RUSH HOUR TIPS
Microwaves very in cooking power and times, so you might have to experiment a little.
For fun you can try seasoning your chips with other than plain salt. You might try a taco seasoning salt, Cajun spice, or a garlic and onion salt, or popcorn salt!
Also when slicing the potato the peel may be left on or removed—your choice.

RUSH HOUR VARIATION
An alternative way to cook your chips is on a greased cookie sheet in a preheated 400-degree oven. Again, arrange the very thin potato slices in a single layer and bake until lightly brown. When the chips are done, carefully remove the hot cookie sheet, using pot holders to protect your hands. Sprinkle the chips with salt and enjoy.

JANUARY 10

Mambone's Pork Chops
6 to 8 servings

INGREDIENTS
6 to 8 lean pork chops, about 1-inch thick
½ cup flour
1½ teaspoons dry mustard
½ teaspoon garlic powder
2 tablespoons oil
1 (10.75 ounce) can chicken and rice soup
1 teaspoon salt, or to taste

Mix flour and seasonings. Dredge pork chops in the flour mixed with seasonings. Brown chops in oil in a large skillet. Place the browned chops into the slow cooker. Add the can of soup. Cover with lid and cook on low for 6-8 hours, or high setting 3½ hours. Serve with applesauce.

RUSH HOUR TIP
When using dried herbs (such as parsley, oregano, thyme, basil, etc.) crumble them between your fingers to release extra flavor.

Facts about "The Other White Meat"

Pork producers have listened to consumers' preferences and concerns. Since the 1980s, the fat content of pork has been dramatically reduced. For example, the most popular selection of pork, the tenderloin is now 42% lower in fat. This was achieved through: improved breeding and feeding practices and better trimming of fat, both at the processors and in the stores. Pork is a source of protein, iron, zinc, and B-vitamins. *- Source National Pork Council*

JANUARY 11
Family Favorite French Dip
8+ servings

INGREDIENTS
1 (3 pound) beef roast (eye, rump or sirloin tip)
Cook's Note: utilize your grocery store sale
1 large onion, sliced
2 cups beef broth
Water
6 pepper corns
1 bay leaf
Garlic cloves, smashed (use several, or to taste)
Salt and pepper to taste at end of cooking
1 to 2 loaves crusty French bread, or individual hard rolls

Place sliced onion in slow cooker. Lay the roast on the onions. Pour the beef broth over the roast and add the spices. Add water until the roast is covered. Cover with lid and cook on high 5 to 6 hours, or low 10 to 12 hours, adding more water if necessary to keep the roast covered. Remove meat from crock-style pot and let stand 5 to 10 minutes before slicing. Slice the meat across the grain. Set aside and keep warm. Strain the liquid (removing onion, pepper corns, garlic, and bay leaf). Skim off any excess fat, making a nice 'dipping broth'. Return broth to slow cooker. Add meat slices back into pot and juices to keep moist. (You can add more water or broth if necessary to make more 'au jus' for dipping.) Adjust seasonings with salt and pepper to taste. Serve the meat warm as sandwiches on French bread, with the dipping sauce provided in bowls on the side.

RUSH HOUR TIP
A fun serving suggestion when using French bread for sandwiches is to split the whole loaf down the middle, horizontally. Pile on the meat slices and close back up, making a giant sandwich. Let everyone slice off a portion-size to their liking and 'customize' their sandwich from a selection of condiments, spreads, and dips, you've provided on the side.

JANUARY 12

Betty's Spaghetti
4 to 6 family-style servings

Tonight feels like a spaghetti night to me. Here is our family recipe inherited down from my mom from her mom. It is very simple, but oh so good. I think this recipe's wonderful taste has something to do with bringing it to the table "family style" in a great big "spaghetti bowl"! This recipe makes enough for a family of 4 with some leftovers for lunch the next day. The sauce may be doubled, tripled, etc., as needed—and frozen for convenience dinners. Just pull out a carton of sauce, boil up some fresh pasta, and serve.

INGREDIENTS
1 pound lean ground beef
1 medium to large onion, diced

Spices to taste, to include:
  Parsley flakes, crushed
  Garlic cloves, smashed and minced (or garlic powder)
  Salt and pepper
  Sweet basil flakes, crushed

1 (28 ounce) can stewed whole tomatoes, with juice
1 (6 ounce) can tomato paste
A pinch or two of sugar
1 teaspoon crushed oregano
1 package sliced fresh mushrooms, sautéed (or can used canned)
A box of spaghetti noodles, cooked al dente at time of serving
A large Italian style, spaghetti bowl
Grated Parmesan for garnish

In a large pot or Dutch oven brown the meat with the list of spices and onion. Then stir in the canned tomatoes (with their juice) and the tomato paste along with the oregano. Add the sautéed (or canned) mushrooms last. Simmer, covered but vented, on low for at least one hour, or "the longer the better" to thicken the sauce and meld the flavors. (My mom's mom used to let it gently simmer all afternoon.) With a wooden spoon, break up the tomatoes as the sauce cooks. At time of serving arrange your al dente pasta in a large shallow bowl. Pour the sauce over the noodles and toss slightly. Serve "family style" with grated Parmesan cheese on the side.

RUSH HOUR TIPS FOR PASTA SUCCESS

Save salting and peppering for later in the cooking process, as salt and pepper (like most of the spices) intensify during extended cooking. Adjust the seasoning at the very end of cooking to your liking.

Fresh Parmesan cheese makes a wonderful garnish. With your potato peeler, shave paper-thin slices of Parmesan cheese and sprinkle them on top of the spaghetti in the serving bowl. Or pass the fresh Parmesan on the side, as this addition might be a little sharp in taste for children.

Most chefs suggest cooking your pasta in at least 4 quarts of rolling-boiling, salted water per pound of pasta. This large amount of water helps disperse the starch and makes the pasta less sticky. Using your largest pot and using a large amount of water is very important in controlling the final texture of your pasta.

Cook your pasta just until al dente (firm or slightly chewy)—not soft and mushy.

Drain your pasta into a colander (carefully and away from you) but don't rinse it. Toss it immediately with your prepared sauce (to prevent sticking) and serve. Or toss the drained pasta with a few tablespoons of olive oil (to prevent sticking) and hold in a warmed bowl until your sauce is ready.

If you are making pasta for a cold salad—do rinse it in cold water to stop the cooking process. Make sure the pasta is dried well before you use it in the salad, or it will not blend with/or will dilute the dressing.

Did you know that the variety of shapes, sizes, thickness, textures and the size of the holes all have to do with developing how the pasta blends with and tastes with its prospective sauce? Each style of pasta has been designed to go with a certain sauce.

JANUARY 13

Shrimp de Jonghe
6 servings

Rich, buttery, and rather formal, this makes a special dinner when you need a little pampering. If you are making a "dinner for two" just cut the recipe in half. I guarantee you'll split the third portion between you.

INGREDIENTS
3 pounds uncooked shrimp, cleaned and de-veined, tails removed
Salt and pepper to taste
½ cup consommé or white wine
6 cloves of garlic, smashed to release flavor
1 cup butter
2 cups dry bread crumbs
6 tablespoons minced fresh parsley

Preheat oven to 400 degrees. Divide the shrimp into 6 individual baking dishes or ramekins. Season with salt and pepper. Drizzle the consommé or wine over the shrimp. In a saucepan cook the garlic in the butter until the butter just begins to bubble and brown. Remove the garlic. Add the bread crumbs and parsley and mix well. Distribute the crumb mixture over the shrimp in the 6 baking dishes. Bake the shrimp for approximately 15 minutes, until cooked through and shrimp are opaque. Do not over cook. Serve hot and bubbly along with a loaf of French bread.

RUSH HOUR TIP
Rather than fussing with raw shrimp, use flash-frozen, already cleaned shrimp from the frozen section of your butcher case. Thawing and cooking instructions will be on the package.

A Thought for Today
THE COMFORTS OF HOME
"He is happiest, be he king or peasant,
who finds peace in his own home."
~Goethe

JANUARY 14

Pork Chop and Sweet Potato Casserole
6 servings

Granted this dinner takes 1½ hours to cook, but it is "rush hour quick" to assemble and pop into the oven. Go surf the net while it's baking, or help the kids with their homework. While dinner's cooking you've gotten your chores done and you will be ready to relax with a nice meal.

INGREDIENTS
6 large slices (½ inch thick) of sweet potato, discard peel
6 thin slices of orange, peel left on
6 pork chops
Salt and pepper to taste
½ cup brown sugar

Preheat oven to 350 degrees. Place sweet potato slices in a non-stick sprayed baking dish. Top the potatoes with the orange slices and then the pork chops. Season with salt and pepper. Then sprinkle on the brown sugar. Cover the casserole with foil and pop into the oven. Bake for 1½ hours, uncovering for the last half hour.

Managing Plastic Wrap

Here's a tip for keeping your plastic wrap "manageable." Store it in the refrigerator and it will be much easier to handle while unrolling and using. Cold plastic wrap is less likely to bunch up on itself ... thus eliminating the need for 18 yards of tangled wrap, an extra pair of hands, and two sailor knots for each dish of leftover

JANUARY 15
Rustic Pork Chop Casserole
4 servings

Pork chops were on sale this week, so what can I say ... two nights in a row ... but completely different tastes.

INGREDIENTS
4 pork chops
A dusting of flour
2 cloves of garlic, smashed and minced for flavor
Salt and pepper to taste
1/2 teaspoon of dried oregano, crushed between fingers
4 large potatoes, sliced
1 large onion, sliced into rings
1 1/2 cups sour cream
1 teaspoon salt
1/2 teaspoon dry mustard

Preheat oven to 350 degrees. Roll the pork chops in flour to coat. Over medium heat brown the chops in a little hot oil along with the garlic for flavor. Season with salt and pepper to taste. Meanwhile arrange the sliced potatoes in a non-stick sprayed baking dish. Top with the browned pork chops. Season the chops with the oregano. Lay the onion rings over the chops. Blend the sour cream with the additional salt and the dry mustard and pour over the assembled casserole. Bake for 1 1/2 hours.

RUSH HOUR WISDOM
Be sure to take advantage of your market's sales. Sometimes I go to the store with a preconceived notion of what I am having for dinner and then change my mind when I see what is on sale! This week the sales were flash frozen shrimp (thus Tuesday's recipe) and pork chops (thus Wednesday's and Thursday's recipes).

Weekly Challenge

RECREATE THE FAMILY DINNER HOUR

At the turn of the millennium I wrote a very well received book called *Back to Basics, 101 ideas for strengthening our children and our families,* ISBN 1891400487. Sometimes when I feel my own family getting off track, or that we are spinning our wheels as each year gets more complex and offers more challenges for our growth; as each family member enters into new endeavors and our over-all family unit evolves, I make time to sit back and take stock of what I wrote several years ago and re-align my priorities. I go "back to my basics."

I find in the hustle and bustle of today, it is easy to lose sight of our most basic priorities and what is truly important. One "basic" I had written about was the return to a family dinner hour. So today take the phone off the hook, unplug the play station, close the computer, turn off the TV, hide the remote, turn off the pager, pocket the PC, let the charge run down on the cell phone, turn off the intercom, the DVD and the VCR, turn off the copier, ignore the fax machine, hide the keys to the car, the snow mobile, the all-terrain vehicle, the motorcycle, forget about the convenience food in the freezer, turn off the noisy dishwasher, the blender, the food processor and the malt mixer ... and just slow down a little ... Take a deep breath and put a family favorite casserole in the oven, and while it's cooking take the dog for a walk, or build a snowman with the kids, or have a family-hour in front of the fireplace, with a game of Scrabble before dinner ... Tomorrow the fax will come back on, you will re-plug in the TV, your Palm Pilot will still work, your phone will still ring , the car will still run, the VCR will still record...but wasn't it nice to take a breather...and just relax with your family!! And it wasn't even a holiday! It was just an ordinary mid-weekday's night spent doing ordinary things. Actually they were anything but ordinary--you were reconnecting--with your family, returning to the basics of hearth and home for an hour-and-a-half of undivided attention and quality family time.

JANUARY 16
Old Fashioned Roast Chicken #1
4 to 6 servings

Often in our quest to find new and exotic tastes we overlook the simple recipes of our past. This recipe is truly a "back to basics," down-home staple to reintroduce to the family dinner hour. How can anything so easy taste so good? Basic, flavorful, and economical to boot, roast chicken warms the soul on a cold winter night.

INGREDIENTS
1 (3 to 4 pound) roasting chicken, left whole
Salt and freshly ground black pepper
2 tablespoons butter, softened
Stuffing of choice (optional)(use a mix, make your own, or omit)

Preheat oven to 400 degrees. Wash chicken; wipe clean and pat dry both inside and out. Salt and pepper the cavity of the chicken. Fill with stuffing, if desired. (I roast mine un-stuffed.) Truss the chicken by tucking the wings back under the shoulders and tying the legs together with a bit of string. Place chicken in a roasting pan and rub with salt and pepper. Then spread the chicken with the softened butter. Roast for approximately 1½ hours, basting occasionally with more butter or using the pan juices. When done, juices should run clear when chicken is pierced at thickest point. Remove chicken to heated platter and let sit while making gravy from the pan juices. To make pan gravy add a little water or broth to the pan juices. Stir over moderate heat to bring up all the browned bits in the pan. Thicken with a mixture of flour and water (shaken in a jar) if desired. Simmer for a bit longer to thicken, and season with additional salt and pepper to taste.

RUSH HOUR TIP
The secret to this recipe is the roasting at high temperature (400 degrees). This makes for succulent chicken on the inside, crispy skin on the outside.

Old Fashioned Roast Chicken #2
4 to 6 servings

For a bolder taste (instead of the salt and pepper version in the previous recipe) you can rub the chicken with this Dry Spice Rub, a mixture of:

INGREDIENTS
1 teaspoon garlic powder
1 teaspoon crushed fennel seed
½ teaspoon thyme
2 teaspoons freshly ground black pepper
1 tablespoon paprika
½ teaspoon oregano
½ teaspoon salt

Mix all together to form a "dry spice rub" for the chicken. Rub chicken to coat (in place of salt and pepper) and continue as in recipe #1.

Chicken Tips

When adding chicken to a recipe that calls for a measured amount, determine how much chicken is needed by using the following standard: one pound of boneless chicken = approximately 3 cups of cubed chicken.

Covered chicken takes longer to cook in the oven than uncovered chicken.

Cutting meat across the grain will create more tender cuts of meat.

When preparing a dish with a long cooking time, try to use dark meat. Dark meat will stay moist longer than white.

Let roasted chicken rest for 10 to 15 minutes before carving to allow juices to be distributed throughout the meat.

To keep breast area of chicken from drying out during roasting, place a piece of foil over this area.

JANUARY 17

Knock. Knock…Who's there?
Gorilla…Gorilla who?
Gorilla me a cheese sandwich please.
…Well, how about a corn dog instead?
(Impress your kids with home made corn dogs!)

Home Made Corn Dogs
A KIDS IN THE KITCHEN RECIPE
8 servings

INGREDIENTS
1 cup Bisquick®
2 tablespoons yellow cornmeal
¼ teaspoon paprika
½ teaspoon dry mustard
A very small smidge of cayenne
1 egg, slightly beaten
½ cup milk
8 to 10 hotdogs
Wooden skewers, to complete the effect

Mix the Bisquick®, cornmeal, and seasonings together. Stir in the egg and milk to make a batter. Dip the hotdogs into the batter to coat. Fry the battered hotdogs in deep, hot (375 degree) oil for 2 to 3 minutes to heat the hotdogs and brown the batter. Insert wooden skewers into the ends of the 'corn dogs' for easy eating. Serve with plenty of ketchup and plenty of kids.

Knock. Knock…Who's there?
Banana…Banana who?
Knock. Knock…Who's there?
Banana…Banana who?
Knock. Knock…Who's there?
Banana…Banana who?
Knock. Knock…Who's there?
Orange …Orange who?
Orange you glad I didn't say banana!

JANUARY 18

Grandma Wendy's Sautéed Bananas as a Vegetable
Use 1 banana per serving

Okay—okay—enough of the banana jokes—here's the real deal...
Tired of serving the same old veggie? Surprise your family (especially your children) with this side dish!

Variation # 1
Firm, under ripe bananas (nice and yellow, no brown spots)
Butter
Salt and pepper

Peel bananas and leave whole. Sauté in butter until golden brown on all sides, gently turning with a spatula. Bananas should be softened and tender when done, but still hold their shape. Very lightly season with salt and pepper. Serve warm in place of a vegetable. Make at least 1 banana per person.

Grandma Says Make that Vegetable into Dessert
Tired of serving the same old dessert? Surprise your family with this sophisticated treat!

Variation # 2
Firm, underipe bananas (nice and yellow, no brown spots)
Butter
Brown sugar
Sour cream

Sprinkle with 2 or 3 tablespoons of dark brown sugar as you are sautéing the bananas. Omit salt and pepper. Sauté until bananas are well glazed, but again don't overcook. You want the bananas to still hold their shape and be just warmed through and glazed. Serve warm. Can garnish with a dollop of sour cream, if desired.

> **Bananas:** Bananas are the most popular fruit in America. Americans eat 33 pounds of bananas per person a year! That equals about one banana every three days for each person in the U.S. Keep it up...they are rich in vitamin C, fiber, and potassium. Source: Dole

JANUARY 19

Joan's Chicken Parisian
6 servings

INGREDIENTS
6 medium chicken breasts
Salt and pepper
Paprika
½ cup dry white wine or vermouth or broth
1 (10.5 ounce) can condensed cream of mushroom soup
1 (4 ounce) can sliced mushrooms, drained
1 cup dairy sour cream, mixed with
¼ cup flour (be sure to see Cook's Note that follows)

Sprinkle chicken breasts lightly with salt, pepper, and paprika. Place into slow cooker crockery-style pot. Mix together the white wine, soup, mushrooms, and the flour-thickened sour cream. Pour over chicken breasts in the pot. Sprinkle with additional paprika. Cover with lid and cook on low setting 6 to 8 hours. Serve chicken and sauce over rice or noodles.

Cook's Note: If you elect to shorten cooking time and cook this dish on high setting, for 2 ½ to 3½ hours, you must add the thickened sour cream during the last 30 minutes of cooking, to minimize the chances of your sauce separating! The flour also helps to keep the sour cream from "breaking."

Setting A Table "Parisian" Table
Get out the linen napkins and have your kids set the table. Fold the napkins into fancy folds and place in the center of each plate. (There are even books on napkin folding! Check out your local library, or bargain bin at your local book store.) Or flare-out the napkins and place in long stemmed glasses. Put a pitcher of ice water, flavored with lemon slices, on the table to accompany your dinner. Kids love to drink out of "special glasses" and you'll add to your daily water quotient as well! Everyone will feel like they're in Paris ... with their long stemmed glasses and linen napkins.

JANUARY 20

Blueberry Cinnamon Muffins
12 to 16 Muffins

INGREDIENTS
¾ cup unbleached all-purpose flour
¾ cup whole-wheat flour
¾ cup natural sugar
1 teaspoon cinnamon
¼ teaspoon baking soda
3 tablespoons melted butter
1 large egg, beaten
1 cup plain yogurt
2 cups blueberries

Preheat oven to 400 degrees. Grease muffin tins. In a large bowl, mix all dry ingredients. Stir in butter, egg, and yogurt. Add blueberries. Fill muffin tins 2/3 full. Bake for 15 to 20 minutes.

RUSH HOUR TIPS for Muffin Success
1. Always preheat your oven and bake on the middle rack for even baking.
2. Always grease or non-stick spray your muffin tins for easy removal of the muffins. Or, as I prefer, use the traditional paper baking cups to line your muffin tins.
3. For optimum baking fill the muffin cups ¾ full—or if you want very large, puffy muffins fill the wells just to the top. If you do this, make sure you grease the top of the muffin tin as well.
4. For tender muffins, always sparingly blend your ingredients—stirring just until blended (batter may still be lumpy). Over working your batter will make for tough muffins.

Bonus Muffins for Breakfast
Make a double batch of muffins and freeze half. (Baked breads and muffins keep well in the freezer for about two months.) Cool the muffins completely before freezing and freeze in airtight-plastic containers or airtight- plastic bags. Label and date. When taking muffins directly from the freezer for re-heating, unwrap and heat in 350-degree oven for 10 to15 minutes. How luxurious to have homemade muffins on hand for an impromptu addition to a meal—especially at breakfast time.

JANUARY 21
Mix-It-Up Meatloaf
6 to 8 servings

Meatloaf is one of those wonderful recipes with which you can mix-up a variety of ingredients and spices to vary the flavor and texture of the loaf. Exact measurements can fall by the wayside. Be creative: try adding a handful of chopped raisins, or chopped green olives, or melt cheese over the top, instead of the usual ketchup or chili sauce. Try mixing in a packet of Taco Seasoning Mix in place of the salt, pepper and other spices. Use cubed rye bread instead of white bread and add a little oregano and dill to the recipe. Some recipes even mix in a little applesauce instead of milk! Sneak in a tablespoon of ground flax seed for your family's health.

INGREDIENTS
1½ pounds lean ground beef
½ pound ground pork (or use all beef)
1 medium onion, diced
2 to 4 garlic cloves, mashed and minced, to taste
½ cup of chili sauce
1 tablespoon prepared horseradish
Salt and pepper to taste
Dash of Worcestershire
2 to 3 slices of day old bread, cubed or crumbed (or ½ cup dry bread crumbs)
1 extra-large egg (or use 2 small eggs),
½ cup milk (optional)
¼ cup additional chili sauce for the top of the meat loaf.

Preheat oven to 350 degrees. Lightly toss all ingredients together (accept for the additional ¼ cup chili sauce) until well blended, but don't overwork the blending. Then lightly form the loaf into a non-stick sprayed baking dish or loaf pan. Bake in center of oven for approximately 1 hour and 15 minutes, glazing the top of the loaf with the additional ¼ cup chili sauce for the last 15 minutes of baking.

RUSH HOUR TIPS

If you wish to cut down cooking time, divide meat mixture into 2 smaller loaves and bake in 2 loaf pans for approximately 50 minutes.

For a milder meatloaf, omit the horseradish and Worcestershire, and replace the chili sauce with ketchup. Leave the top plain and serve with ketchup on the side.

When mixing your meatloaf do not overwork mixture. You want the meat loaf to stay light and tender, not dense and tough.

A Thought for Today

"Good, better, best, may you never rest, until your good is better, and your better best." ~Anonymous

Homemade Television Dinners

Why not double this recipe and make homemade "TV Dinners" instead of the unhealthy counterparts so often purchased in stores? Pick up some microwave safe plastic containers, or the small disposable foil pans available at the grocery store (purchase a small size that will work for one serving). Store mini-meatloves, wrap well with foil and make sure to mark the date in permanent marker. To make it easy on family members, write the instructions for reheating on the bottom of the package. These meatloafs will keep for 3 months. (They also make a great mini-meal to take to work and reheat in the microwave.)

JANUARY 22

The Nanny's Texas Tacos
4 to 6 servings

This recipe is tall on authentic flavor due to the Nanny's "Texas touch." The secret to its great flavor is the cooking of the green peppers and onions separately with additional seasoning! "Sometimes the simplest touch makes all the difference in a dish!"—Just like the Nanny's "Texas touch" has been such a blessing to our family! I cannot imagine our lives without "our" Nanny!

INGREDIENTS
2 pounds lean ground beef
1 packet of Taco Seasoning Mix
Green peppers, diced or sliced
Onions, diced or sliced
A 2nd packet of Taco Seasoning Mix
Warmed soft flour tortillas or crispy taco shells, or a package of each
Jarred hot pepper slices, served on the side
Grated cheeses, served on the side
Chopped tomato, served on the side
Chopped onion, served on the side
Shredded lettuce, served on the side
Low-fat sour cream and your favorite splash of hot sauce for garnish

In a large pan with a little oil, sauté the ground beef over medium-high heat until browned. While sautéing the meat, mix in the first packet of Taco Seasonings and continue to cook a bit to blend flavors. When done set aside in a serving bowl to keep warm. In a second pan, with a little oil, sauté the onion and green peppers with additional seasoning from the 2nd packet of seasoning-mix (use about half the packet, or to taste).

When this mixture is done, set aside in another bowl and keep warm. (Everything may be held in a 200-degree oven, including your warmed tortillas or taco shells.) When ready to serve, put everything out in separate dishes. Let each person "build their own" according to taste.

Beef Tips

When selecting ground beef, make sure it's fresh and lean, and that the packaging has not been torn, damaged or is leaking ... and of course always check the date on the package. (The meat should not be discolored or breaking down in texture.) Have the checkout girl bag your meat in a separate plastic bag, to avoid contact with other groceries. If you are using frozen ground beef for your recipe make sure you give it adequate time in the refrigerator to thaw (about 12 hours or overnight for a 1-pound package). Make sure to prevent raw meat-juice spills in your refrigerator as well, to avoid contamination with other foods. This goes for all raw meats and poultry too. Be sure to clean up any spills right away.

Remember that frozen beef should never be defrosted at room temperature. Harmful bacteria may grow rapidly under such conditions. To thaw any meat, place it in the refrigerator. Keep in mind that larger cuts will need significant time to defrost. Store meat on a low shelf on a wide platter to catch any juices while thawing.

Weekly Challenge

POST-HOLIDAY RESOLUTIONS

If you are like me, the holidays snuck up ever so quickly last year! You would think after 30 Christmases I would remember to prepare in advance—however, each year Christmas seems to pop out of nowhere and is over before I know it. I find myself scrambling for extra time to make that extra meal I want to donate; the volunteer work I'd like to do; and the homemade gift calendars with the family photos where I only make it to March...you know the drill!

So this year, I have decided to sit down right now after the Holidays and list out the major things I want to accomplish for next Christmas! Here are a few:

1. Complete a family calendar. Find a family-significant photo for each month, scan them in or take them to the local office store for copying. Many copy centers now offer calendar making services. The only service called Snapfish (www.snapfish.com) also offers an easy calendar making method.

2. Frame some favorite family photos for my closest family members and friends.

3. Finish a family video tape that I have been working on for year after year after year!

I then resolved that all of my goals will be accomplished by October—instead of trying to start them December 1 and finish in time. What goals do you want to set for your next holiday season? Go ahead and design them now, scheduling them in on your calendar with plenty of time to spare. Make your Holiday-giving last the whole year 'round by working on these special gifts a few hours each month.

Include your kids in the projects too. Grandparents will love handmade gifts from little hands—a framed piece of artwork, a handwritten story, or a replicated recipe—the more sentimental the better!

JANUARY 23

Samantha's Fancy Rainbow Jell-O ® Mold
A KIDS IN THE KITCHEN RECIPE

Kids love to help in the kitchen and my daughter has concocted her favorite combination of jell-O ® mold. Let your kids show their creativity by "inventing" a dessert or dish of their own. They will serve it with such pride and bask in your compliments.

INGREDIENTS
Berry blue
Lime green
Lemon yellow
Orange flavor
Strawberry red
A clear glass bowl (if you have one)

Make each jell-O® according to instructions, in order given. Let the first jell-O set up in the bowl, before you start the next. When you are finished you will have a "rainbow" arrangement of jell-O® layers. When serving, make sure you scoop into all the layers for best effect. You can optionally garnish with whipped topping and rainbow sprinkles.

Mandarin Mold
ANOTHER KID FRIENDLY RECIPE

INGREDIENTS
Orange flavored gelatin
Canned Mandarin orange sections, with juice reserved

Make your gelatin according to package instructions—only substitute the reserved canned Mandarin juices for an equal portion of the water called for on the gelatin box. Fold in the mandarin orange sections and let set in refrigerator till molded, firm, and jiggly.

JANUARY 24

The Rush Hour Cook's Quick-to-Mix,
Long-to-Cook Italian Roast

8 servings

INGREDIENTS
1 (3 pound) beef round roast
1 onion, sliced
2 garlic cloves, minced
½ teaspoon salt
½ teaspoon pepper
1 (8 ounce) can tomato sauce
1 package Italian salad dressing mix
Kaiser rolls at serving time

Place sliced onion in bottom of slow cooker crockery-style pot. Add roast. Top with remaining ingredients. Cover with lid and cook on high setting for 5 hours, or until meat is fork tender. Slice or shred and serve on Kaiser Rolls.

RUSH HOUR TIP
Garlic may be easily peeled by removing individual cloves from the head and smashing under the broad side of the blade of a chef's knife. The garlic will 'smoosh' right out of the peel, as you put pressure on the side of the blade with the heel of your hand.

A Mini-Spa Retreat

As we near the end of January, it's the perfect time to take a break! Log onto www.spaindex.com to find a collection of wonderful recipes for home spa treatments. You will feel pampered and renewed with simple ingredients and recipes you can make at home!

JANUARY 25

Judy Brown's Indiana Salad
6 servings

Lose one of your beaters? Ready to throw out your old hand mixer and buy a new one? Never fear—Chef Judy from Midland, Michigan is here with a very unusual recipe that calls for mixing with one beater!

INGREDIENTS
½ cup milk
½ cup sugar
8 ounces cream cheese, softened
9 ounces Cool Whip®
1 can crushed pineapple, drained really, really dry, overnight and then
   squeeze and squeeze and squeeze to get out all juice

Mix milk and sugar and stir until dissolved. Add cream cheese and whip with only 1 beater. Then stir in well-drained pineapple and lastly, Cool Whip®. Voila! Indiana salad … made right in Judy Brown's kitchen in Midland, Michigan. (Sometime we'll have to ask Judy why her recipe is called Indiana salad, when she lives in Michigan.)

A Thought for Today
"Ask yourself… what do I truly want to do this year
Dig for your answer. Then do it."
~ Brook Noel

JANUARY 26
The Perfect Party Pitas...and more
48 pieces

With the Superbowl just around the corner, today we will highlight some fun treats to serve during the game. If you aren't a football fiend, never fear—throw an "After Holiday Get-Together" instead. Have a few friends over and recount your favorite moments of the past year and your hopes for the upcoming year. This Party Pita recipe offers a tasty and healthier alternative to the traditional chip combinations usually offered.

INGREDIENTS
6 pita bread pockets
¼ cup olive oil
½ teaspoon ground black pepper
½ teaspoon garlic salt
¼ teaspoon dried basil

Preheat oven to 400 degrees. Slice each pita bread into 8 triangles and place pita slices on a cookie sheet. Combine the olive oil and spices in a small bowl and brush mixture over each chip. Bake for 5 to 7 minutes, or until crispy. Serve plain or for an extra added treat serve with a carton of your favorite commercially made Hummus Dip.

RUSH HOUR TIP
Hummus Dip is a great alternative to all those salsas and cheese dips we've been eating over the holidays. Made with chickpeas, sesame seeds, and olive oil, pre-made, deli-style Hummus comes in a variety of flavors such as garlic, roasted pepper, basil, etc., and is wonderful served with warm pita bread or pita chips. So surprise your guests with this out-of-the-ordinary Mediterranean dip the next time you want to serve a munchie. Hummus (already made) can readily be found in the deli or cheese section of your favorite market.

PARTY PLEASERS GALORE!
Check out the following dates for additional party faves: March 28, October 11 through 13.

JANUARY 27
Healthy Mashed Sweet Potatoes
6 servings

Often overlooked, we think of serving sweet potatoes just for the Holidays, when all through the year sweet potatoes can make a nice alternative to our ever-popular, every-day, mashed-potato side-dish. Mashed sweet potatoes are a wonderful companion to any grilled meats any time of the year.

INGREDIENTS
4 sweet potatoes, peeled and cut into chunks
1 ½ cups sugar-free apple sauce
1 tablespoon sugar-free maple syrup
½ teaspoon ground cinnamon
¼ teaspoon ground nutmeg

Boil sweet potatoes in water until tender. Drain and mash them with a large fork, potato masher, or electric mixer until smooth. Blend in remaining ingredients. Serve as a tasty alternative to mashed potatoes.

RUSH HOUR AT HOME ALONE DINNER
If you are cooking for yourself some evening and want an easy, vegetarian single dinner … just microwave a large sweet potato until tender. (Cooking times will very due to size of potato and power of microwave.) Pierce the skin of the potato with a fork several times before placing in microwave. Cook on high approximately 4 to 8 minutes. When potato is cooked and tender, "plump" it open and add a little butter along with salt and freshly cracked pepper. Then pop open one of those "600-million diet cokes consumed daily" (see trivia below) and serve in a fancy glass over ice cubes. Add a mixed green salad to complete your light and tasty dinner.

RUSH HOUR TRIVIA
Q: How many Coca-Colas® will be consumed worldwide during the next hour?

(a) 17-million
(b) 27-million
(c) 37-million

A: About 27-million. That's over 600-million per day!

JANUARY 28
Peppered Sirloin Steak
4 to 6 servings

This recipe makes enough marinade for approximately 2 pounds of meat. For serving size estimate ¼ to ½ pound steak per person.

INGREDIENTS
½ cup olive oil
¼ cup soy sauce
1 teaspoon freshly cracked black pepper, or to taste (Freshly crushing black peppercorns will give this the best flavor! The more you use, the zestier your recipe.)
½ teaspoon garlic salt
1 large (approximately 2 pound) sirloin steak, or use individual strip steaks (1 per person)

Combine all ingredients except steak into a large Zip-loc®-style plastic bag. Shake bag to mix ingredients well. Add steak and seal bag. Place in refrigerator for at least 30 minutes, but can marinate up to overnight. Remove steak from marinade and discard the marinade. Preheat broiler. Broil large steak approximately 8 to 10 minutes per side, or to desired doneness. Broil individual steaks to everyone's liking, approximately 5 to 8 minutes per side, again depending on thickness.

RUSH HOUR VARIATION
For a tasty variation add a tablespoon of Dijon style mustard to the marinade.

RUSH HOUR TIPS
Looking to prolong the life of your garlic? Store the garlic bulbs at room temperature instead of in the refrigerator.

When determining amounts of meat needed for a recipe, I usually plan at least ¼ pound per person or serving.

JANUARY 29
A Different Kind of Spaghetti
A KID-FRIENDLY RECIPE
4 to 6 family-style servings

What kid doesn't love spaghetti? Here's a tomato-less (sort-of-carbonara-style) version just right for all tastes.

INGREDIENTS
1 (16 ounce) package spaghetti noodles
½ pound bacon, cooked and crumbled
½ pound ham, cooked and cubed
2 cloves garlic, minced
5 tablespoons olive oil
Salt and pepper to taste
Grated Parmesan cheese, to pass at time of serving

Prepare spaghetti according to package directions. Meanwhile combine remaining ingredients, except for Parmesan cheese, salt, and pepper. Pour mixture over the cooked and drained spaghetti and toss to combine. Serve immediately. Serve the Parmesan cheese, salt, and pepper on the side and let each person flavor and season to their liking.

RUSH HOUR WISDOM
When all else fails this is a fool-proof, kid friendly dinner for the finickiest of eaters!

A Thought for Today
"The best of miracles are often wrapped in
the smallest packages of day to day living."
~ Wendy Louise

Weekly Challenge

RESOLUTION REFRESHER

How have you been doing with your New Year Resolutions? If you are anything like me you may be starting to waiver or teeter. Why not start a club to keep you on track? Joining forces with others who have similar goals can be a great way to stay motivated when our willpower runs low. If you don't have local friends with similar goals, consider starting an online goal group. You can easily set up a free e-mail group with chat and message board through Yahoo®... just go to www.yahoogroups.com I recently started a book group with six friends and we are posting our questions and comments through Yahoo®.

Another motivational-booster is to align your goal with a cause. If you are trying to walk several times a week, why not aim to walk in this year's Avon Walks for a Cure. Located throughout the country, these walks help raise money for breast-cancer research and awareness. You can learn more about their program at www.avonwalk.org or by calling 877 WALK AVON.

Take a moment to jot down your own personal resolutions:

_____

_____

_____

_____

_____

_____

JANUARY 30
Chili Pepper Pasta Dinner
4 servings

INGREDIENTS
2 medium onions, coarsely chopped
5 chili peppers
2 cloves garlic, minced
28 ounces plum tomatoes, Italian style
15 ounces prepared chili, either beef or turkey-style
8 ounces linguini or spaghetti

For sauce place onions and peppers into a skillet. Cover and cook over high heat until onions are transparent and pepper skins are browned on all sides. Remove peppers; peel and discard skin and seeds; chop and return to pan. Stir in tomatoes and chili. Cook over medium heat, stirring occasionally, 15 to 20 minutes. Meanwhile, cook pasta according to package directions, drain and reserve. Serve sauce over pasta.

RUSH HOUR TIP
When working with chili peppers, always, always wash your hands immediately after handling the peppers, or wear gloves during handling. Never rub your eyes or mouth with out washing your hands. As a contact-lens wearer, I speak from experience on this one! I atually keep disposable plastic gloves for this purpose.

Where on earth did pasta come from?

Popular legend has it that Marco Polo introduced pasta to Italy following his exploration of the Far East in the late 13th century; however, we can trace pasta back as far as the fourth century B.C., where an Etruscan tomb showed a group of natives making what appears to be pasta. The Chinese were making a noodle-like food as early as 3000 B.C. And Greek mythology suggests that the Greek God Vulcan invented a device that made strings of dough (the first spaghetti!).
Source: www.ilovapasta.org

JANUARY 31
Beef Bake
6 servings

INGREDIENTS
1 pound ground beef
½ cup chopped onions
½ teaspoon salt
¼ teaspoon pepper
1 to ¾ cups water
1 cup barbecue sauce
2 cups Minute Rice ® uncooked
1 cup shredded Cheddar cheese

Brown meat and onion in large skillet; drain. Add water and barbecue sauce to skillet. Bring to boil. Stir in rice; cover. Cook on low heat for 5 minutes. Sprinkle with cheese and serve.

FEBRUARY 1

The Rush Hour Cook's Dijon Potatoes

8 servings

INGREDIENTS
8 baking potatoes, peeled and sliced thin
5 tablespoons flour
2 ½ cups milk
½ to ¾ cup Dijon-style mustard, or to taste
5 tablespoons butter
1 cup shredded Swiss cheese
Salt and white pepper to taste, toward end of cooking

In a sauce pan make a blended roux of the butter and flour, cooking for a few minutes. Slowly add the milk, stirring all the while. Cook gently until sauce thickens. Add in the mustard. Set aside. Place the sliced potatoes into a greased slow cooker crockery-style pot. Pour the sauce over the potatoes and stir to mix. Cover with lid and cook on high setting for 1 hour, then reduce to low setting for 4 to 6 hours more, or until potatoes are tender. At beginning of last hour of cooking adjust seasoning with salt and white pepper if necessary. Then sprinkle the shredded Swiss cheese on the top, re-cover, and continue to cook for that last hour.

A Thought for Today

"Too few people understand a really good sandwich."
~James Beard, noted chef

For the next several days I would like to share some of my favorite sandwich recipes with you. Sometimes going back to such a simple thing as a sandwich recipe can bring new and innovative combinations to your cooking, or kick start a new idea for using-up leftovers. This week why don't you search your own recipe collections for a forgotten or overlooked sandwich recipe or two; add a bowl of soup or a favorite gelatin mold, and you have an easy and tasty dinner made from true comfort food.

FEBRUARY 2

Tuna Melt Sandwiches

6 servings

My husband loves tuna-fish salad sandwiches so this recipe is for him. Serve these sandwiches along with a bowl of tomato soup and you will have a quick and warming dinner. Add a fruit salad for a complete meal.

INGREDIENTS
2 (6.5 ounce) cans of water packed tuna, drained
¼ cup pickle relish
1 to 2 ribs of celery, de-veined and chopped
1 tablespoon lemon juice
Salt and pepper to taste
½ cup low fat mayonnaise
6 American cheese slices
2 toasted bread slices, per sandwich

Preheat oven to 350 degrees. Mix first six ingredients together to make your tuna filling. Toast the bread slices. Place the bottom slices of toast on a baking sheet, spread with tuna filling and then top with a slice of cheese. Bake for 5 to 10 minutes until the cheese melts and is warm and bubbly. Top with a second piece of toast and serve. (Or you may serve the sandwich "open-faced" if you prefer—not topping it with the second piece of toast.)

RUSH HOUR VARIATIONS
In place of bread slices, toast English muffins, pita bread, or thick French bread slices. In place of (or added to) the celery, use a chopped tart apple in the filling and sharp Cheddar cheese for your cheese choice. Instead of the American cheese slices substitute Swiss, Colby, Mozzarella, or Provolone!

It has been said that the sandwich was "invented" in 1762 by John Montague, The Earl of Sandwich. During a card game, from which he didn't want to be interrupted, he asked that his meat and cheese be layered between two hunks of bread—creating a meal that could be picked up with one hand, while still playing cards with the other! The idea caught on and this newly invented "portable-style" meal became all the rage.

FEBRUARY 3
Sara's Ten Layer Taco Wraps
10 servings

Sandwiches can come in all sizes and combinations and lately the "wrap" has been added to this category. The following recipe would be great for a party and you could let each person build their own.

INGREDIENTS
1 (1 ounce) packet taco seasoning mix
1 (16 ounce) can refried beans
1 (8 ounce) package cream cheese, softened (I use low fat)
1 (16 ounce) container sour cream (I use low fat)
1 (16 ounce) jar salsa (you choose the heat)
1 large tomato, chopped
1 green or yellow bell pepper, chopped
1 Spanish red onion, chopped
Shredded iceberg lettuce or individual leaves of leaf lettuce
1 (6 ounce) can sliced black olives, drained
2 cups shredded Cheddar cheese
Jarred hot chili-pepper slices, drained
10 soft tortillas of choice (have a variety on hand if you are serving for a party)

Start with your favorite soft tortilla (don't hesitate to use some of the new flavors, like sun dried tomato) and build your wrap in the following order. First blend the refried beans with the taco seasoning mix and spread a layer of this mixture on the tortilla. Then mix the sour cream and softened cream cheese together, and spread some over the refried beans. Continue building your layers, adding ingredients in the order listed. Roll it up and it's ready to eat.

RUSH HOUR VARIATION
For those who don't like refried beans or vegetarian-style sandwiches, you could also offer, or substitute, a mix of sautéed ground beef and taco seasoning mix for your first layer.

Did You Know?
Did you know that in Spansih, the word "taco" is a generic word similar to how we use sandwich?

FEBRUARY 4
The Monte Cristo Sandwich

INGREDIENTS
2 slices of bread per sandwich
Sliced, cooked turkey (from the deli)
1 generous slice Swiss cheese per sandwich (I like Swiss lace-style Swiss
   cheese from the deli)
Thinly sliced, lean ham (from the deli)
1 egg, beaten
Jellied cranberry sauce, at serving time

Preheat a non-stick frying pan with a little butter or non-stick cooking spray over medium heat. Gently dip one side of the first bread slice in the egg and arrange egg-side down in the pan. Quickly build your sandwich, laying on the turkey, then the cheese, then the ham. Dip the second slice of bread into the beaten egg and place on top of the sandwich, egg side out. Gently sauté the sandwich, turning once until both sides are browned to your liking, the sandwich is warmed through, and the cheese is melting. Serve immediately. Serve jellied cranberry sauce on the side, as a traditional garnish for this sandwich.

The History of Sliced Bread

Have you ever heard the saying "—the best thing since sliced bread?" Well, pre-sliced bread wasn't even invented until 1912 and then wasn't widely used until 1928, when Otto Rohwedder finally perfected his bread-slicer to also wrap the loaf once sliced, thus keeping the bread fresh and soft. Although the modern day pop-up toaster was invented around 1919 by one Charles Strite, it wasn't commonl used until the Wonder Bread Company popularized pre-sliced bread around 1930. Suddenly the sandwich knew no boundaries and a new convenience food was born...sliced, packaged, anc ready for sandwich making.

FEBRUARY 5
The Whitehall Sandwich
Served with Mornay Sauce

This recipe is the ultimate in sandwiches—a dinner in itself. Served "open face" with a side of steamed broccoli, The Whitehall Sandwich, with its luscious sauce, is good enough for a formal lunch or dinner—truly "the best thing since sliced bread…" This is as close as I have come to replicating the sandwich I remember enjoying at the CAA in Chicago as a young girl. *Wendy Louise*

INGREDIENTS
2 slices buttered toast per sandwich
Thinly sliced lean ham
Thinly sliced Swiss lace cheese
Sautéed mushrooms, optional (or used canned and drained)
A recipe of Mornay Sauce (don't let the name scare you—just a basic
    white sauce with Parmesan cheese added, see accompanying recipe
    that follows)
Grated Parmesan for garnish

On a broiler safe platter, individual casserole dish, or baking ramekin, arrange two pieces of buttered toast side by side per sandwich. Top with thinly sliced ham, thinly sliced cheese, and sautéed mushrooms. Drizzle Mornay Sauce over sandwich to cover. Sprinkle with grated Parmesan. Broil or bake just long enough to heat thoroughly, and bubble and brown the sauce-covered top and edges. Gently remove the sandwich to a warm plate using a wide spatula, or serve as is if using individual ramekins. Serve warm with a side of steamed broccoli or a contrasting fruit salad.

Mornay Sauce
yield 1 cup

INGREDIENTS
2 to 3 tablespoons butter
1 cup (give or take) of milk, to reach desired thickness
1/4 teaspoon salt
1/4 cup Parmesan cheese
A pinch of nutmeg (optional)

In saucepan, over low heat, melt butter and whisk in flour, making what is called a "roux." Cook the roux for a minute or two just until it starts to turn golden.

Continue to cook and stir over low heat while whisking in milk, stirring until sauce arrives at consistency you desire. You can thin or thicken sauce simply by adjusting amount of milk used. Voila! In a matter of minutes you have just made a basic white sauce, or as they say in France, a Béchamel Sauce. To this sauce, add ¼ cup Parmesan cheese and a pinch of nutmeg, blending until smooth. You now have what is called Mornay Sauce, in this case ready to use in your Whitehall Sandwich Recipe.

RUSH HOUR WISDOM

Now that you know how to make a Basic White Sauce (or as the French call it, Béchamel Sauce), here are some suggestions for converting that basic sauce to fit other dishes. So the next time you are thinking of opening a can of cream soup to make a sauce, think again

To one cup of homemade basic white sauce add:
  For Mornay Sauce: ¼ cup Parmesan and a pinch of nutmeg.
  For Mustard Sauce: 1 tablespoon of Dijon mustard.
  For Cheese Sauce: Gently blend in ½ cup shredded Cheddar cheese.
  For Curry Sauce: ½ teaspoon curry powder and a pinch of ginger.
  For Veloute Sauce: Substitute chicken broth in place of the milk.

According to the <u>Washington Post</u>, the USA sandwich business was worth $105 billion US in sales in 2003, with a 6% annual growth.

Weekly Challenge

SOLVING THE CLUB CARD BLUES

The other day I opened my purse to discover 300 discount cards (and I'm probably not exaggerating) to different stores. Between all my "earn 500 points reward cards" and my "buy 10 coffees, get one free cards" it seemed I would need to carry an extra purse! To stay organized and maximize savings, I purchased an index card box with A-Z letter dividers and filed each card under the applicable store name. I keep this box on the hall table by my keys so I can grab the cards I will be using for that day's errands. Then I return them back into the file, along with my keys when I come home.

Many stores allow you to just give your number, instead of actually scanning your card. For these stores, consider storing your club numbers in a small address book that will easily fit in your purse, rather than stuffing it full of cards … only to frantically at the counter for the needed card.

Savings Online

Speaking of club cards and savings, you might want to check out Coupon Chief at www.couponchief.com They offer a great variety of savings opportunities!

A Thought for Today
KEEPING IN TOUCH
"In cooking, as in all the arts,
simplicity is the sign of perfection."
~Curnonsky

And what could be more simple—or more perfect—than a jelly sandwich—on soft, crust-less white bread! ... especially if you are eight years old!

FEBRUARY 6

A KIDS IN THE KITCHEN RECIPE
Samantha's Perfectly Precious
Bread and Butter-Butter "Tea Sandwiches"

INGREDIENTS
2 slices of soft white bread, crusts removed, per serving
Just the right amount of softened butter
Just the right amount of Grape Jelly
And/or sometimes just the right amount of peanut butter

Assemble sandwich as desired and then cut into quarters, or "tea size" sandwiches. (Sometimes whole wheat bread is acceptable, since the crusts have been removed—but Wonder® or Bunny® bread is preferable.) Serve with a tall glass of cold milk (even though they are called tea sandwiches...)

RUSH HOUR VARIATIONS
Have your child substitute softened cream cheese in place of the butter and/or peanut butter. The simple combination of cream cheese and fruit jelly or jam is delicious!

Another combo ... cream cheese with crushed (drained) pineapple.

Or how about this combo ... peanut butter and thinly sliced banana.

For fun get out the cookie cutters and cut the crust-less sandwiches into a variety of mini-shapes to make the sandwiches even more special.

FEBRUARY 7
Chili Tortillas
Makes 6 tortillas (with a good amount of filling)

INGREDIENTS

1 (28 ounce) can Chili or 1½ cups homemade chili—my definite
  preference. (I love to make HUGE batches of chili and freeze a bunch
  for future use and this recipe as well.)
½ cup of water
1 cup Minute Rice®
6 flour tortillas
Cheddar cheese, shredded, for garnish
Tomatoes, chopped, for garnish
Green onions or white onions, sliced or diced, for garnish
Sour Cream, at serving time
Guacamole, at serving time

Bring chili and water to a boil in a large saucepan. Stir in Minute Rice®, cover
and cook on low heat for 5 minutes. Spoon chili mixture into tortillas and wrap.
Serve warm with toppings of choice.

Rice is Nice!
You can make rice in a flash with one dish and a microwave. Simply
place 1 cup of rice with 2 cups of hot water. Cook on high for about
9-10 minutes. For brown rice, use the same ratio but cook for 15-
20 minutes. To add more taste, use a tablespoon or two of bouillon
granules or add ½ cup of frozen peas after cooking, cover and let
peas warm for 5 minutes. Cubed ham is another quick and easy
addition! When I was first married, I used to always use chicken
broth instead of water to cook instant rice. Then add peas, ham,
and miscellaneous. While my husband eventually told me this was
getting old, he played along for a while and it remains a common
side dish.

FEBRUARY 8

Manly Man Chili Fries
6 servings

This recipe ranked very high on my brother's scale of comfort foods—whenever he got together with the guys, and a sporting event was involved, out came the chili fries.

INGREDIENTS
1 package frozen French fries (32 ounce bag would cover 6 servings)
   baked in the oven according to package instructions
Homemade chili (or your favorite jarred brand), heated through
Shredded Cheddar cheese (or a jarred Taco Cheese Sauce-Dip, for those
   who like it spicy)

Cook fries according to package directions. While warm, arrange in serving bowls and top with a generous portion of warm homemade chili. Top off with some shredded Cheddar cheese (or a cheesy-sauce/or dip of your choice). Pop each bowl in the microwave, or back into the oven, just long enough to melt the cheese on top. Serve immediately.

RUSH HOUR KITCHEN TIPS
Your dishwasher got the blues? ...Try using plain, old white vinegar in your dishwasher's rinse compartment instead of an expensive rinse solution for a nice clean, sparkling dish run!

I also throw my kitchen-scrub-brush in the dishwasher from time to time, just to keep it sanitized and prolong its scrubbing life. Annnnd don't forget your hand-held can opener once in a while…it needs a scrubbing too!

FEBRUARY 9

Patty Morell's Cherry Dessert
6 to 8 servings

Red and sweet and easy, this makes a perfect dessert to be included in our selection of sweet temptations as we approach Valentine's Day.

INGREDIENTS
2 cans cherry pie filling
1 standard yellow layer cake mix
1/3 cup melted butter
Vanilla ice-cream or whipped topping, as serving time

Spread the 2 cans of pie filling evenly in the bottom of a lightly, non-stick sprayed 13 X 9-inch baking pan. Sprinkle on 1 standard cake mix, straight out of the box. Drizzle the melted butter over the cake mix. Bake at 350 degrees for 45 minutes. Serve the cherry dessert warm, topped with vanilla ice cream or whipped cream.

Add Some Spice to Your Life!
More for fun than a Freudian study, here are what some popular herbs represent:

Basil	Love (or hate)
Bay	Victory
Lavender	Acknowledgement
Fennel	Praise
Caraway	Retention
Marjoram	Happiness
Mint	Wisdom
Rosemary	Remembrance
Sage	Long Life
Thyme	Bravery

So the next time you are feeling under the weather, stock up on the marjoram!

FEBRUARY 10

Ham Slice Dinner
4 servings

INGREDIENTS

1 (¾ to 1-inch thick) fully-cooked ham slice
Non-stick spray or a bit of fat from the trimmed ham
Serve with Sweet Surprise Rice (see recipe that follows)

To prepare ham for cooking trim off excess fat and cut slits around the outside edge of the ham slice (this will help prevent the edges from curling as you cook it). Spray the bottom of a non-stick frying pan with a little cooking spray (or instead, rub the pan with a small piece of the trimmed fat). Gently brown the ham slice about 3 to 5 minutes on each side, until lightly browned and heated through. (Remember the ham is already cooked, so you just want to heat it.) Serve with Sweet Surprise Rice as your side dish.

RUSH HOUR VARIATION
For extra flavor you can spread a little Dijon-style mustard and brown sugar on the ham while heating it, to form a glaze.

Sweet Surprise Rice
4 servings

INGREDIENTS

White or brown rice (use your favorite instant-style rice), use enough for 4
  servings
Mixed-dried fruit (like a trail-mix variety that is all fruit, coconut and nuts,
  but no candy)

Boil up the rice according to package instructions. Meanwhile chop the dried-fruit mix into small, dice-size pieces. When the rice is done, mix the fruit (about ½ cup) into the hot-cooked rice. Cover tightly, remove from heat, and let the fruit steam in the rice for a few minutes to soften. The fruit will soften just enough, yet remain a little chewy. Serve the sweet rice as a contrast with the salty ham.

FEBRUARY 11
Ron's Pudding Cake
A KID-FRIENDLY RECIPE
8 servings

This cake needs to chill and set for at least 6 hours before serving to your sweetie.

INGREDIENTS
1 yellow layer cake, boxed mix
1 small box jell-O ®, (use a red flavor, such as cherry or strawberry for Valentine's Day), prepared according to package instructions
Whipped cream or ready-made whipped topping

Bake the cake, following package instructions and using a 13 X 9–inch baking pan. When the cake has cooled pierce the cake randomly with tines of a fork. Pour on Jell-O ® (that has been prepared according to its package instructions). Pour the gelatin around and into the holes in the cake. Let the dessert chill and set at least 6 hours in the refrigerator before serving. Top with whipped cream or whipped topping

A Thought for Today
KEEPING IN TOUCH
"True friends are those who really know you but love you anyway."
~Edna Buchanan

Today would be a great time to review correspondence with a few of your true-blue friends. While you're at it dig out your Christmas-card list and send off a few Valentines to some distant friends. They'll be both delightfully surprised and so pleased to get a note from you—especially if they didn't hear from you over the Holidays.

FEBRUARY 12

Judy Brown's Strawberry Pizza
A KIDS IN THE KITCHEN RECIPE

Whether down in the Florida Keys, or back up north in Midland Michigan, this is a favorite dessert in the Brown's Household.

INGREDIENTS
1 cup flour
¼ cup sugar
1 stick margarine
1 can Eagle brand® milk
1 (8 ounce) package cream cheese
1/3 cup lemon juice
1 quart fresh strawberries
4 tablespoons cornstarch
Whipped topping (optional)

Mix flour, sugar, and margarine together and spread on pizza pan or in a 9 X 13 –inch pan. Bake 10 to 12 minutes at 350 degrees. Set aside and let cool. Meanwhile mix milk, cream cheese, and lemon juice together. Spread on cooled "crust." In a saucepan cook the strawberries and cornstarch together until thick. Cool. Spread on top of cream cheese filling. As an optional final touch, spread a thin layer of whipped topping over entire pizza before serving. Cut into wedges as if you were serving pizza.

Click for Savings
Looking for a way to save money without clipping coupons? Try www.valuepage.com This online site allows you to enter your zip code, choose a supermarket, browse their weekly sales and specials, and then click the items you would like to save on. Print your list, hand it to the cashier and you will receive Web Bucks good for any purchase on your next visit Note: Even if you consider yourself an Internet Novice, don't be afraid of this site. I promise it is simple and assessable to even the most inexperienced. After all, this is a Rush Hour Cook™ book—I promise not to include anything that takes more time than it's worth! Visit coolsavings.com for other great savings opportunities.

Weekly Challenge

CONNECT WITH ONE ANOTHER

"No matter what you've done for yourself or for humanity, if you can't look back on having given love and attention to your own family, what have you really accomplished...?"
~Lee Iacocca, Automobile Manufacturing Executive

Taking Lee Iacocca's words to heart, let's turn this whole week into "Sweets Week." As Valentines Day approaches, let the feelings of the season sweep over you. Say "I love you" outloud, rather than just thinking it. When given the chance, be an attentive listener, putting down your magazine or turning off the TV and/or computer screen while the person is talking to you. Make time to sit down and engage in conversation (actual sentences back and forth) not grunts and nods as you, or they, dash out the door or look back over a shoulder. Make eye contact. Tell a joke. Make yourself and those around you laugh. Have fun. Be a kid again. Lighten-up! This is Valentine's Week ... a time to show our sweetest attentions. Say "I love you" outloud, again ... it's a sentence that bears repeating time and time again., for no one ever tires of hearing it!

FEBRUARY 13
Strawberry Yogurt Dip
Served with Fresh Fruit

INGREDIENTS
1 ½ cups low-fat whipped topping
1 (8 ounce) container low-fat strawberry yogurt
½ cup fresh strawberries, chopped, and sweetened with a little sugar
Assorted fresh fruit (including additional fresh strawberries, bite size
   pieces of banana, pineapple, peaches, etc.) for dipping
Wafer cookies, for dipping

Mix together first 3 ingredients and serve as a dip with assorted bite-sized fresh fruit and wafer cookies for dipping. Or, use the same ingredients to assemble as a fancy parfait dessert (see below).

The Rush Hour Cook's
Fancy Valentine Parfaits

INGREDIENTS (same as for previous recipe)

In the bottom of your prettiest stem-ware glasses place a little of the Strawberry Yogurt Dip. Layer on some freshly cut strawberries and freshly cut banana. Top with more yogurt dip. Repeat layers. Garnish with whipped topping and place each glass on a doily-lined dessert plate. Garnish the plate with fancy-style wafer cookies, to be dipped into the parfait.

RUSH HOUR TIP
When storing fresh strawberries loosen the wrapping on the package and store the berries un-washed in the refrigerator. Wash the berries just before using. Pat berries dry if leaving whole. If slicing them, sprinkle with sugar to sweeten. If the berries are very ripe at time of purchase, immediately wash and sprinkle with a little sugar before storing. Use promptly.

A Thought for Today

The first valentines were hand-crafted tokens of affection exchanged during Victorian times in England. As the trend caught on and printing methods became more sophisticated the Stationery Firm of Joseph Addenbrooke developed the commercially printed valentine card around 1830. From the 1840's through the 1860's the valentine got fancier and fancier as embossing, folding, pleating, printing, and layering techniques became increasingly elaborate. It is said that the first commercial American valentines were produced in Worcester, Massachusetts around 1847. Sought out for their beauty, charming graphics, and romantic sentiments of the era, many people enjoy collecting the older valentines yet today.

FEBRUARY 14

Valentine Heart Cake
A KIDS IN THE KITCHEN RECIPE
12 Servings

This is a fun dessert for your kids to help you with. Not only is it deliciously edible, it's a "geometry lesson" as well.

INGREDIENTS
1 standard, boxed layer-cake mix (your favorite flavor)
1 container of white frosting, or 1 box white frosting mix
Red food coloring
1 (8 x 8–inch) square cake pan
1 (8–inch) round cake pan
Spatula

Baking the cake:
Prepare the cake mix according to package instructions and pour one half of the batter in the square pan, and the other half in the round pan. (Be sure to butter and flour the pans before you fill them with the cake batter. This coating of the pans prevents sticking and making the cakes difficult to remove after they are baked.) Pre-heat your oven and bake the cake according to package instructions on the box.

Carefully remove the pans from the oven, using pot holders and cool the square cake and the round cake completely before removing from pans and handling.

Assembling the cake:
Place the square cake on a platter and rotate it, until you have a tip pointed toward what is going to be the bottom (of the heart). Cut the round cake in half and carefully place each half-circle against a top (8–inch) side of the cake … kind of like assembling a puzzle. The result will be a single layer cake in the shape of a heart.

Frosting the cake:
Mix a few drops of red food coloring into your white frosting to make a valentine-colored frosting. Using your spatula gently frost the cake, filling in any dips and valleys along the edges to make an evenly frosted, heart-shaped cake. You want to be gentle when doing this, so you don't tear the cake or jumble unwanted crumbs into the frosting. You can then embellish your cake with fresh strawberries, a written message, or assorted sprinkles.

RUSH HOUR TIP
If the frosting is too stiff to spread easily, add water, milk, cream, or fruit juice, blending in 1 tablespoon at a time until you arrive at a spread-able consistency.

Take a Break

How about having a little "Post-Valentine-Time" after the big day. What nice thing can you do for yourself today? Maybe it's carving out a half hour to exercise or to take a brisk walk with the dog. Or you could dash out and pick up that new book you've been wanting to read; find a cozy, quiet corner and start chapter one. Maybe it's a trip to your favorite make-up counter, or the purchase of a new perfume. Or, maybe it's a matinee-escape to see that new movie that's out. Whatever you choose…TAKE SOME TIME OUT FOR YOU, you, you … yes you!!

FEBRUARY 15

Bobbie Brown's Chicken Strips

How can something so simple be so good…but, let me tell you, "It is!" (Recipe submitted by an admiring Judy Brown)

INGREDIENTS
Boneless, skinless chicken breasts cut into strips
Buttermilk
Self-rising flour
Salt and pepper to taste.

Soak chicken strips in buttermilk several hours. Roll in self-rising flour to coat. Salt and pepper to taste. Fry until golden brown. Enjoy! Enjoy! Enjoy!

RUSH HOUR TIP
Fry the chicken strips in 350–degree canola oil, or as old-fashioned as the above recipe is, a mixture of melted Crisco® and ½ stick butter—for the crispiest chicken you can imagine. Drain on paper towels before serving.

You can even "double-dip" in the buttermilk and flour, for extra heavy coating! You must use self-rising flour for this recipe.

FEBRUARY 16

Me-Mamma's Minestrone
8 servings

INGREDIENTS
1 pound lean ground beef
1 medium onion, chopped
2 cloves garlic, mashed and minced
1 to 2 tablespoons olive oil
1 to 2 teaspoons Italian seasoning
2 cups water
2 teaspoons beef bouillon granules
2 stalks celery, sliced diagonally
1 medium zucchini, sliced, skin left on
1 cup shredded cabbage (for convenience I use ready-made coleslaw mix)
1 (28 ounce) can stewed tomatoes, with their juice
1 (8 ounce) can kidney beans, un-drained (optional, I happen to not like beans)
1 (8 ounce) can yellow corn, un-drained
1 cup elbow macaroni, uncooked
Salt and pepper to taste

In a Dutch oven or large soup pot, cook the ground beef and onion in 1 or 2 tablespoons of olive oil until beef is brown. Drain off any excess fat. Add the garlic and Italian seasoning and cook 2 minutes more. Add remaining ingredients (except salt and pepper), stir to mix, and heat to boiling. Reduce heat and cover. Simmer the soup for about 15 minutes, or until macaroni is tender. Adjust seasonings with salt and pepper to taste.

RUSH HOUR TIP
For a healthy variation substitute ground turkey in place of the beef and proceed with recipe.

FEBRUARY 17

Cathie's Pink Lemonade Pie

"Pretty in Pink," this makes for one refreshing pie!

INGREDIENTS
1 (ready made) Graham cracker crust/pie shell, baked and cooled
2 large cans Frozen Pink Lemonade, softened
2 cans Eagle Brand® condensed milk
8 ounces Cool Whip®

If you elect to bake your own graham cracker crust, follow package directions and cool completely before filling. Mix the pink lemonade and condensed milk together until blended. Lightly fold in the whipped topping until all is blended well. Pour into prepared pie crust and chill for at least 4 to 6 hours before serving. Best to chill overnight if possible. Garnish with more whipped topping at time of serving.

A Thought for Today

"That it will never come again is what
makes life so sweet."
~ Emily Dickinson

Freezing Facts

Most soups and stews can easily be frozen for quick preparation later. When freezing make sure to leave an inch of space near the top of the container for any liquid that expands as it freezes. Also, use a black Sharpie® permanent marker to label containers and the date frozen. This will help avoid "mystery dinner." Another bright freezing idea is to prepare extra servings that can intentionally be saved for another day (I call these right-overs instead of left-overs.) For best reheating results, undercook these dishes slightly before freezing.

FEBRUARY 18

Skinny Cheese-y Noodle Bake
A KID FRIENDLY RECIPE
6 servings

INGREDIENTS
1 (8 ounce) package noodles, cooked and drained
1 cup low-fat cottage cheese
1 cup shredded, low-fat Cheddar cheese
¼ cup grated Parmesan cheese
¾ cup low-fat sour cream
1 teaspoon Worcestershire sauce
½ teaspoon salt
¼ teaspoon white pepper
1 whole egg, lightly beaten
2 egg whites, beaten softly-stiff
Paprika
Additional low-fat sour cream, at serving time

Preheat oven to 350 degrees. Mix the cooked noodles with the 3 cheeses, sour cream, Worcestershire, and salt and pepper. Mix in the whole-beaten egg and then gently fold in the egg whites. Pour the mixture into a non-stick sprayed baking dish. Dust top with a sprinkling of paprika. Bake 35 to 45 minutes, until center is set and edges are golden brown. Remove from oven and let set 5 minutes before serving. Garnish each serving with additional sour cream.

RUSH HOUR WISDOM:
Wondering how much uncooked pasta you'll need? See below.

Small to medium pasta shapes ... 8 oz. uncooked = 4 cups cooked
(Elbow Macaroni, Medium Shells, Rotini)

Long pasta shapes ... 8 oz. uncooked or 1 1/2 inch diameter bunch=4 cups cooked

Egg Noodles ... 8 oz. uncooked = 2 1/2 cups cooked

FEBRUARY 19

Ham and Rice Salad
6 to 8 servings

INGREDIENTS
1 cup ready to cook, instant-style brown rice
2 cups cooked ham, cut in julienne strips
1 (15 ounce) can pineapple chunks, drained (reserve juice for another
  recipe)
1 cup seedless green grapes, halved
½ cup vinaigrette salad dressing of choice
1 tablespoon finely minced onion, or more to taste
1 teaspoon zest from an orange
½ cup cashew pieces

Cook rice according to package directions and set aside to cool. Mix ham, pine-apple, and grapes together and toss with the cooled rice. In a screw-top jar mix the onion and orange zest with your favorite vinaigrette salad dressing and shake to mix well. Pour the dressing over rice mixture and toss to coat all. Mix in cashew pieces. Cover and chill to meld all flavors. Spoon individual servings onto large romaine lettuce leaves. Serve with warm bread or muffins to complete the meal.

Good to the Last Drop

When using canned fruits, save the drained juices to use in another recipe. For example the drained pineapple juice (from this recipe) could be added to flavor a yellow-cake mix or a blender-smoothie. Drained canned-fruit juices can be used in place of water in gelatin molds. Drained juices can be mixed with brown sugar to make a glaze for pork or ham, or even baked chicken.

Weekly Challenge

CONQUER MORNING MADNESS
"Those who have found tranquility are calm and
pleasant to be with." ~Zen saying, excerpted from
A Thousand Paths to Tranquility

Since our day is greatly dependent on how we begin our mornings,
give yourself some extra time to calmly organize and get your kids
off to school. Maybe get up 15 to 30 minutes earlier so you can have
a quiet cup of coffee or tea before you wake your children and get
them going. Morning should be a pleasant time ... not a mad dash
and scramble to get everyone directed down their path for the day.
Everyone will feel so much better, all the day through, by getting a
confident and calming send-off first thing in the morning ...

FEBRUARY 20

Ice Cream Muffins
A KIDS IN THE KITCHEN RECIPE
6 to 8 muffins

INGREDIENTS
1 cup self-rising flour
1 cup vanilla ice cream, softened
A muffin baking tin
Paper muffin-tin baking cups

Preheat oven to 350 degrees. In a bowl stir together the flour (it must be self-rising flour for the recipe to work) and the softened ice cream. Stir just until moistened. Do not over mix the batter! Pour into paper lined muffin tins, filling each ¾ full. Bake for 20 minutes. Remember to use a pot holder when removing muffins from oven. Let muffins cool and enjoy! Eat plain or lightly frost with the following glaze.

Easy Glaze for Muffins
INGREDIENTS
A small bowl
A dinner fork
½ cup powdered sugar
½ tablespoon of softened butter or margarine
1 to 3 teaspoons of milk or water, added a teaspoon at a time

In a small bowl stir together powdered sugar, softened butter, and milk or water with a dinner fork. Make a smooth, well-blended glaze. (Glaze is a term for a thin type of frosting.) You can add a little more powdered sugar to thicken the frosting, or add a few drops more of milk to thin the frosting to arrive at the thickness you like.

RUSH HOUR TIP
You can mix in a few drops of vanilla extract, maple extract, almond extract, or lemon, or orange extract to flavor the glaze, if you wish.

FEBRUARY 21

Chicken-Rice-Broccoli Casserole
aux LeNormand

6 servings

INGREDIENTS
1 (10 ounce) package frozen broccoli spears, chopped
1 cup grated Velveeta® cheese, divided
2 cups cubed cooked chicken
Salt and pepper to taste
1 cup cooked rice
2 tablespoons butter
2 tablespoons flour
1 cup milk
1 tablespoon lemon juice
1 cup sour cream

Cook broccoli according to package directions; drain well. Arrange chopped broccoli in 13 x 9 x 2–inch baking dish. Sprinkle with half the cheese. Top with cubed chicken. Season with salt and pepper. Spoon on the cooked rice. In a saucepan melt butter over low heat. Blend in flour and then milk, making a sauce. Cook, stirring constantly, over medium heat until mixture thickens and bubbles. Remove from heat. Stir in lemon juice and fold in sour cream. Pour over chicken-rice mixture. Sprinkle top of casserole with remaining cheese. Bake at 400 degrees for 15 to 20 minutes.

RUSH HOUR TIP
Broccoli and chicken, sauce and rice—dare I say more!—and what a great way to use up leftover chicken! Thank you Audra, for this wonderful recipe.

A Thought for Today
FROM THE HEART
"You cannot live a perfect day without doing something for
someone who will never be able to repay you."
~John Wooden, College Basketball Coach

FEBRUARY 22
MaryAnn's "Husband's Delight"
4 to 6 servings

Make every day Valentines Day with this husband-pleasing recipe!

INGREDIENTS
1 pound ground beef
2 (15 ounce) cans tomato sauce
1 teaspoon salt
1 teaspoon pepper
1 teaspoon garlic salt
1 medium onion, chopped
1 ½ small packages cream cheese, softened
8 ounces sour cream
1 (8 ounce) package of noodles, cooked and drained
Grated cheese (your choice)

Brown ground beef; drain off excess fat. Add tomato sauce and seasonings; mix well. Combine onion, cream cheese, and sour cream; mix well. Layer noodles, beef, and sour cream mixtures into a lightly greased casserole dish. Top with grated cheese. (Can pre-assemble up to this point and store in fridge.) Bake at 350 degrees for 20 minutes, if ingredients are already warm. Bake at 350 degrees, 35 minutes if pulling from the fridge.

RUSH HOUR WISDOM
Don't be afraid to experiment with this one...Add some chopped green bell pepper and a little paprika and turn this into a Hungarian Goulash Variation (of sorts) ... You could even add a can of mushrooms for a Stroganoff-type taste!

RUSH HOUR TIP
For convenience assemble your casserole the night before (or even in the morning before you go to work). Store, covered, in the fridge. When you get home after work, pop it in the oven and relax until it's ready to serve. Add an additional 15 minutes cooking time if going directly from fridge to oven.

FEBRUARY 23

Soy-Sketti
A KID FRIENDLY RECIPE
6 servings

INGREDIENTS
1 pound spaghetti
¼ cup soy sauce
1/3 cup rice wine vinegar
2 cups chicken, cooked and shredded

Cook spaghetti according to package directions, drain. Heat rice wine vinegar, soy sauce, and chicken in small saucepan over medium-low heat until heated through. Toss with the spaghetti and serve.

RUSH HOUR TIP
When using soy sauce in recipes, don't forget about the health-conscious lite-salt version.

A Thought for Today
WHEN PUT TO THE MEASURE…
"…Be not afraid of greatness: some are born great, some achieve greatness, and some have greatness thrust upon them." ~William Shakespeare

Our greatness can even be expressed in the way we cook…be it a casserole…or an extravagant dinner, a hamburger or a steak, an artful salad or a lowly potato patty… banana boats or just a plate of fresh fruit…good food, lovingly prepared, and artfully presented, is always nothing but great!

FEBRUARY 24

Brook's Easy Pasta Toss
4 servings

For a quick, light and tasty vegetarian dinner, serve this easy-meatless recipe along with a nice salad and warmed bread or rolls.

INGREDIENTS
16 ounces linguine noodles
½ cup butter
3 tablespoons fresh parsley, chopped
1/8 cup Dijon-style mustard
2 tablespoons lemon juice
3 cloves garlic, minced
Salt and pepper to taste

Prepare pasta according to package directions. Drain and reserve, keeping warm. Melt butter in pan over medium heat. Stir in parsley, mustard, lemon juice, and garlic. Heat for 2 to 3 minutes. Toss sauce with pasta and then salt and pepper to taste.

Preparing Perfect Pasta

For perfectly cooked pasta noodles, be sure to cook them in a deep, large pot of boiling, salted water. Do not crowd pasta in the pot. The more water the better, as this draws the starch away from the noodles. Do not overcook; leaving noodles firm and al dente—there is nothing worse than mushy noodles as the feature of your main dish. Drain and toss immediately with companion sauce to avoid gummy and sticky noodles. If not putting into sauce right away, toss cooked noodles with a little olive oil or butter to coat very lightly.

FEBRUARY 25

Lemon Angel-Hair Pasta
A KID FRIENDLY RECIPE
4 servings

INGREDIENTS
6 ounces angel-hair pasta
2 teaspoons olive oil
4 garlic cloves
¼ cup minced fresh parsley (or to taste if making for kids. My daughter
  accepts no "green specks" in her sauce!)
2 tablespoons fresh lemon juice
¼ teaspoon salt
Pinch of pepper
Parmesan cheese, for garnish

Cook angel-hair pasta in boiling water for 3 minutes. Drain. Meanwhile, in medium skillet cook garlic cloves in oil. Crush garlic with fork and cook 2-3 minutes or until tender. Add cooked angel-hair, parsley, lemon juice, pepper and salt; toss to coat. Serve warm and pass the Parmesan.

A Thought for Today

"Life is like an ever-shifting kaleidoscope--a slight change, and all patterns alter" ~Sharon Salzberg, Cofounder, Insight Meditation Society.

What slight changes you have done for yourself lately? Think about how a happier "you" reflects into the fabric of your family, creating a happier "kaleidoscope" of day-to-day living experiences for all! The change can be as little as always, always, ALWAYS leaving your car keys in the same place every evening when you come home ... only to conveniently find them every morning again when you need them! Or the change can be as big as up-dating your family mission statement, with a new goal, a new plan, or a rejuvenated addendum.

FEBRUARY 26

Okay, okay—your family is probably ready for some steak right about now. So you choose the steak and I'll provide the mashed potato recipe.

Mash-it Garlic Potatoes
6 servings

INGREDIENTS
5 large baking potatoes
3 tablespoons butter
½ cup sour cream
2 tablespoons minced garlic
1/8 teaspoon salt
½ cup milk, more or less depending on your preference (This would be a good time to try out some buttermilk, see tip below)

Bring several quarts of water to a boil in Dutch oven or other large pot. Wash potatoes thoroughly. Peel and cut into quarters (or leave skins on if you like) and cook for 10 to 15 minutes, or until tender when pierced with a fork. Drain and transfer potatoes to mixing bowl. Add remaining ingredients and mix to desired consistency with an electric mixer.

RUSH HOUR TIP
When using recipes for cakes (especially chocolate cake), mashed potatoes, dips and sauces that call for milk, try substituting buttermilk in place of the regular milk called for, for a great taste treat.

Put Your Best Spud Forward...

Small Potatoes are best for use in salads.

Medium Potatoes work well for just about anything—mashed, baked, fried, you name it.

Large potatoes are ideal for French fries or the "meal-in-itself" baked potato.

Weekly Challenge

GRATITUDE

"Gratitude lights up what is already there. You don't necessarily have anything more or different, but suddenly you actually see what is. And because you can see, you no longer take it for granted. You're just standing in your yard, but suddenly you realize, Oh, there's the first flower of spring struggling to emerge from the snow; Oh, there's a deer emerging from the brush; Oh, there's the measuring cup you've been looking for that your daughter was using to make mud pies. It's just your ordinary old backyard, but suddenly you are filled with happiness, thankfulness, and joy." ~excerpt from *Attitudes of Gratitude, how to receive and give joy every day of your life*, by M. J. Ryan.

What are you grateful for? What little things bring a smile to your face? What ordinary occurrences make you deliriously happy? When the 'winter doldrums' of late February begin to get you down, take a moment to 're-discover' the everyday subtleties that make you happiest. What cute thing has your child done lately, or what creative dinner did you whip up on the spur of the moment, who phoned after you had them on your mind... Did your violets just bloom decorating the ledge of a winter-window sill? This week "light up" your thoughts with what is already around you and chase those winter-blahs away!

FEBRUARY 27
"Finger" Jell-O®
A KIDS IN THE KITCHEN RECIPE

Simple, slimy, scrumptious, silly, slick, and stupendously-satisfying. I remember my brother and me making this when we were little.

INGREDIENTS
4 envelopes Knox® gelatin
3 (3 ounce) packages jell-O® gelatin, you pick the flavor
4 cups boiling water
A shallow pan or dish
A long-handled spoon or wire whisk

Put gelatins in a shallow dish that has been positioned on a stable counter top. Carefully pour on the boiling water (or have an adult help you). Mix the gelatins with the boiling water until dissolved, stirring constantly and gently with a long-handled spoon or wire whisk. Once the gelatin is totally dissolved have an adult carefully transfer the warm dish to the refrigerator, so you don't spill. Refrigerate till jiggle-y firm and set. Serve cold. Cut into fun-size pieces and pick up with your fingers to eat.

FEBRUARY 28
MaryAnn's Rushin' Rice Bake
4 to 6 servings

INGREDIENTS
I pound hamburger
I onion, chopped
I (15 ounce) can tomatoes
I (15 ounce) can peas, drained
I cup cooked rice
Salt and pepper to taste

Fry hamburger and chopped onion until brown. Put tomatoes, peas, and cooked rice into a greased casserole dish. Add meat. Season with salt and pepper to taste. Rush it to the oven and bake for I hour at 325 degrees.

MARCH 1
Sara's "Greek" Tortilla Wraps

Tuesday is usually Taco Day at our house and this week I've decided to take on my best friend Sara's version of "tacos" as prepared at her house.

INGREDIENTS
Sun dried tomato tortillas, warmed
Roasted red pepper hummus
Leaf lettuce
Diced cucumber
Diced red onion
Feta cheese
Greek dressing, Vinaigrette dressing, or Olive oil

Start with a flavored tortilla (Sara's favorite—sun dried tomato). Layer on hummus, lettuce, cucumber, red onion, and then feta cheese. Drizzle with a little vinaigrette or olive oil. Roll it up and "it's a wrap."

RUSH HOUR TIP

This tip comes from my friend Sara, who is a rather adventuresome cook. She suggests replacing regular soft tortillas with some of the great flavored varieties available today. Although today's recipe features a whole new slant on tacos, I've followed her suggestion with my own standard-family-recipe, much to everyone's delight. Flavored soft tortillas make a wonderful addition to any recipe!

MARCH 2
Lacy Basinger's Easy Lasagna
4 to 6 servings

This "make-my-day-perfect" recipe comes from a rush-hour reader in Grenada, Mississippi, who has lasagna down to a science.

INGREDIENTS
1 pound ground chuck
Minced garlic, to taste
1 (8 ounce) can tomato sauce
Pinch of oregano
1 (8 ounce) package cream cheese, softened
16 ounces of sour cream
5 green onions, chopped
3 cups shredded mozzarella cheese
5 lasagna noodles, cooked to package instructions (*or use no boil variety for preparation ease and add directly to casserole)

In a pan brown meat with garlic and drain off any excess fat. Add tomato sauce and oregano; simmer for 1 hour. In a bowl mix softened cream cheese, sour cream and chopped onion together. Spray bottom and sides of a 9 x 13-inch Pyrex®-style baking dish with non-stick cooking spray. Line bottom of dish with either cooked noodles, or as Lacy suggests with the no-boil variety. Layer on meat mixture, then cream cheese-mixture, then top with the shredded mozzarella cheese. Cover with foil and bake for 1 hour in a 325–degree oven. Serve to the receipt of rave reviews!

RUSH HOUR TIP
Take Lacy up on her tip about no-boil noodles … they are the best thing since the noodle machine!

Pasta Popularity
Ever wonder what pasta is the most popular? According to the *American Pasta Report*, 40 percent of respondents say spaghetti is their personal favorite, followed by lasagne (12%), macaroni and cheese (6%), fettuccine (6%), linguine (3%), elbows (3%), pasta salad (3%), and angel hair (2%).

MARCH 3
The Rush's Beef Roast with Onion-Mushroom Gravy
6 to 8 servings

Although hints of spring have glimmered our way, winter-weather still hangs on. Leaving me with thoughts of a simmering beef roast and rich gravy for dinner tonight. I guess old Punxsutawney Phil really did see his shadow back in February.

INGREDIENTS
3 to 4 pound beef roast, trimmed of excess fat
1 envelope dry onion soup mix
2 tablespoons A-1 Sauce®
2 (10.5 ounce) cans cream of mushroom soup
1 soup can water
1 onion, chopped
2 cups fresh sliced mushrooms
Salt and pepper to taste
Mashed potatoes at serving time

Place roast in slow cooker. Combine next 5 ingredients and pour over roast. Cover with lid and cook on high setting for 7 to 9 hours, while you are off doing something else. Add sliced mushrooms last hour of cooking and adjust seasoning to taste with salt and pepper. Serve with mountains of mashed potatoes and gravy from the crock.

RUSH HOUR TIP
Be sure to cook up a large enough roast so you can serve leftovers tomorrow night! While you are at it, also make extra mashed potatoes for the recipe I am going share with you tomorrow!

A Thought for Today
A PURPOSE DRIVEN LIFE...
"Be life long or short, its completeness depends on what it was
lived for." ~David Starr Jordan

MARCH 4

Mother's Potato Patties
4 servings

This recipe was a favorite when my mom was a little girl, and then when my brother and I were growing up. Now my husband and daughter are big mashed-potato fans too, so the recipe lives on!

INGREDIENTS
2 cups leftover, yesterday's mashed potatoes
1 egg, beaten
Salt and pepper to taste
½ pie plate of flour or bread crumbs
Grated Parmesan cheese, optional
1 to 2 tablespoons cooking oil
1 to 2 tablespoons butter

In a bowl, using a fork, mix the leftover, cooked mashed potatoes with the egg just until blended. With your hands form about ½-cupfuls into individual patties. Season with a little salt and pepper and gently dredge each patty in the pie plate of flour or bread crumbs. Heat the cooking oil and butter in the pan and add the patties. Sauté on each side, carefully turning once, until golden brown and heated through. (Patties will break apart easily, so gently turn and/or remove from pan using a spatula for support.) Add more butter to the pan as/or if needed. Sprinkle with Parmesan cheese (optional) toward end of cooking. Serve warm with left-over meat and gravy. Or serve potato patties as a side dish with a completely new meal.

RUSH HOUR TIP
Take advantage of leftovers to create not only a convenient meal, but an economical one as well. This recipe uses leftovers from yesterday's meal to give you a delicious new twist!

MARCH 5

The other day, my mom reminded me about these two desserts I used to make as a kid—I guess I've always been a Rush Hour Cook at heart! Hmmm, think I'll go make some right now!

Brook's Banana Boats
A KIDS IN THE KITCHEN RECIPE #1
1 banana per serving

INGREDIENTS
1 banana per person, with peel
Mini marshmallows
Chocolate chips
Aluminum foil
A camp fire, fireplace, or pre-heated oven

To make the banana boats:
Pull back peel on banana, but don't remove. Make a slit, lengthwise in each banana. Fill with mini marshmallows and chocolate chips. Replace peel around banana. Wrap each banana individually in foil. Bake over coals 5 minutes, until gooey. Carefully remove bananas from fire with long handled tongs. Remove foil, pull back peel, and serve warm and gooey.

Brook's Nutty Frozen Bananas
A KIDS IN THE KITCHEN RECIPE #2
1 banana per serving

INGREDIENTS
1 banana per person, peel removed
A plate of chocolate syrup
A plate of crushed nuts (or "jimmies" if you
   don't like nuts)
Aluminum foil or plastic wrap
A freezer

Remove peel entirely from banana. Roll the banana in chocolate syrup to coat; then roll in the crushed nuts or "jimmies." Wrap individually in foil or plastic wrap and freeze. Serve frozen, but slightly thawed.

Weekly Challenge

KIND AND COURTEOUS

What can I do today, or this week, to help a friend, a school mate, a co-worker, a fellow church member, the bus driver, the mail man, my next door neighbor, my boss, the check-out girl at the grocery store, my dog, my cat, the baby sitter, my mother, the gal that does my nails? The list is endless! What random act of kindness can I bestow on someone's day to make it just a little brighter, a little better, for absolutely no reason at all, except that today is today! The gift can be anything: maybe being a good listener or telling a joke, running an errand for a sick or aging neighbor, stopping to get a 'Starbucks' for a coffee-loving-friend, dropping off a homemade batch of muffins or a pot of soup, fixing a broken toy, this list too, can be endless. Pick someone and pick something and go to it! Since the recipient will never be able to repay you above and beyond the satisfaction you will automatically feel on your "now perfect day (see Thought for the Day).

MARCH 6
Audra LeNormand's Easy Ravioli Casserole
6 servings

INGREDIENTS
1 pound Italian Sausage, removed of casing, cooked, crumbled, and drained
1 (28 ounce) jar spaghetti sauce
A dash of Italian Seasoning Spice Mix
2 cloves garlic, minced
1 (13 to 16 ounce) package frozen large ravioli, thawed
1 (8 ounce) package shredded mozzarella cheese

Preheat oven to 375 degrees. Mix cooked Italian sausage with spaghetti sauce in a bowl. Add Italian seasonings and garlic. In a greased, glass casserole dish spoon 1 cup of the spaghetti-sauce mixture. Top with half of the ravioli, half of the remaining sauce, and half of the cheese. Repeat layers. Bake, uncovered, for 30 minutes until bubbly and cheese on top is golden. Audra says to serve with a salad and garlic bread, just like they do in Liberty, Texas.

RUSH HOUR TIP
Always preheat your oven to the desired temperature before you place your casserole in the oven. If the casserole is chilled from being in the fridge, you might want to start with a little hotter oven, and then lower temperature after 15 minutes or so. Or add 15 minutes to cooking time, if using one temperature.

A Thought for Today
UNCONDITIONAL ACCEPTANCE
"Of course there is no formula for success except, perhaps, an unconditional acceptance of life and what it brings." ~Arthur Rubenstein, composer and conductor

MARCH 7

Audra's Pecan Chicken aux LeNormand
6 servings

Audra, set a place at your table for me... I'm coming to dinner tonight!

INGREDIENTS
3 whole chicken breasts, halved, boned, skinned and flattened
6 tablespoons butter, melted
3 tablespoons Dijon mustard
1 ½ cup ground pecans
¼ cup butter
¾ cup chicken broth
2/3 cup sour cream
1 package stuffing mix
Salt and pepper
Garlic powder

Prepare stuffing mix. Divide among chicken breasts, then roll up and fasten with a toothpick. Season with garlic powder, salt and pepper. Blend together melted butter and mustard. Coat chicken in mixture and roll in pecans. In large skillet brown chicken in butter all over. Add chicken broth and simmer until chicken is tender. Remove chicken to platter, blend sour cream into skillet drippings. Heat and spoon over chicken.

RUSH HOUR TIP
To pound chicken breasts thin, place between layers of waxed paper and pound with the back of a wooden spoon or with a wooden mallet, or even gently with a hammer, if you have nothing else!

Chicken Savings
When cooking with chicken breasts, check out your local Cost-co or Sam's Club for incredible prices! They sell 10 pound bags of chicken breasts that taste phenomonal and cost much less than purchasing at the local store. You can also purchase individually packaged chicken breasts at great prices, too!

MARCH 8
Audra (We Love Your Recipes)
Coca-Cola® Salad

INGREDIENTS

1 can pitted dark sweet cherries
1 can crushed pineapple
1 (8 ounce) package cream cheese, cut into cubes
1 box black cherry gelatin
1 box cherry gelatin
1 (12 ounce) can Coca Cola®
1 cup chopped pecans

Drain cherries and pineapple, reserving juices. Boil juices with enough water to make the 2 cups required to make gelatin. Dissolve gelatin in boiling mixture. Add enough water to the cola to make the 2 cups required to add to the gelatin. Add cola/water-mixture gently to gelatin to avoid foaming. Once mixed skim foam off top and refrigerate until "soft-set." Stir in cherries, pineapple, nuts, and the cream cheese (that has been cut into small cubes). Chill until set.

A Thought for Today
DIAMONDS IN THE ROUGH
"A diamond is a chunk of coal made good under pressure..."
~ excerpted from *A Thousand Paths to Tranquility*

Just think about it, something as common as a lump of coal can become as beautiful and crystal clear, as strong and enduring, as valuable and fine as a diamond. Our children are "diamonds in the rough," diamonds waiting to happen, and with our encouragement and guidance we can make them the best they can be. Today is never too early to implement new understanding and open communication with our children, helping them to become the best they can be.

MARCH 9

Mother's Meat Loaf
6 to 8 servings

INGREDIENTS
1 ½ pounds lean ground *beef, (makes 1 loaf)
1 small to medium onion, chopped
2 to 3 slices of day old bread, cubed
1 teaspoon Worcestershire sauce
1 tablespoon prepared horse radish or ¼ teaspoon Tabasco®
½ teaspoon salt
½ teaspoon pepper
Additional herbs, such as a pinch of dried oregano, parsley, garlic, etc.
¼ cup ketchup
1 egg, slightly beaten
BBQ Sauce, ketchup, or Cheddar cheese slices (for last 10 minutes of
   cooking)

Lightly toss all ingredients (meat through egg) together, mixing well, but do not overwork—you want your meatloaf to be tender—not dense and heavy. Gently form mixture into a loaf and pat into a 9 X 5 -inch bread loaf pan. Bake at 350 degrees for about 1 ¼ to 1 ½ hours. Last 10 minutes of baking top the loaf with Barbecue sauce, or ketchup, or Cheddar cheese slices to melt and coat the top. Serve warm slices for main entrée for dinner—save leftovers for lunch-box sandwiches. Double recipe and freeze, depending on desired amount of leftovers.

RUSH HOUR TIP
A "meat loaf mixture" of 1/3 beef, 1/3 pork, 1/3 veal can also be used in place of all-beef. You will find this mixture pre-packaged in your butcher section.

MARCH 10
Chicken and Rice Casserole a la Audra
4 to 6 servings

INGREDIENTS
1 (10 ounce) package frozen broccoli spears (chopped)
1 cup grated Velveeta® cheese, divided
2 cups cubed cooked chicken
Salt and pepper to taste
1 cup cooked rice
2 tablespoons butter
2 tablespoons flour
1 cup milk
1 tablespoon lemon juice
1 cup sour cream

Cook broccoli according to package directions; drain well. Arrange chopped broccoli in 13 X 9 X 2 –inch baking dish. Sprinkle with half the cheese. Top with cubed chicken. Season with salt and pepper. Spoon on the cooked rice. In a saucepan melt butter over low heat. Blend in flour and then milk. Cook, stirring constantly, over medium heat until mixture thickens and bubbles. Remove from heat. Stir in lemon juice and fold in sour cream. Pour over chicken-rice mixture. Sprinkle top of casserole with remaining cheese. Bake at 400 degrees for 15 to 20 minutes.

MARCH 11

Rock Cornish Game Hens
4 servings as written (1 game hen per person)

INGREDIENTS
4 Rock Cornish game hens, thawed
1 stick butter, melted
2 teaspoons kosher salt
3/4 teaspoon freshly-cracked black pepper
1 teaspoon paprika
1 jar red currant jelly

Place game hens in slow cooker crockery-style pot. Drizzle melted butter over hens. Sprinkle with salt, pepper and paprika. Cover with lid and cook on high setting for 4 hours. Spoon currant jelly over each hen, letting the jelly melt and glaze each bird. Return lid to slow cooker and continue cooking on the high setting for 2 to 3 hours more, or until hens are extremely tender and glazed. Serve up with all the 'fixins' for a festive feast.

Make Any Day a Holiday!
Cornish game hens are one of the most overlooked values in the meat department today. Plump, tasty, and elegant, wow your friends, or impress the in-laws with these little charmers!

"Make any day a holiday"...think of Cornish game hens as "mini turkeys" and cook up one per person.

Family too small to cook a large turkey? Serve each person their own "mini turkey" with all the extras on the side, for a culinary-savvy banquet.

Alone for a Holiday?—cook one up for yourself, or invite a neighbor and make two. Bake two sweet potatoes in the microwave, open a can of cranberry sauce, add a jarred, spiced peach-half and voila—you never even touched your oven and you've made a Festive Banquet for Two, an every day meal with a twist, a company savvy dinner, a March-Madness-Meal...you get my drift...

MARCH 12

Josie-Lynn's Gingerbread Muffins
I dozen

Have a box of baking mix sitting in your pantry? Josie-Lynn Belmont from Woodbine, Georgia has a great idea for transforming your mix into something other than the usual pancakes or waffles. Try her tasty recipe as breakfast muffins, dessert, or even to keep on hand for a delightful snack. She says she "came up with this recipe as a way to use up baking mix before it turned stale."

INGREDIENTS
2 cups store bought, boxed baking mix
½ teaspoon ground cinnamon
½ teaspoon ground ginger
¼ teaspoon ground cloves
¼ cup sugar
I egg
¼ cup vegetable oil
½ cup milk
½ cup molasses

Heat oven to 375 degrees. In a large mixing bowl, combine the dry ingredients. Then stir in egg, oil, milk, and molasses until all dry ingredients are absorbed. Fill paper-baking cup lined-muffin tins half full. Sprinkle tops with a little extra sugar and cinnamon. Bake at 375 degrees for about 20 minutes, or until muffins test done. This recipe makes I dozen muffins. Serve warm or cold, as muffins, or as a dessert with a topping of whipped cream.

Weekly Challenge

INSTANT SAVINGS INSTEAD OF INSTANT COFFEE
If you eliminated just one of your daily coffee-kiosk-lattes, five times a week, you could save around 16 dollars a week, which adds up to 65 dollars a month, which quickly mounts to 780 dollars a year X 10 years = 7,800.00. Interesting notion...cutting down on that caffeine. Your heart and your wallet will thank you.

MARCH 13

Vickie's Cheesy Hashbrown Casserole

6 to 8 servings

INGREDIENTS
1 (10.5 ounce) can creamy potato soup
1 cup sour cream
1 tablespoon flour
½ teaspoon garlic powder
1 (24 ounce) package frozen hash brown potatoes
2 cups shredded Cheddar cheese
1/3 cup grated Parmesan cheese
Paprika

Preheat oven to 350 degrees. In a bowl combine soup, sour cream, flour, and garlic powder. Stir in frozen potatoes and Cheddar cheese. Pour into a greased 9x13-inch baking dish. Sprinkle with grated Parmesan and a dusting of paprika. Bake uncovered at 350 degrees for 50 to 60 minutes, or until potatoes are done.

RUSH HOUR TIP

For variation Vickie Eastham from Casselberry, Florida adds sliced of cubed, cooked ham, turkey, or chicken, as well as a favorite chopped or mixed vegetable to turn her recipe from a side dish into a one-dish meal.

MARCH 14

Choose-Your-Way-Basic-Chicken
4 to 6 servings

BASIC INGREDIENTS
1 (3 pound) chicken, cut up
½ cup flour
1 teaspoon paprika
½ teaspoon salt
½ teaspoon pepper
Vegetable oil

Heat oil in skillet (with a tight-fitting cover for later) over medium-high heat. Coat chicken and cook until brown on all sides, about 10 minutes. Reduce heat, cover, and simmer for about 30 to 35 minutes, turning occasionally. Remove cover for last five minutes of cooking to crisp the chicken.

Choose-Your-Way-Breaded-Chicken
Roll chicken in basic flour mixture, then beaten egg. Next, mix 1 cup dry bread crumbs with ¼ teaspoon salt and roll chicken in this mixture. Cook as above.

Choose-Your-Way-Super-Crunchy-Chicken
Replace basic flour in above recipe with ¾ cup crushed cornflakes. Melt enough margarine or butter in a bowl to dip chicken and then dredge in crushed cereal. Cook as above.

MARCH 15
Aunt Jo's Creamy Lime Mold

INGREDIENTS
1 (3 ounce) package lime gelatin
¼ teaspoon salt
1 ½ cups boiling water
1 cup sour cream
½ cup slivered almonds
1 cup crushed pineapple, drained

Stir and dissolve lime gelatin and salt in the boiling water. Chill. When gelatin begins to set, fold in sour cream, almonds, and pineapple until evenly mixed. Refrigerate until firmly set.

A Thought for Today
"BENEFICIARIES"

"The discovery of a new recipe can do more for the happiness of mankind than the discovery of a new star." ~said the housewife to the astronomer

MARCH 16

Steamed Broccoli or Asparagus
Served With Lemon Wedges, Lemon Butter, or Hollandaise Sauce

When I think of Spring, I think of asparagus, and broccoli, and the fresh produce of the coming season ... Surely Punxsutawney Phil is releasing his slumbering grip by now!

INGREDIENTS

Fresh broccoli or asparagus, by the bunch, trimmed and ready for
   cooking (estimate ¼ pound of vegetable per serving).

Steam vegetables until just tender, in a colander or strainer placed above 1-inch of boiling water in a deep-covered pot. Or poach vegetable of choice, standing up-right in 1-inch of boiling water, in a deep-covered pot. The cooking process should take about 8 to 10 minutes—you want the vegetables to be tender-crisp, not soft and mushy. (In other words, don't boil the freshness right out of them!) Place on a warm platter and drizzle with one of the following: Lemon Wedges, Lemon Butter, or Hollandaise.

RUSH HOUR TIPS

When selecting fresh broccoli and/or asparagus look for tight (not rubbery), full bodied (not de-hydrated), and richly (not pale) colored stalks, heads and/or spear-tips. Avoid "tired" or wilted looking vegetables. Tops (heads) of broccoli should be compact and dark green (no yellowing)—tips of asparagus spears should be closed tight and deep in color. When trimming broccoli, cut off tough bottom-third of stalks, trim off side-stem-leaves, and leave stalk with head intact. Slice thicker broccoli stalks (with their heads) into half, vertically. Trimming fresh vegetables to an even size allows for more uniform poaching, steaming, and cooking. When trimming asparagus, the bottom of each stalk will automatically "snap off" at the proper spot. Steam or poach your fresh vegetables just until fork-tender. Vegetables that are over-cooked will lose their fresh texture, bright color, and their inherent vitamin value! Save any cooking water that's left-over to flavor a soup or sauce in a future recipe.

3 Toppings for Steamed Asparagus or Broccoli

Lemon Wedges

Drizzle cooked vegetable of choice with fresh lemon juice. Sprinkle with a little salt and freshly cracked pepper. Serve extra lemon wedges on the side for garnish and additional taste.

Lemon Butter

Mix together melted butter with fresh lemon juice and drizzle over cooked vegetable of choice. Season with salt, a little freshly cracked pepper, minced parsley, and crisped bacon bits (if you wish).

Hollandaise Sauce Supreme

Convenient hollandaise sauces are available by the mix or ready-made at your market, but for a real taste treat, try my Aunt Joan's wonderful recipe!

INGREDIENTS (for Auntie Joan's Hollandaise Sauce Supreme)
3 egg yolks, at room temperature
2 tablespoons fresh lemon juice
½ teaspoon salt
Dash of cayenne
1 teaspoon dry mustard
1 tablespoon hot water
1 stick butter, melted to bubbling but not brown, warm

Combine room-temperature egg yolks, lemon juice, salt, cayenne, and dry mustard in blender and blend well. Continue blending and add in the 1 tablespoon hot water. (This will 'temper' the mixture to receive the warm butter without curdling the eggs.) Continue blending on high, while drizzling in the melted butter. Serve immediately, over steamed broccoli or asparagus.

A Thought for Today
IT'S ALL ABOUT FAMILY
"Call it a clan, call it a network, call it a tribe, call it a family. Whatever you call it, whoever you are, you need one." ~Jane Howard

I think Jane Howard is trying to express just how important our family is to each of us, and each of us in turn to our family! Let's not waste a day, without making our family first and foremost in our thoughts, energies, and joys. Tonight, at dinner time, let's share our day and rejoice in the special-ness each one of us brings to our family's dinner table.

MARCH 17
St. Paddy's Day Olive-Cheese Cookies
2 dozen

This recipe makes 2 dozen 'cocktail-cookies,' so let's have a dinner party—it's St. Paddy's Day—whether you are Irish or not! (Don't forget to dye your accompanying cocktail or bottled water green, with a few drops of food coloring. Or dye a tray of ice cubes green and serve mineral water in tall stemmed glasses over the colored cubes. Add a slice of fresh lime to the rim of the glass to complete your green theme.)

INGREDIENTS
6 tablespoons softened butter
1 1/3 cups grated Cheddar cheese
1 ½ teaspoons parsley flakes
1/8 teaspoon onion powder
Dash cayenne
2/3 cup flour
24 pimento-stuffed green olives

Preheat oven to 400 degrees. Cream together softened butter and Cheddar cheese until smooth and blended. Add in the spices (parsley flakes, onion powder, and cayenne) to blend. Gradually add and mix in the flour until a smooth 'short dough' is formed. Blend well but don't over work dough. Drop by teaspoonfuls onto un-greased cookie sheet. Press an olive into center of each 'cookie'. Bake for 15 to 20 minutes. Serve warm, right from the oven. (To keep warm, serve from a cloth-napkin lined basket. I guarantee you won't be able to eat just one!)

A Thought for Tonight or Any Night
CREATE A MEMORY NIGHT
Get out a bunch of old photographs and set one next to each person's place setting. Have each person remember and tell stories about that time in their life. Add a lot of giggling, good food, and fun. Or use baby photos as 'place cards' and have everybody guess 'who sits where'. This is a great theme to use for any holiday, party, or festive family dinner.

MARCH 18

Spinach-Fettuccini Alfredo-Style
4 to 6 servings

INGREDIENTS

1 (8 ounce) package spinach flavored fettuccini noodles, cooked to package instructions, drained, kept warm, and 1 cup of cooking water reserved

1/3 cup butter, melted and kept warm

½ cup grated Parmesan cheese, room temperature

2 ounces of Gruyere or Swiss cheese, finely grated, room temperature

½ cup cream, room temperature

A small amount of reserved starch water, only if needed

½ teaspoon white pepper, or to taste

Fresh parsley, for garnish

Fresh chives, for garnish

Cook spinach-flavored Fettuccini noodles until al dente, per package instructions. Drain well. Immediately toss pasta with the melted butter. Then toss with the grated Parmesan and Gruyere until melted and combined. Add the cream, a little white pepper, and toss once again—add any reserved-starch water if needed, to adjust texture. Transfer all to a warm bowl. Sprinkle with minced-fresh parsley and minced chives. Serve.

Sauce it Up! Pasta Tips

When boiling and draining pasta, reserve a cup of the resultant starchy water. This water can be added to sauces to refine their consistency and make the sauce adhere more easily to the pasta.

When making white sauces, Alfredo sauces, and creamy sauces, use white pepper instead of black—your mother-in-law will be very impressed.

MARCH 19

Wendy Louise's Chicken Parmigiana
4 servings

Fried up in the skillet till crusty and golden, covered with pasta sauce and melted cheese, this recipe has pleased my family many a time.

4 boneless, skinless chicken breasts, pounded thin
½ pie plate of flour
1 egg, lightly beaten with 1 tablespoon water, in a shallow dish
½ pie plate dry bread crumbs (or Japanese bread crumbs)
A little olive oil
1 to 2 tablespoons butter
Tomato-based pasta sauce, your choice of brands
½ cup shredded mozzarella cheese
Parmesan cheese
Cooked pasta, at serving time (optional)

Pound chicken breasts to flatten. Dredge in pie plate of flour and then dip in beaten egg mixture. Roll in breadcrumbs to coat evenly and well. Heat olive oil and butter in your skillet on a medium-high heat setting to 350 degrees. Gently add chicken and sauté/fry on each side until golden brown. Turn down heat setting slightly and continue cooking until chicken is cooked through and juices run clear. (Cooking times will vary with thickness and size of the pounded meat.) Add a little more oil if necessary, to prevent sticking. Spread a coating of pasta sauce on top of each chicken piece. Top with mozzarella cheese and a sprinkle of Parmesan. Cover and continue cooking until all is hot and cheese is melt-y. Serve "as is" or on a bed of pasta. Add your favorite salad to complete the meal.

RUSH HOUR TIPS

Using a mixture of olive or cooking oil along with the butter keeps the butter from burning at high temperatures.

If you are dieting and are concerned about 'portion control' cut the pounded chicken breasts in half—extending the serving capability of this recipe to 8 portions. Add a generous side of steamed broccoli with lemon wedges or a side of steamed fresh green beans to extend the dish. Plating your entrée (rather than serving 'family style') and adding steamed vegetables on the side is a great way to 'portion control' the amount you eat.

Weekly Challenge

HOW TIMES CHANGE

I thought it would be fun to have a "trivial pursuit week" concerning food. When I "pursued" some of these odd facts I realized how cooking (and eating) have changed and recipes have 'modernized' over the years. Aren't we lucky today to have so much variety and convenience at our disposal? I even just think back about my mom (and her mom!) and how many things they had to make from scratch, or hadn't even been introduced to yet (like TV dinners ... well, there was no TV yet). Or, new fangled, electric refrigerators, still being called 'ice boxes' out of habit. Or, only bottled soda in 8-ounce, returnable-bottle six-packs that were religiously taken back to the store and sent back to the factory for reuse! Or, only certain produce being limited to a specific season. My, how times have changed!

So the recipes for this week will be geared around history and trivia. Okay, so that isn't exactly a challenge, but maybe a chance, to pause and reflect about how fortunate we are to have such wonderful supermarkets and specialty shops today, to ease our 365 daily-dilemma of ... "What's for dinner tonight?"

MARCH 20
Kickin' Lemon Garlic Baked Chicken
8 servings

INGREDIENTS:
2 chickens, giblets removed, each cut into eight pieces (have the butcher do this for you)
3 tablespoons extra virgin olive oil
½ cup fresh lemon juice
10 garlic cloves, minced (yes I said ten)
Salt
Freshly ground pepper

Preheat oven to 375 degrees. In a bowl, whisk the oil, lemon juice, and garlic. Place the chicken in a large roasting pan. Pour the marinade over chicken and turn to coat. Let marinate 20 minutes (or more). Arrange chicken, skin side up, on a baking sheet. Season with salt and pepper and place in the oven. Bake for 1 hour or until chicken is cooked through, basting occasionally with pan juices.

Rush Hour Trivia
On this day in 1733 carbonated water was invented; cornstarch was patented in 1841, by a one Orlando Jones (see March 22 recipe); and 113 years later the first Regional Shopping Mall Opened in Southfield Michigan, only to have today, kiosks selling carbonated beverage and cornstarch-thickened-foods to weary shoppers and mall-walkers, finding their way to the 'food court.' (Just a little food trivia I thought you might want to know.)

MARCH 21

Monterey Chicken Enchiladas
6 servings

INGREDIENTS:
2 tablespoons olive oil
1 cup chopped onion
2 cloves minced garlic
1 can diced green chilies
2 (14.5 ounce) cans chopped tomatoes
1½ teaspoons cumin
1 teaspoon oregano
1 tablespoon chili powder
1/8 teaspoon cayenne
1 teaspoon sugar
2 cups cooked, diced chicken breast
1 cup Monterey Jack cheese, shredded
6 corn or wheat tortillas
Sour cream
Salt and pepper to taste

In a large skillet, heat the oil. Add the onion and garlic, cooking until opaque. Add the tomatoes, green chilies, and spices and cook for 10 minutes. Pour ½ of the sauce over the bottom of a medium casserole dish. Stir chicken into remaining sauce to form a filling. Spoon chicken filling evenly onto 6 tortillas and roll up. Place seam-side down in the casserole dish and cover with the cheese. Bake at 350 degrees for 10 minutes until cheese melts and casserole is warm throughout. Top with sour cream.

RUSH HOUR TIP
If you want a traditional enchilada sauce, purée sauce with a stick blender before assembling and baking.

RUSH HOUR TRIVIA
The first Taco Bell opened its doors to our Mexican tastes in 1962, in the great state of California. As of today there are 6500 Taco Bells in the United States alone.

MARCH 22
Mom's Lemon/Lime Meringue Pie

INGREDIENTS (for the crust)
1 (9-inch) store-bought (a convenience old Orlando Jones didn't have in his pie making days!) pie-shell, "blind-baked" according to package instructions.

INGREDIENTS (for the filling)
1 ½ cups sugar
1/3 cup (of Orlando Jones' patented invention) cornstarch
1 1/3 cups water
3 eggs separated, yolks lightly beaten, whites set aside for meringue
3 tablespoons butter, softened or melted
1 tablespoon grated lemon or lime zest (or mixture thereof)
½ cup juice from fresh lemons or limes (or mixture thereof)

INGREDIENTS (for the meringue topping)
The 3 egg whites
¼ teaspoon cream of tartar
6 tablespoons of sugar
½ teaspoon of vanilla

Bake pie shell according to package instructions and set aside. While you are making your filling, preheat oven to 400 degrees. To make filling, mix together sugar and cornstarch in a saucepan. Over medium heat and stirring all the while, gradually stir in the water. Continue to stir and cook over medium heat until mixture dissolves and thickens, and comes to a boil. Boil and stir an additional minute. Remove from heat and stir about ½ of the hot mixture into the beaten egg yolks (to temper them) and then stir the tempered-egg mixture back into the remaining mixture in the sauce pan. Stir and heat filling for an additional minute, and then remove from heat. Stir in butter, then lemon (or lime) zest, then lemon (or lime) juice. Blend well. Pour completed filling into the baked pie shell. Set aside to let cool. While pie is cooling, prepare meringue for topping. To prepare meringue, with an electric mixer, beat egg whites and cream of tartar until foamy. Gradually add in the sugar, continuing to beat until stiff and glossy. Beat in vanilla. The meringue should form stiff, glossy peaks—do not under beat. Spread the meringue on top of the lemon filling, completely covering the filling and out to the edges of the crust. Touching the meringue to the crust, helps to prevent shrinkage and shifting of the meringue while baking. Swirl a few peaks into the meringue. Put completed pie in 400-degree oven and bake 8 to 12 minutes, or until meringue is just set and just delicately brown. You do not want to over cook. Cool the pie on a rack away from drafts. Allow to cool before eating. Refrigerate any leftover pie.

RUSH HOUR TIP

"Blind baking" means pre-baking an empty pie shell and cooling it before adding a filling that you are not baking in the shell itself. In this case we are making our lemon filling in a saucepan, pouring it into the pre-baked pie shell, followed by baking the meringue topping for a short time—thus the need for a "blind-baked shell."

MARCH 23
Old Fashioned Dessert Smoothie

INGREDIENTS
1 cup cranberry juice
½ cup orange juice
1 to 2 cups vanilla ice cream, slightly softened
Fresh strawberry for garnish

Put all in blender and blend until smooth. You can add or subtract ice cream to get the thickness you desire. Also try peach, strawberry, cherry, or other fruit-flavored ice creams for a variety of tastes. Serve as a party treat in Dixie® cups, or in tall glasses along with a straw and a spoon and topped with a fresh strawberry. Remember no slurping!

Rush Hour Trivia

The Dixie Cup was invented on this day in 1912. The spoon was also invented on this date, approximately three thousand eight hundred and twelve years before...so no excuses for slurping any more!

MARCH 24

Barbara's Perfect Pecan Pie
8 slices

INGREDIENTS
Pastry for 1 (8-inch) one crust pie
1 (packed) cup brown sugar
½ cup granulated sugar
1 tablespoon flour
2 eggs
2 tablespoons milk
1 teaspoon vanilla extract
½ cup butter, melted
1 cup chopped pecans
Rich vanilla ice cream, at serving time

Pre-heat oven to 375 degrees. In a bowl, mix together the sugars and the flour. Beat in the eggs, milk, vanilla extract, and melted butter, in that order, until all is blended well. Fold in the chopped pecans. Pour the filling into 8-inch pie shell. Bake 40 to 50 minutes in a 375-degree oven, or until filling is set. Serve pie warm with rich vanilla ice cream on the side.

RUSH HOUR TIP
The rich, smooth, vanilla ice cream is such a delicious foil to the warm, very sweet, and crunchy pie. Serve small slices because this dessert is, as I say, very rich. This pie also tastes wonderful warmed up the next day.

RUSH HOUR TRIVIA
Today precedes National Pecan Day. Tomorrow will be the 230th anniversary of George Washington's planting of his pecan trees, given to him by Thomas Jefferson. So in honor of the pecan I present you with this scrumptious pie, to be enjoyed today ... and even better, a second slice tomorrow.

MARCH 25

TV Dinners
A KIDS IN THE KITCHEN BIT OF TRIVIA

It is hard to believe, but the first color television came off the assembly line only 50 years ago today. I'm sure it didn't take long before people were consulting their TV Guides®, pulling up their TV tray tables and enjoying their TV dinners while watching a favorite TV show in "living color."

So tonight, carry on the tradition—get out the snack tables—tune in your favorite show—and serve your family "TV dinners"! Your only task will be to pick a favorite flavor for each member of your family!

Although they are not called TV dinners any more, what a selection of frozen meals we have to pick from today. There has to be one for each member of our family...lean ones for the diet conscious; robust ones for the super hungry; low fat, no fat, no salt, etc., etc., for the health conscious; vegetarian ones and cosmopolitan fair and international tastes—everything from beef bourguignon to meat loaf, roasted turkey breast with sweet potatoes to fettuccini Alfredo with broccoli—all neatly packaged for microwave cooking. How far we have come from those first standard dinners, in their little aluminum compartments of fried chicken, yellow kernel corn, and mashed potatoes, foil wrapped and ready for the oven. (The only thing you are not allowed to pick out today is frozen pizza...try to stick with "TV dinner"- full meal-style items for the complete effect for your old fashioned, family TV night.)

After you have picked out your frozen dinners, go over to the frozen-dessert section and see what can tempt you there. And when is the last time you made one of those Jiffy Pops®—better pick up one of those too—an old fashioned TV night wouldn't be complete without a magical, Jiffy Pop® pop corn cooked up on the stove top.

MARCH 26

FOOD TRIVIA HOLIDAY
A KIDS IN THE KITCHEN DAY PROJECT

March 26th has been allocated as Make-up Your Own Holiday Day! So kids, in keeping with our food trivia theme, put on your 'thinking caps' and your 'cooking aprons' and mastermind your own special Food Trivia Holiday. Think up something really special, that your family makes—something that you really like and have your Mom and/or Dad help you make it. Also think up some cool, trivial facts and history that go along with the recipe.

For example, we have a special family-pancake recipe that my grandmother devised during "the great depression," when certain food supplies were scarce and rationed. Anyway, everybody got so used to eating the old recipe, and liking it, that the recipe was passed down. My mother used to make these and now I do too. When my friends would come over, they would always ask her to make "those pancakes." Every once in a while I still get a craving for what I've always called "Skinny Pancakes." This recipe makes about 4, maybe 5 large semi-crepe style pancakes. (Usually each person eats at least 2 and the 3rd fills them up.)

"Skinny Pancakes"
4 to 6 pancakes

INGREDIENTS
A bowl and a wire whisk or fork
1 cup of flour
1 cup of milk
1 egg
1 hollow palm's worth of salt (i.e. fill the cupped palm of your hand)
A non-stick frying pan and some non-stick spray (or butter)
A large spoon, or a ladle, or like a ¼ measuring cup (with which to scoop batter from the bowl into the pan)
A spatula or pancake turner (for flipping the pancakes)
Pot holders (for handling the hot pan and any hot plates or platters)
Butter and Sugar or Cinnamon Sugar (my favorite) at serving time.

In a bowl mix together the flour, milk, egg, and salt to form a smooth, but not too thick (and not too thin) batter. A fork or wire whisk works really well for blending. Over medium heat, pre-heat your non-stick frying pan with a little butter, or use non-stick spray. Scoop or ladle out about ¼ cup of batter and pour it into the pan. Rotate the pan in a circular motion, so the batter spreads out around the bottom of the pan, forming a thin pancake about 1/8 thick and as large as you can spread it in the pan. Cook very quickly. When top of pancake is no longer looking wet or shiny and has set, flip the pancake and cook another minute on the second side. With your spatula or long handled turner, carefully remove pancake to a warm plate, spread with butter and sprinkle with sugar. Roll up, jelly roll fashion and eat immediately. As you cook each additional pancake, re-coat your pan with non-stick spray or a little butter to melt, and then pour in batter and spread to form another pancake. You can hold pancakes in a 200-degree oven (on an oven-safe platter) to keep warm, until all are done. Just remember to use your pot holder when you remove the plate from the oven to the table.

RUSH HOUR TIP
These pancakes are also excellent smothered in warm maple syrup.

MARCH 27
Zucchini-Corn Party Salsa
about 3 cups

INGREDIENTS
1 medium red onion, finely chopped
1 tablespoon sugar
1 cup red wine vinegar (to be drained later)
1 medium zucchini, scrubbed and diced
1 cup corn (can use canned, frozen or fresh)
1 teaspoon olive oil
1 teaspoon salt
1 teaspoon pepper
Tortilla chips, at serving time

Combine onion, sugar, and vinegar, and marinate for 30 minutes. Drain off vinegar. Set aside. Sauté zucchini until soft. Set aside. Toss all with remaining ingredients. Serve salsa chilled or warm with your favorite tortilla chips.

Weekly Challenge

LET'S THROW A PARTY

Looking for a reason to throw a party? You don't need to look far. Here are a few of my favorite ideas:

1. Your boss gets fired (unless I am the boss being fired).
2. Your child has their first "on the pot" experience.
3. Your mother-in-law is going to visit someone else this summer.
4. You got a new blender.
5. You have all kinds of food in your fridge which you will never eat by yourself if you want to fit into your shorts this year.
6. You found out your ex-boyfriend, a.k.a. the love of your life, has been divorced and remarried three times and gained 50 pounds and is unemployed.
7. You learned how to reset the clock and time on both your microwave oven and VCR.
8. Your child ate four bites of vegetables without a 15 minute preamble on human torture.
9. You got something fixed before the warranty expired.
10. The price of gasoline dropped more than a nickel.

MARCH 28
3 PARTY PERFECT DIPS

Baked Onion-Cheese Party Dip

INGREDIENTS
3 cups onion, chopped
2 cups Hellmann's® mayonnaise
2 cups Swiss cheese, grated
2 cups Parmesan cheese, grated
¼ teaspoon white pepper
½ teaspoon cayenne pepper

Preheat oven to 350 degrees. In a large bowl, combine onion, mayonnaise, Swiss cheese, Parmesan, white pepper, and cayenne pepper. Spoon into rectangular baking dish. Bake 25 to 30 minutes. Serve warm with sliced crusty bread or crackers.

Mi Salsa Su Salsa

INGREDIENTS
3 large tomatoes, chopped
1 medium onion, diced
1 ½ tablespoons fresh cilantro (or flat leaf parsley)
2 teaspoons fresh lime juice
1 tablespoon olive oil
Salt and pepper to taste
Cucumber, peeled, seeded, and chopped (optional)

In a medium bowl combine tomatoes, onion, cilantro, lime juice, and olive oil. Salt and pepper to taste. Serve with corn chips. For crunchier salsa, add cucumber.

Guacamole Ole!

INGREDIENTS
2 ripe avocados
1 tablespoon red onion, minced
2 garlic cloves, minced
½ cup tomatoes, seeded and chopped

Juice of half a lime
1 tablespoon flat leaf parsley (cilantro)
Pinch of cayenne
Salt and pepper to taste

In a bowl mash flesh of avocados along with red onion, garlic, tomatoes, cilantro, lime juice, and cayenne. Salt and pepper to taste. Serve with corn chips.

RUSH HOUR WISDOM
Avocados are so good for you because they contain mono-unsaturated fats ... in other words, healthy fats.

MARCH 29

A Thought for Today
Stressful week? Treat yourself to a mid-week treat!
Here's a "recipe" to add soothing luxury to your bath.

"Take-a-Break" Fizzing Bath Bombs
2 tablespoons cornstarch
2 tablespoons citric acid (sold as Fruit Fresh in the US)
¼ cup baking soda
3 tablespoon coconut oil
½ teaspoon fragrance oil (your choice)

In bowl, mix together cornstarch, citric acid, and baking soda. Melt coconut oil and add fragrance. Slowly drizzle oils into powder mixture. Mix well. Scoop out by scant ¼ cup, roll into balls. Let sit for 2 to 3 hours, and check to see if the balls have lost their shape. Reshape if necessary. Let dry for 48 hours. Wrap in clear plastic wrap, or colored wrap for gift giving. To use, just place in bath as water fills tub.

MARCH 30

Kay Edward's Cocoa Mix
Makes a lot, but you use it up quick

16 ounces Nestles Quick®
11 ounces (2 ½ cups) Coffee Mate®
1 pound confectioners' sugar
4 cups powdered milk

Combine all ingredients in large bowl,
stirring well. Store in airtight container.
To make one cup, spoon two heaping
tablespoons of mix into a mug. Add one
cup boiling water, stir until well blended.

RUSH HOUR WISDOM
For coffee lovers, blend 2 parts Kay's mix with 1 part instant coffee.

RUSH HOUR GIFT IDEA
Fill a cute jar with Kay's Cocoa Mix; decorate jar; present as a gift … great for
hostess gift, spontaneously needed present at the last minute, holiday gift giving,
etc. Add a cute mug and a tin of cookies.

MARCH 31

Cat's Slow Simmered Meatballs

Makes a bunch

Cathie Rosemann, from Texas knows how to cook for a party in the Dallas/Ft. Worth area...and she proves it's not all Tex/Mex style!

INGREDIENTS

3 pounds lean ground beef
2 medium eggs
1 cup bread crumbs
Salt and pepper to taste
1 bottle Heinz® chili sauce
1 can whole cranberry sauce
1 can cranberry juice
2 cans spicy bloody Mary mix

Mix together beef, eggs, and bread crumbs, and season with salt and pepper to taste. Form meat mixture into small meatballs. Brown in skillet and drain off grease. Mix together last 4 ingredients to make a sauce and pour over meatballs. Cover and slow cook (at 300 degrees) for about 6 hours. (That translates to high setting on your crockery pot.)

Save those Meatballs!

Meatballs this good should be savored! Make an extra batch for the freezer. The trick to successfully freezing meatballs is to lay them on a cookie tray lined with waxed paper. Freeze. Once frozen, transer to freezer-safe bags. This avoids the problem of one big meatball! This tip comes from my friend Deborah Taylor-Hough, author of Frozen Assets: how to cook for a day and eat for a month. She is the expert on all things bulk-cooking!

APRIL 1

A Thought for Today

The first of April, some do say
Is set apart for All Fools' Day
But why the people call it so
Nor I, nor they themselves do know
But on this day are people sent
On purpose for pure merriment."
~Poor Robin's Almanac, 1790,
concerning April Fool's Day

It has been thought that All Fools' Day originated with the reformation of the old European calendar over 400 years ago. New Years Day, and all its merriment, had always been celebrated on April 1st–probably, and logically, in tandem with the Spring Equinox and the return of spring and its new growing season. When reforming the calendar, the Pope decreed New Years Day be changed to January 1st. Obviously, with the poor communications of the day, people remained unaware of the change…thus continuing to act out foolishness and merriment on April 1st as if it were still the start of a new year.

Vicki's Macaroni Cheese Twist
4 to 6 servings

INGREDIENTS
½ cup green bell pepper, diced
1 clove garlic, minced
½ cup chopped onion
1 tablespoon olive oil
2 (8 ounce) cans tomato sauce
1 cup water
½ teaspoon dried oregano
2 tablespoons dried parsley
4 ounces processed American cheese, cubed
16 ounces corkscrew pasta, cooked and drained

In saucepan, sauté green pepper, garlic, and onion in olive oil until tender. Stir in tomato sauce, water, oregano, and parsley. Simmer 20 minutes. Meanwhile cook and drain corkscrew pasta, according to package instructions. Mix cheese cubes and cooked pasta together in a large serving bowl. Pour sauce over all and serve. And Vicki Lanzendorf from Madison, Wisconsin says don't forget to pass the Parmesan cheese!

APRIL 2

Vicki's Peanut Butter Cup Bars
A KIDS IN THE KITCHEN RECIPE

Here's a semi-no-cook recipe from Vicki Lanzendorf, of Madison, Wisconsin who enjoys making this tasty treat with her children.

INGREDIENTS
2 sticks margarine
1 cup peanut butter
1 ½ cups graham cracker crumbs
3 cups sifted powdered sugar
1 (12 ounce) package milk chocolate chips

In a microwave-safe bowl, microwave margarine and peanut butter, until butter melts and peanut butter becomes very soft. This will take about 2 minutes. Stir to mix. Add the graham cracker crumbs and powdered sugar and stir again to mix well. Spread the mixture into the bottom of a 9 X 13-inch pan. Melt the chocolate chips (again you could use the microwave) and spread over the peanut butter mixture in the pan. Refrigerate for about 20 minutes, just until chocolate appears "dry" (but is still soft). Immediately cut into squares. Cut cookies while still warm, because if the chocolate gets too hard, the cookies will break when cut. Store in refrigerator.

Weekly Challenge

EASTER, EGGS, AND SAFETY 101
As Easter approaches we all begin to think eggs, eggs, and more EGGS. Plus they are usually on sale. So let's have an "Eggs-travagant Week" featuring delicious egg recipes and some refreshers on safety, use, and storage.

APRIL 3
"Egg-stonishing" Custard Pie
6 to 8 servings

INGREDIENTS
1 (9-inch) store bought pie shell (or homemade if you wish)
4 eggs, beaten lightly
2 ½ cups whole milk
½ cup sugar
1 teaspoon vanilla
Pinch of salt
¼ teaspoon ground nutmeg
Whipped cream or whipped topping, at serving time
A dusting of additional nutmeg, at serving time

Preheat oven to 450 degrees and place baking rack in lower middle of oven. In a medium size bowl, beat together the eggs, milk, sugar, vanilla, salt, and nutmeg until well incorporated. Carefully pour the filling into the pie shell and carefully place on oven rack. Bake for 20 minutes at 450 degrees. Reduce oven temperature to 350 degrees and continue baking until, knife inserted in center of custard comes out clean—about an additional 10 to 15 minutes. Store finished pie in refrigerator until well chilled. Serve chilled. Top with whipped cream and a dusting of nutmeg at serving time. Store any leftover pie back in refrigerator.

Buying Eggs

Buy eggs from a refrigerated store shelf. Check the carton for any cracked shells and damaged eggs—avoid these. Immediately refrigerate eggs upon returning home. Raw eggs may be stored, in their shell, in your refrigerator for 5 weeks—hardboiled eggs, in their shell only 1 week. Raw eggs that have been un-shelled for a recipe (for example, leftover raw yolks or whites, from dividing eggs for a recipe) may only be saved for 2 days maximum. And most importantly eggs, cooked or uncooked, should not be left un-refrigerated more than 2 hours!

APRIL 4
"Mex-egg-an" Scramble
6 to 8 servings

INGREDIENTS
6 to 8 corn tortillas cut into wedges
Canola oil to cover bottom of pan
2 to 3 green onions, including tops, diced
6 eggs, beaten
1 cup shredded Mexican-style cheese (such as a Monterey Jack that includes
    hot peppers)
Chunky-style tomato salsa (your choice, your heat)
Sour cream

Cut tortillas into wedges and cook, stirring frequently, in heated oil just until crisped. Reduce heat slightly and add the onions to the pan, cooking for just a minute. Pour beaten eggs into the pan, over and around the tortillas. Cook, as if you are scrambling eggs, lifting edges and making room for uncooked egg to flow to the edges. When eggs are thoroughly cooked and set but still moist, sprinkle shredded cheese over all. Continue to cook until cheese melts. Cut into 4 to 6 wedges and serve warm, topped with salsa and sour cream.

RUSH HOUR TIP
Serve cooked eggs and cooked-egg dishes immediately. Promptly refrigerate any leftovers and use them within 2 days. Egg dishes that have been left at room temperature (for example at a party or buffet) should be discarded after 2 hours.

APRIL 5
Individual "Eggs-travagantly" Baked Custards
6 servings

Old fashioned … delicate … what could speak more of Easter.

INGREDIENTS
3 large eggs, slightly beaten
¼ teaspoon salt
1/3 cup sugar
2 ½ cups *scalded whole milk
1 teaspoon vanilla
Dust with nutmeg for garnish
Whipped cream, optional

Combine eggs, salt, and sugar. Slowly whisk in scalded milk, stirring constantly Add vanilla. Pour into individual custard cups (or miniature baking ramekins). Sprinkle each with a dusting of nutmeg. Arrange custard cups in a baking pan filled with 1 inch of hot water (this is called a 'water bath') and place in 350–degree oven. Bake for 30 to 35 minutes, or until knife inserted in center comes out clean.

RUSH HOUR TIPS
To scald milk—heat in small sauce pan just until milk begins to foam, but not boil and form a "skin." Skim off skin before using.

RUSH HOUR BONUS RECIPE
"Egg-y" Custard Pie
8 servings

INGREDIENTS
1 custard recipe from above
1 (9-inch) pie shell, ready for baking (I use a store-bought crust)

Carefully pour individual custard recipe into pie shell (instead of individual cups). Dust with nutmeg. On center rack of oven bake at 450 degrees for 20 minutes. Lower temperature to 350 and bake 15 to 20 minutes more, or until knife inserted in center comes out clean.

Always serve cooked egg dishes immediately. Store any leftovers promptly in the refrigerator and use up within a period of 2 days. As I said before, do not buy any eggs that are already cracked in the carton—this is an invitation for Salmonella bacteria just waiting to happen. If you accidentally crack an egg yourself, use it immediately for cooking or discard it. Storing un-shelled eggs in the refrigerator only slows bacterial exposure, it dose not inhibit it completely. Salmonella can be destroyed by cooking eggs to a temperature of 140 degrees for at least 3 minutes...*as a side note, it has become recommended to "coddle" or slightly poach eggs (at least two minutes) for use in Caesar Salad—that classic of salads that calls for a raw egg and anchovies in the dressing.

A Thought for Today

"Life is a great big canvas; throw
all the paint on it you can."
~Danny Kaye, Entertainer

APRIL 6

"Eggs-quisite" Quiche
8 servings

INGREDIENTS
1 (9-inch) store bought pie shell, pre-baked according to package instructions
1 cup shredded Monterey Jack cheese
1 to 2 green onions, including tops, chopped
8 slices of bacon, cooked crisp, drained of any excess fat, and crumbled
4 eggs, lightly beaten
½ cup half-and-half (cream)
1 to 2 dashes of hot sauce (such as Tabasco®)
1 tablespoon butter, melted
Salt and pepper to taste

Sprinkle cheese, green onions, and cooked bacon crumbles into the pie shell. Lightly beat eggs and then blend in cream, hot sauce, and melted butter. Salt and pepper to taste and pour over ingredients already in pie shell. Bake on center rack in 375-degree oven for 45 minutes, or until knife inserted in center pulls out clean. Cut into wedges and serve warm.

RUSH HOUR TIPS
Store fresh eggs, refrigerated, point down in their carton. This will center the yolk within the white—making for more attractive eggs, when hard-cooked. Cook your eggs (point down) in water brought to simmering…not a rolling boil. Over-cooking at high temperature will cause greenish-surfaced dry yolks and rubbery, shrunken egg whites.

To perfectly simmer hard-cooked eggs: Place your desired number of eggs in a pot. Cover with cold water to at least 1-inch above the eggs. Heat rapidly to just a boil. Remove pot from heat and cover immediately. Let eggs "stand" 15 to17 minutes in the hot water. Immediately cool eggs in cold water to prevent further cooking. You can do this by putting the pot under cold running tap water. Your eggs are now ready for a favorite recipe such as deviled eggs, egg salad for sandwiches, sliced egg garnish on salads, or just peeling, rolling in salt and enjoying as is. From your tender-loving care the eggs should be moist yet firm, the whites not rubbery and the yolks perfectly colored and perfectly situated smack dab in the center of the white. For safety's sake do not leave eggs out at room temperature for longer than 2 hours.

Okay…you boiled some of your eggs…you put 'em back into the fridge and now you can't tell which ones are which …which are cooked and which are not? Do a "test egg" by spinning it like a top on the counter. A cooked egg will spin like a top...an uncooked egg will wobble...just make sure it doesn't wobble off of the counter and onto your nicely waxed floor.

And for Safety's Sake remember the 2 Hour Rule when coloring and hiding the eggs, using them as decoration, or serving "deviled-style." I would strongly suggest that the "Easter Bunny" bring "Plastic Eggs" to use for his hiding and your hunting! Any dyed eggs that are going to be eaten, pop them back into the fridge, when you are done decorating them.

APRIL 7

Gramma's "Perf-eggtly" Deviled Eggs
Makes a dozen

INGREDIENTS
6 hard boiled eggs
1 tablespoon softened butter
1 tablespoon cream
½ teaspoon dry mustard
Dash cayenne
1 tablespoon anchovy paste
Paprika
Mixed-spring salad greens or watercress, to arrange as nests

Halve eggs, and remove yolks to a small bowl, whites to a platter. Mash yolks to a smooth paste with next five ingredients. Mound filling back into whites and garnish with a sprinkling of paprika for color. Serve the eggs on a pretty bed of mixed-spring salad greens or watercress, arranged like a bird nest. Store in fridge until serving time.

"Egg-stremely" Simple Deviled Eggs

Many variations exist for deviled eggs, with one of the simplest (and mildest flavored) versions being to simply mash yolks with a bit of mayonnaise and a pinch of salt until velvety smooth; fill whites and even forego the paprika! A garnish of a mini-strip of sun dried tomato, or a dab of caviar, or a sprinkling of capers, adds a sophisticated touch for a more adult taste.

APRIL 8

Karl's "Megg-nificent" Muffin Cup Frittatas

Makes a dozen

INGREDIENTS
1 (10 ounce) package frozen chopped spinach, thawed and squeezed dry
3 large eggs
Salt and pepper to taste
¼ to ½ teaspoon cumin (to taste)
¼ cup finely chopped cilantro (or parsley)
1 cup shredded Jack (or mild, white Mexican) cheese (recipe can be made
    with Cheddar also and is excellent)
1 cup small curd cottage cheese
Crumbled. cooked chorizo sausage, optional
Salsa at serving time (optional)

Mix first 7 ingredients together until blended.
Divide mixture into a well-greased muffin
tray. Top each portion with crumbled cooked
chorizo (optional). Bake in 350-degree oven
until cooked through and set, and knife poked
in center comes out clean. This will be about
20 to 30 minutes. Serve warm with a condiment of your favorite salsa on the
side.

APRIL 9

"Egg-cellent" Florentine Pie

8 servings

INGREDIENTS

1 single crust pie shell, ready for baking (use a 9-inch shell)
4 eggs, plus 1 egg yolk
1 cup shredded Swiss or Monterey Jack cheese
1 (10 ounce) package frozen chopped spinach, thawed and squeezed dry
2/3 cup whole milk
2 scallions, including green tops, sliced
¼ teaspoon each: salt and pepper
¼ teaspoon ground nutmeg

With an electric mixer, beat eggs and the extra yolk in a medium size bowl until extremely foamy. Gently stir in remaining 5 ingredients, to blend filling. Pour into pie shell Bake at 325 for approximately 45 minutes, or until knife pierced in center comes out clean.

Egg Tips

When cooking eggs, cooking temperatures need to be kept moderately low to avoid overcooking the eggs and making them tough and rubbery. When boiling, reduce to simmer. When baking use 325 instead of 350. Sauté omelets over medium-high heat. Cook them a little slower over moderate heat, rather than forcing the recipe on a higher heat. Your delicate touch will make for delicate results.

Weekly Challenge

SPRING CLEANING

With Spring well under way it's time to do a little house cleaning, "spiffy-ing-up," and organizing. Champion Press Author, Deborah Taylor-Hough has two books that are just the ticket to help us. The first, her book *A Simple Choice, a practical guide for saving your time, money and sanity* ISBN 1891400495 offers many solutions for tackling the closet, the car, the garage, and the house in general. The author even touches on Garage Sales, Stretching our Budgets, and Creating a Family Mission Statement…while also delving into some kitchen philosophy as well.

Deborah's second book, *Mix & Match Recipes* (ISBN 189140007X) tackles leftovers, odds and ends in our pantries, and inventive ways to use up items in our pantry.

So this week, taking some tips from Deborah, why don't we get a grip on our clutter, a grasp on our budget, a pitch on some give-a-ways to the Salvation Army, and a toss-it-out attitude for what ever is left! "If we're not usin' it, let's lose it to a better cause!"

APRIL 10

Wendy's Use-it-Up French Toast "Buffet"
A KID FRIENDLY RECIPE
Allow 2 to 3 pieces per serving

INGREDIENTS
Assorted day-old-bread ... any kind (see note below)
Eggs, lightly beaten with a bit of *milk (see note below)
Butter
Assorted (clean-out-the-pantry) toppings at serving time (see note below)

Carefully dip your selected bread in the beaten egg mixture to coat and place in non-stick sprayed, non-stick skillet. Over medium heat, sauté the slices, adding butter if you wish, until first side is golden brown. Turn with a spatula and cook second side until golden. If you are using a variety of breads they each might take a different time to cook. You can hold all on a platter in warm (200 degree) oven until all slices are cooked. Bring the warm platter of French toast to the table and offer garnishes of butter, cinnamon sugar, confectioners' sugar, maple syrup, and assorted berry syrups. And to tackle those odds and ends in the pantry you could even add warmed pie filling or canned fruit, plus whipped cream!

RUSH HOUR NOTES
When it comes to bread for my French Toast "Buffet" I've used hamburger buns, French bread, whole wheat and natural grain breads, baguettes, and bratwurst rolls, Texas toast cut bread, and even English muffins. Any leftover bread will do, when you cut it down to size. For Holiday occasions, I've used slices of holiday stolen (Christmas bread), sliced cranberry bread, and after Easter, even split hot-cross-buns (a type of Easter bun).

*For extremely rich French toast substitute half-and-half cream for the milk. Cook over low heat, so egg covering doesn't get tough.

A Thought for Today

"A well stocked-pantry is a girl's best friend."
~ Deborah Taylor-Hough

While we are doing our spring cleaning, let's not forget to take a look at our pantry and kitchen cupboards. I'm sure a little "pitching," organizing, and re-stocking can take place in those areas, and don't forget to check those expiration dates.

.

APRIL 11

Beth Sullivan's Two Cakes for the Price of One
4 to 6 servings for each recipe

Maybe you have a cake mix in the pantry that you need to use up. Use a suggestion from Beth and make two recipes for the price of one.

#1
Preheat oven to 350 degrees. Prepare a packaged yellow cake mix as directed. Lightly grease 2 (8 or 9-inch) square pans. Divide batter evenly between the 2 pans.

Bake one as directed on package instructions. Cool and use for dessert. Embellish with ice cream and toppings of choice, or whipped topping and fruit such as strawberries.

#2
Prepare the second cake for baking. Before putting in oven, sprinkle generously with a mixture of ½ cup brown sugar, 1/8 cup white sugar, and ¼ teaspoon cinnamon on the second batter. Bake this cake 25 to 30 minutes or until done. Serve at breakfast the following morning.

RUSH HOUR WISDOM
Take a tip from the Rush Hour Cook—Always when restocking your pantry put like items together. That way you can take a quick glance to see what you need, rather than searching all over. Put newly purchased items in the back and move older items to the front. That way expiration dates don't get overlooked.

APRIL 12

Darlene's Family Favorite All-Purpose Recipe

6 to 8 servings for breakfast, lunch, or dinner!

Well, now that we've cleaned out the cupboards and organized the pantry, it's time to tackle the refrigerator...One of our Canadian readers, Darlene Ashe, says, "This recipe is great for breakfast or supper too, when it's clean-out-the-fridge-day. It's versatile and everyone loves it."

INGREDIENTS
10 large eggs
2 cups leftover cooked meat, such as sausage, ham, or chicken, cut into
   bite-size pieces
½ cup chopped vegetables, such as onion, corn, tomatoes, or zucchini
1 cup chopped cooked potatoes—any kind, such as leftover fried, baked,
   boiled, hash brown, or even mashed!
Seasonings, a few shakes of each: parsley, oregano, hot sauce, garlic,
   basil, etc., (mix and match as you like)
Cheese, your choice, thinly sliced, grated or shredded

Preheat oven to 375 degrees. Grease or oil a 9 x 11-inch pan and set aside. In a large bowl, mix 10 large eggs; add meat, potatoes and your seasonings of choice, mixing well. Pour mixture into greased baking pan. Top with cheese of your choice. Bake at 375 for 20 to 25 minutes, or until center is set and done, and does not jiggle. Serve with toast, buns, or garlic bread, depending on breakfast, lunch, or dinner.

RUSH HOUR BONUS RECIPE
Change the seasonings to a packet of taco mix, add some chopped hot chilies from that lingering jar in your fridge, and you've turned Darlene's Dish into a Tex-Mex Delight. Garnish with dollops of sour cream and some salsa (from another needs-to-be-used-up jar) and ole! Cut into wedges and serve with a warmed tortilla on the side.

A Thought for Today
BODY MIND CONNECTION
"To get the body in tone, get the mind in tune."
~Zachary Berkovitz, Physician and Writer

APRIL 13

The Rush Hour Cook's (Weekly Wonder) Cheese-y Turkey Casserole

6 servings

Here's another recipe that works well with leftovers—leftover chicken (or even ham) could easily be substituted for the turkey in this casserole. And if you are cleaning out your pantry a different canned cream soup could readily replace the cream of mushroom that is called for. Instant brown rice could replace the white. You could even change your cheese choice. Once again, great tastes, great combos, great savings, can come under many names, while using up "what you have when you have it."

INGREDIENTS

1¼ cups instant white rice
2 cups diced turkey
1 (10.5 ounce) can cream of mushroom soup
¾ cup milk
1 cup seasoned stuffing croutons
1 cup shredded Cheddar cheese

Prepare rice according to package directions. Transfer cooked rice to a greased baking dish. In a medium bowl mix soup and milk well. Add turkey and croutons to soup mixture and stir well. Spread turkey mixture over rice and top with Cheddar cheese. Bake in 350-degree oven for 30 minutes. Serve with your choice of steamed veggies.

RUSH HOUR WISDOM

Think about making one night a week your "Weekly Wonder Casserole Night." Consider it a "budget meal"—a bonus, a freebie—and how great is that on your pocket book? Say ... every Wednesday night ... could be a Weekly Wonder Casserole Night at your house...who would ever guess ... while you are laughing all the way to the bank, you are using up perfectly good leftovers.

APRIL 14

Rush Hour Aztec Salad
4 servings

Here's a recipe to use up a lingering salad dressing along with canned goods from your pantry.

INGREDIENTS
1 package salad mixed-greens
1 can corn, drained
1 can black beans, drained
½ red onion chopped
½ cup tomato vinaigrette dressing

Toss all ingredients in a large salad serving bowl. Serve immediately.

RUSH HOUR WISDOM
Turn this salad into a main dish meal by adding ½ pound cooked chicken.

A Thought for Today
FEELING GOOD
"Happiness is bigger than any bank account."
~David Baird

APRIL 15

Laura's Layered Italian Beef (for sandwiches)

INGREDIENTS

2 to 4 "English Cut" beef roasts

4 to 8 packages of Good Seasons® Original Italian Dressing Mix (You will need 2 packets per each roast.)

Trim roasts of all fat. Put first roast in slow cooker. Sprinkle with 2 packets of seasoning mix. Stack another roast on top of the first one. Sprinkle with 2 more packets of seasoning. Cover and cook for 24 hours on low setting. Do not open lid! When done the meat will be ultra tender—stir with two-pronged fork for a great shredded beef. Serve on your favorite buns for sandwiches. (Laura says, "depending on how many you want to serve, you can do up to 4 roasts in a larger slow cooker—each with two packets of seasoning on top per roast.)

RUSH HOUR TIP

Make this recipe over the weekend and you'll have plenty of sandwich meat for delicious brown-bag lunches all through the week.

APRIL 16
Mom's Stuffed Flank Steak
4 to 6 servings

INGREDIENTS

1 flank steak, the largest you can find
1 package seasoned stuffing-style bread cubes, such as Pepperidge
   Farm® (or make your own with about 4 slices of day-old bread cut into
   cubes, sprinkled with seasonings of choice and sautéed quickly to toast,
   in a little butter and minced onion for flavor.)
Cooking oil (I like to use canola or olive oil)
½ cup water or canned broth

Score the flank steak with a sharp knife, by making a diagonal pattern of slashes across the grain on the surface of one side of the steak. This will help tenderize the meat. Put the stuffing down the center of the steak and roll up jelly-roll fashion, with the scored side facing out. Secure with toothpicks. Brown the steak on all sides in a little oil. Transfer to a slow cooker pot sprayed with cooking spray and add ½ cup water or broth. Cover with lid and cook on low setting 6 to 9 hours, or on high setting 3 ½ to 5 hours. During cooking add small amounts of broth or water if at all necessary. To serve, remove toothpicks and cut meat into ½-inch thick slices. Arrange slices (with their filling) on platter and drizzle with gravy made from the cooking juices. (You can leave the juices alone or thicken them to your liking.) Let each person salt and pepper their serving to taste.

RUSH HOUR TIP
For a spicier version of this same recipe, marinate the scored steak in Italian or Russian-style salad dressing before stuffing. Remove steak from marinade and discard excess marinade. Stuff and roll the steak and proceed per recipe instructions.

APRIL 17
The Bachelor's Perfect Pork Roast
6 to 8 servings

INGREDIENTS
1 (3 to 4 pound) pork roast
1 small to medium onion, sliced
2 (16 ounce) cans whole berry, cranberry sauce

Put roast in slow cooker crockery-pot. Surround with sliced onion. Pour on the cranberry sauce. Cover with lid and slow cook on low for 8 to 12 hours, or until roast is very tender. Or, roast on high setting, approximately half that time. Serve roast, smothered in its "pan juices" with mashed potatoes on the side…or serve as succulent hot pork sandwiches.

Weekly Challenge

DON'T JUST GRAB AND GO …

This weekly challenge is especially for the kids in the family (but we adults can take heed too). Mealtime should be an opportune time for family to gather to communicate and nourish themselves, to bond with wonderful conversation and family favorite recipes. Mealtime should not be regarded as a chore or an interruption in your schedule, a time to just ask Dad for the keys to the car, before you dash out to be with friends, a time to just "grab a bite" and be off to the next task at hand, or dash home and dash out again. Through all the advertising barraged on us through the TV, we've become accustomed to eating power bars while dashing for a taxi, wolfing down power drinks while riding our bikes over impossible terrain, eating drive-thru burgers while speeding down the highway, infusing deli food while rushing from one place to the next. What ever happened to the dining table? And chairs?

APRIL 18

Roberta Epstein's Chicken Trocadero
4 servings

Fry it! Bake it! And season it up bold! Soup it! Cheese it! And enjoy it!

INGREDIENTS
1 stick butter
4 large chicken breast-halves
Garlic powder—Lots!
Onion powder—Lots!
1 can cream of mushroom soup
1 soup can milk
4 thick slices of very good Swiss cheese

Melt butter in electric frying pan set at 350-degree setting. While butter is melting, heavily season chicken breasts. When you think you have enough seasoning on, double it! Lightly brown chicken; keep turning so chicken browns all over. When chicken is browned remove from fry pan and place in oven-proof baking dish. Top each piece of chicken with a cheese slice. Blend soup and milk together thoroughly in a blender, add any remaining sauté butter from the fry pan to blender-mixture and blend again. Pour blended mixture over chicken and *immediately put into 350—degree oven (see tip) to bake for 1 hour, topping will be brown and soft. Serve with its own gravy.

RUSH HOUR TIP
Recipe can be assembled to this point and held for 24 hours in the refrigerator before continuing with the final cooking process ... a convenience for make-ahead-dinner party-dishes. If pulling directly from fridge to pop into the oven be sure to add at least 15 additional minutes to the cooking time.

APRIL 19

With the warmer weather and longer evenings, my husband has been firing up the barbecue-grill lately…and he's always looking for the ultimate BBQ sauce! This award winning recipe (devised by her mother, Tina) has been submitted by Kita Schuehle, of Sabinal, Texas. Kita says her mom's sauce is great on chicken, pork, and especially steaks, and has won many awards in cooking contests— Here is yet another example of how a few simple ingredients can be combined to make a sensational recipe.

Tina's Award Winning 1/3-1/3-1/3 BBQ Sauce
(submitted by Kita Schuele, Sabinal Texas)

INGREDIENTS
1/3 cup catsup
1/3 cup cider vinegar
1/3 cup oil (can use any of the following: olive oil, canola oil, cooking oil,
   vegetable oil, and even bacon grease—or a combination of any there of)
Seasonings to taste (such as Worcestershire sauce, garlic salt, pepper, etc.)

Add all ingredients in a saucepan and simmer gently for a few minutes. For best results, use sauce often while grilling, basting frequently. This sauce is intended to be cooked and glazed onto the meat, not poured on at the end.

APRIL 20
Sindi's Salmon

From the state of Virginia, Sindi sends in this healthy dish using fresh fillets from her favorite fish market.

INGREDIENTS
Fillet of salmon (about 1/3 pound per person)
1 bottle of Whole Foods Lemon Tahini Salad Dressing® (or any salad dressing containing some of the following: oil, vinegar, lemon and/or mustard)

Adjust oven rack to top level and preheat oven to 350 degrees. Lay salmon in pan skin side down. Pour salad dressing over salmon to completely cover the salmon. Cover pan with aluminum foil and put on top rack in oven. Bake for 20 to 25 minutes (timing will depend on thickness of salmon). Remove foil and continue cooking by broiling for 10 minutes more.

RUSH HOUR TIP
Fresh fish is extremely perishable and should be bought chilled (preferably on ice), taken home, and held in coldest part of refrigerator for no more than a day after purchase. If you are not going to use it right away, be sure to transfer the fish to the freezer. When removing fish from its packaged container (or wrapping) it should be rinsed thoroughly and patted dry (with paper toweling) before cooking. If you are thawing fish, do so by placing it directly from the freezer into the fridge. Some recipes even suggest thawing fish in cold milk to remove some of the "fishy taste"—a technique that I have never tried.

APRIL 21

Carolyn Miller's Lemon & Poppy Seed Muffins from Wisconsin

24 Muffins

INGREDIENTS
1 box lemon cake mix
1 cup boiling water
1/2 cup oil
1 small box instant pudding
4 eggs
1/3 cup poppy seeds

Preheat oven to 425 degrees. Mix all ingredients together. Fill paper lined muffin tins 1/2 full. Bake for 15 minutes. Cool for 10 minutes, then remove from pan.

RUSH HOUR VARIATION

Omit poppy seeds and replace with just a touch of zest from a lemon. When cool lightly frost with an icing made from powdered sugar, a dash of milk, and a dash of lemon juice or extract. Or replace poppy seeds with a touch of orange zest and frost with orange-flavored icing—for a multi-citrus-y taste. It is so nice to get away from snacks and treats that are always chocolate, chocolate, and more chocolate!

Five uses for muffins, other than breakfast:

1. A snack after school
2. Include in your brown bag lunch
3. Invite a friend over for afternoon tea and muffins
4. Include in a gift basket, along with spiced tea for a convalescing friend
5 Serve alongside a refreshing salad and a tall glass of iced tea for a light lunch

APRIL 22

Granny Faye's Apple Dumplings
16 Dumplings

Submitted by Victoria Beckham of Fort Worth, Texas, this recipe uses a surprising combination of convenience foods to turn every-day apple dumplings into extraordinary apple dumplings.

INGREDIENTS
2 cans crescent-style rolls
2 large Granny Smith apples
2 sticks butter
1 ½ cups sugar
1 (12 ounce) can Mountain Dew® soda pop (do not use diet)

Spray a baking pan with non-stick cooking spray and set aside. Preheat oven to 350 degrees. While oven is heating peel and core the 2 apples. Cut each apple into 8 wedges. Set aside. Separate rolls and flatten. Place wedge of apple on large end of roll—roll up and place in baking pan. Melt the butter and sugar and pour over apple-rolls. Pour Mountain Dew over this. Bake in 350-degree oven for 45 minutes, basting during cooking. Remove from oven. Separate rolls from pan. Return to oven for an additional few minutes. Excellent served with ice cream.

A Thought for Today
"Travel and change of place impart new vigor to the mind"
~Seneca, Roman Philosopher and Statesman

Even if we're just traveling from the kitchen out to the backyard to have a picnic, a change of place can bring new enjoyment to our dining. Fresh air might just be one of the greatest "spices" we can add to our meal.

APRIL 23

This meal is great for outdoor cooking and is especially easy for kids to help make. Make the packages at home, store in fridge or freezer, transport them in a cooler, and then toss on a grill or a campfire when you are ready for a delicious and easy dinner. Be sure to pick a great location for your picnic (even if it's just your back yard) to enjoy your "change of place" meal!

Campfire-Meal in a Foil-Packet
A KIDS IN THE KITCHEN RECIPE
1 foil packet per person

INGREDIENTS
Lean ground beef, shaped into generous hamburger patties
Diced or sliced potatoes
Diced or sliced carrots
Salt and pepper to taste, and/or a mixed seasoning like Mrs. Dash® if
  you wish
A little butter, optional
Aluminum foil
Campfire, outdoor grill, fireplace, (or lastly the oven, for a rainy day picnic)

Lay out a double thickness of aluminum foil for each dinner. Form hamburger patties and season with salt, pepper, and any seasonings of choice. For each dinner, place a hamburger patty on the foil. Surround the patty with sliced potatoes and carrots on the side. You may dot on a few dabs of butter over all if you wish. (You may also add additional veggies, if you wish, like diced onion and corn.) Wrap up each dinner, folding the foil envelope-style, to make a nice neat packet with sealed edges. Store in fridge, and then in a cooler until ready to cook over your campfire. Lay packets on a grill or directly on coals to cook. Cooking times will very according to fire temperature, but probably about 10 to 12 minutes is good. (You can always check for doneness and wrap it back up again.) When done to your liking, unwrap and enjoy right out of the packet.

Weekly Challenge

ON A SCALE OF ONE TO TEN...

Well...how are we all doing when we jump on that scale these days? (Remember our New Year Resolutions to eat healthier, and happier, and make a return to fitness?) I don't know about you, but I've added a couple of unwanted pounds over the winter. So, I thought some wonderful salad meals might be in order. The next time you think "comfort food" think "salad," and how "comfortable you'll feel" when you buy that new little sun dress in a smaller size! Your hubbie can probably benefit from this regimen too, (even though he might not admit it) so I've even included a "manly-man" salad in this week's menu. Our weekly challenge: scale down on calories...scale up on fitness.

APRIL 24
Marily's Sweet Oil and Vinegar for Tossed Salad
makes 1 batch

INGREDIENTS
1 shot glass sugar
1 shot glass salad oil of choice
1½ shot glasses vinegar of choice
Salt
Pepper
Paprika
Dry Mustard

In bottom of screw-top jar place the sugar. Add the oil. Pour on the vinegar. Shake in salt until it sinks in a ball. Crack in pepper to cover the surface. Then paprika to cover the surface. Then dry mustard to generously cover the surface. Cover jar and shake to blend well. Serve dressing at room temperature, tossed lightly with mixed-salad greens and fixings of choice.

RUSH HOUR TIP
The no-fail formula for making this dressing is to add the ingredients in the order listed and to sprinkle in the salt just until it sinks in a ball, and the rest of the season-ing until they generously cover the surface. Be sure to re-shake the dressing just before using.

A Thought for Today
"Nothing tastes as good as thin feels."
~Anonymous

APRIL 25

Mother's Sunny Summer Salad
A KID FRIENDLY RECIPE
6 to 8 servings

I remember eating this salad as a child. It was a great way for my mother to get me to eat my veggies! I was always so pleased when I saw one of these little, individual-serving-size molds jiggling at my place setting, along with its little dab of creamy mayonnaise on top.

INGREDIENTS
1 (3 ounce) package lemon-flavored gelatin
2 tablespoons lemon juice
Pinch of salt
1 cup diced celery
1 cup shredded cabbage
1 cup shredded carrots
Mayonnaise, at time of serving (optional) for garnish
Paprika, at serving time (optional)

Prepare gelatin according to package directions and stir in lemon juice and salt. Place in refrigerator to start to set. As it starts to firm, stir in the veggies so they are mixed through the whole gelatin, and don't fall to the bottom. At this point you can put the salad into individual-serving-size molds, 1 large mold, or a pretty glass serving dish, to refrigerate until firm. Garnish each serving with a little dab of mayonnaise and slight sprinkle of paprika

---

Come Out.. Come Out... Wherever You Are!
To easily un-mold gelatin, turn mold upside down on serving plate, platter, or dish. Soak a kitchen towel in hot water, wring it out, and wrap around the mold. Jiggle the mold, until you hear the gelatin inside release and plunk onto the plate. Lift up the mold and voila! You're ready to garnish and serve. Some people like to pre-spray their mold with non-stick spray before originally filling with recipe—as this also eases the un-molding procedure.

APRIL 26

The Rush Hour Cook's Asparagus Salad
6 servings

INGREDIENTS

1 pound fresh asparagus
1 head leaf lettuce, washed and dried with paper toweling
3 tablespoons juice, freshly squeezed from a lemon
3 tablespoons raspberry vinaigrette (select a fat-free variety at your
   market)
Freshly cracked pepper
1 package crumbled blue cheese (or if you are not a blue cheese fan,
   substitute shaved Parmesan curls or slices of soft, fresh mozzarella)

In a large pot, bring a deep amount of water to a boil. (Did you know that they actually make an 'asparagus pot' just for this purpose?—but it certainly isn't necessary to have one.) Have a large bowl of ice water on the counter for later use. Trim asparagus by "snapping off" the tough end of each spear. (Spears will naturally break at the point they are meant to.) Trim off any unwanted scales from the sides of the stalks with a potato peeler. Plunge trimmed asparagus into the boiling water, and simmer until just crisp-tender…about 4 minutes or so. Do not over cook! Remove asparagus and plunge into the cold ice water to stop any further cooking and hold the bright color. Set aside. In a small lidded jar, shake together lemon juice and raspberry vinaigrette. Set aside. Remove asparagus from ice water and drain well, patting dry with paper toweling. Arrange on individual salad plates lined with leaf lettuce. Drizzle dressing over all. Season with a little fresh cracked pepper. Sprinkle on crumbled blue cheese, or garnish with your cheese of choice and serve. Accompany with optional servings of good French bread and unsalted butter; and optional, portion-controlled servings of meat, chicken, or fish.

A Thought for Today
THE ART MAKING SALAD

My mother taught me that there is an art to making salads. It is the attention to detail, that makes your salad great! Did you know that salad dressing 'rolls off' wet greens, rather than adhering to their surface ... leaving an oil-slick in the bottom of the bowl! Did you know that dressings should be served at room temperature for maximum mixing and maximum flavor? How about the fact that only about 1 to 2 tablespoons of dressing is needed per salad ... rather than slathering on half the bottle! Salads should be lightly "dressed" at the very last minute and tossed only until their greens become glossy. When garnishing a salad with nuts, toast the nuts first in a dry pan, or spread in a single layer on a cookie sheet and toast in the oven, as this releases their flavor and keeps the nuts crisp and crunchy in the salad. These few details can take an ordinary, ho-hum salad to delicately delicious! Thanks Mom!

APRIL 27
Tomato Bread
8 servings

This yummy bread makes a nice accompaniment for any salad.

INGREDIENTS
½ loaf French bread
2 fresh tomatoes, chopped
1 tablespoon olive oil
1 tablespoon crushed oregano
Sprinkling of Parmesan cheese

Preheat broiler. Cut French bread into 8 (1-inch) slices. Place on baking sheet and broil 1 to 2 minutes on each side, or just until lightly browned. Meanwhile, combine tomatoes, oil and oregano in small bowl. Remove bread from broiler and spread each slice with tomato mixture. Sprinkle with Parmesan cheese. Serve with one of this week's great salads.

APRIL 28

Turkey Super Supper Salad

4 to 6 servings

INGREDIENTS
3 to 4 cups cooked turkey, cut into bite size pieces
1 cup seedless green grapes, cut into halves
2 stalks celery, sliced
2 green onions, including tops, sliced
1 (8 ounce) can water chestnuts, drained and sliced thin
1 cup lemon flavored low-fat yogurt
1 to 2 tablespoons low-salt soy sauce, to taste
Leaf lettuce, at serving time
Cantaloupe and/or honeydew melon slices, at serving time

Mix first 5 ingredients together in a glass bowl. Set aside. Mix yogurt and soy sauce together to make dressing. Add to turkey mixture and toss well. Cover salad with plastic wrap and store in refrigerator for at least an hour to blend flavors. Toss again at serving time and serve mounded on leaf lettuce. Garnish with slices of melon on the side. Add optional bread or muffins (sticking to your portion control) to complete the meal.

A Thought for Today

THE SLOW BURN...

Did you know that you burn about 2 calories per minute while you are bowling, about 6 calories per minute while gardening or hiking, around 8 per minute while taking a brisk walk, 9 per minute playing tennis, 12 calories per minute jogging, and back down to 3 per minute while golfing (with a cart). Ah-hum, and how many calories do we take-in per minute while eating!? Just a little food for thought...

A Thought for Today

What do they say: "Real men don't eat quiche?"…and would just as soon forget the salad too! Well, we'll see how they feel when they go to put on last season's shorts and go out to mow the lawn! Today's recipe is for them…our manly-men, who might just need to shed a pound or two, too.

APRIL 29

Low-Cal Lo-Fat Manly-Man Fajita Salad

4 to 6 servings

INGREDIENTS

I pound boneless beef steak, trimmed of fat (use sirloin or flank steak)
I tablespoon Canola or olive oil
I red bell pepper, ribbed, seeded and cut into strips
I yellow bell pepper, ribbed, seeded and cut into strips
I orange bell pepper, ribbed, seeded and cut into strips
Mixed salad greens of choice
1/3 to ½ cup fat-free, Italian style salad dressing of choice
2 green onions, with tops, sliced, at serving time
Low-fat sour cream, at serving time
Low-fat tortillas or pita-bread, at serving time

Trim any excess fat from steak. Cut into stir-fry size strips, making sure to cut across grain of meat. (This will keep the meat tender.) In one tablespoon of oil, fast-sauté the beef strips, just until browned—maybe 3 minutes, or so. Do not over cook. Remove from pan and reserve. Add bell peppers to pan and sauté until crisp-tender. Mix peppers with the reserved beef and place on salad greens. Drizzle on salad-dressing. Garnish with sour cream and a sprinkling of green onion. Serve with a basket of warmed low-fat tortillas or pita breads.

RUSH HOUR WISDOM

For perfect salad greens, wash lettuce leaves in advance and pat dry with paper toweling. Store in the fridge wrapped in paper toweling and then in a plastic bag; or you can place patted-dry greens directly into salad bowl and top with a layer of damp paper toweling (if using that same day)—you want dry-damp, not soggy-sodden, storage. (Lettuce has to breathe a little.) For convenience take advantage of all the wonderful pre-mixed, pre-washed, pre-packaged salad greens available at our markets today. (I personally like the "spring-mixed" baby greens mixed with additional romaine.)

A Thought for Today
THE VALUE OF LAUGHTER
"A complete re-evaluation takes place in our physical and mental
being when we've laughed and had some fun."
~Catherine Ponder, American Motivational Writer

APRIL 30

I hope you've had some fun this week, with my thoughts about salad recipes and
their importance in our "quality control" over our eating habits.

Family-Favorite Fruit Cocktail Salad
A KIDS IN THE KITCHEN RECIPE
estimate 1 cup salad per serving

Admittedly, this recipe is far from new, but is such a stand-by—and what a favorite with kids. Truly a timeless classic that deserves to be served again and
again…and if you use low-cal, it falls right into our healthy-salad-week. (In the
winter I make my salad with fruit cocktail and other canned fruits from the
pantry—while in the summer, I utilize all the fresh fruits of the season.)

INGREDIENTS
Canned fruit cocktail, drained well (use a low-cal)
Sliced Banana
Mini marshmallows
Whipped topping (use a low-cal)

Mix together fruit and marshmallows. Fold in whipped topping. Chill in fridge
until serving time. Measurements and proportions don't really matter … just
what you can find and what you like … feel free to add any fruits (fresh or
canned) that you like.

Weekly Challenge

NEW BEGINNINGS...

The month of May... a new month, new beginnings, new challenges...a perfect time to "refresh" and "re-invigorate" our personal-living skills.

"Ready to turn over a healthy new leaf?" As you are out in the yard raking up all those leaves from last year, sprucing up the lawn or patio, planting your beautiful gardens, and removing all that dead mulch...why not think about tending your own "personal garden."

Click on the web site: www.womeninwellness.com and "turn over a new leaf" with Carrie Myers Smith, a Champion Press author and wellness-coach, who shares her personal experiences and knowledge-gained for exercise-science and healthful-well being, while using gentle and proven coaching methods.

MAY 1

Let's kick off our wellness campaign with a light dinner, Rush Hour Cook style, using an entrée of Mushroom Rice and adding a nice raspberry-vinaigrette salad using mixed spring greens and a low-cal dressing. Add a loaf of crusty French bread to complete your meatless dinner. Bring a pitcher of iced water, spiked with lemon slices, to your table and serve in your best stemmed glasses. Top off the meal with a refreshing lemon sorbet (from your favorite market), garnished with a sliced strawberry or slices of kiwi, and a wafer cookie on the side (to satisfy your sweet tooth).

The Rush Hour Cook's Marvelous Mushroom Rice
6 side servings

INGREDIENTS
2 cups uncooked white rice
1 (10.75-ounce) can condensed cream of mushroom soup
1 cup vegetable broth
1/8 cup water
1 cup fresh sliced mushrooms or 1 (4 ounce) can mushrooms, drained
1 teaspoon dried oregano
¼ cup butter, melted
¼ teaspoon salt
1/8 teaspoon pepper

Preheat oven to 350 degrees. Stir rice, soup and broth together in a 2 quart casserole dish. Blend in all other ingredients. Bake for 35 to 40 minutes, or until rice is tender.

MAY 2

Glorious Green Beans
4 Servings

INGREDIENTS
1 pound fresh green beans, washed and ends trimmed
1/8 cup slivered almonds (toasted, stove-top in a dry pan)
1/8 cup red wine vinegar
Water

Fill saucepan with 1 to 2 inches of water and bring to a boil. Cut green beans into 2-inch pieces and place in steamer or colander, and place over water in saucepan. Cover and steam for 5 to 6 minutes, or until just crisp-tender. Transfer beans to serving bowl. Toss with red wine vinegar and sliced almonds.

A Thought for Today
GETTING RID OF THE BAGGAGE...

Take a tip from the Rush Hour Cook and Carrie Myers Smith's motto...*Real women. Real life. Real solutions.* At Carrie's site www.womeninwellness.com you'll find loads of health tips, a free newsletter, a free goal-setting course and more. When we take our 'old baggage' and recycle it, it may look like something new, but it's still old baggage...just newly repackaged. "If you are going to join this (wellness) journey, you need to start fresh, start over, without all that old mucky-muck. It just goops everything up and gets in the way..."

"What kind of old baggage are you holding onto? Will you allow old hurts and un-forgiveness to hold you back from being the woman you were intended to be? What do you need to do to get rid of your old baggage...?"

~Carrie Myers Smith

MAY 3
Garden Parsnips Plain and Simple
cook up a pan full

My Grandfather used to grow parsnips (amongst the peonies) in his back yard. He'd pick them fresh and cook them up (starchy and sweet) for many a summer dinner. To this day they are one of my mom's favorites, and now my family's.

INGREDIENTS
Fresh parsnips, peeled and cut into very thin julienne strips
Butter (preferably clarified)
Dash of salt and pepper

If you buy your parsnips from the grocery store, be sure to pare off the waxy coating on the outside. (This is used to keep the parsnips fresh during extended storage.) Pare the snips and julienne into very thin strips. Sauté slowly in butter until (about 15 to 20 minutes) tender and golden brown. Parsnips will be sweet and tender, yet kind of chewy. Season with a little salt and pepper.

Time Management Tips for Mom:

Practice the five-minute rule: If something can be done in 5 minutes or less, do it right away versus adding it to your to-do list.

Create a Daily Action List: Let's face it, we will never get everything done on our to-do lists. Identify and choose 3 Power To-Do's each day to complete no matter what.

Mark It: Post a half dry-erase, half-corkboard in a central location of your home. Assign each family member a dry-erase color. Let children (and spouses) be responsible for writing down their calendar. Use the corkboard area for posting messages and notes.

Mom's In Box: Make an in-box for children to place permissions slips, notes, and any other information mom needs to review. This will teach children responsibility while saving you the "backpack" search.

MAY 4
Old Fashioned Parsnip Patties
1 patty per person

INGREDIENTS
Grandfather's garden-picked parsnips, peeled and cut into chunks
Water
Salt and pepper
Butter
Flour or dry breadcrumbs, for dredging

Prepare parsnips as if you are preparing potatoes for mashing. Boil snips in water until fork-tender-soft and ready for mashing. Drain. With an electric beater, mash until smooth, adding seasonings of salt and pepper and a little butter. Form mashed parsnips into patties. Dredge patties in flour or fine, dry breadcrumbs to coat both sides. Melt butter to cover bottom of skillet. On a medium heat setting, sauté patties until golden brown on both sides and warmed through. Add more butter as necessary. Serve warm.

RUSH HOUR WISDOM
Store-bought parsnips work just as well as garden grown, and make this recipe available, year 'round. Rather intimidating looking, with their waxy covering, it is hard to believe they can be so sweet and delectable. Be sure to remove all outer waxy covering if you are using store-bought "snips" before you start cooking. Your potato peeler will work wonderfully to scrape off the waxy coating along with the outer peel of the snips.

A Thought for Today
"Behavioral changes require four basic steps:
desire, choice, planning and action."
~ Carrie Myers Smith

MAY 5

The Rush Hour Cook's Chicken Fettuccini Dijon

4 servings

INGREDIENTS
1 cup fat-free sour cream
2 tablespoons Dijon-style mustard
4 boneless, skinless chicken breasts
½ pound mushrooms, sliced
6 ounces fettuccini
Salt and pepper to taste

Prepare fettuccini according to package directions and keep warm. Stir sour cream and mustard together in small bowl. Spray a skillet with cooking spray. Cook chicken breasts over medium heat, 8 to 10 minutes, or until chicken is cooked through and no longer pink. Remove chicken and cover to keep warm. Add mushrooms and a bit of water to skillet. Cover and cook over medium heat until soft, 2 to 3 minutes. Add sour cream/mustard mixture to mushrooms and heat, being careful not to boil. Return chicken to skillet and gently mix together. Divide fettuccini equally on serving plates and top with chicken mixture. Salt and pepper to taste.

MAY 6

Rockin' Rotini

6 servings

INGREDIENTS
12 ounces tri-colored rotini pasta
1 cup diced deli salami
1 cup diced provolone cheese
1 cup fat-free Italian salad dressing

Cook rotini pasta to package directions, drain and rinse with cold water. Add other ingredients and toss to mix. Cover and refrigerate until serving time.

MAY 7

Rush Hour Quick Quesadilla Bites
A KIDS IN THE KITCHEN RECIPE
4 servings

INGREDIENTS
1 ½ cups mozzarella cheese
1 cup cooked chicken, shredded
8 flour tortillas (I like to use healthy whole wheat tortillas)
½ teaspoon cayenne pepper

Sprinkle mozzarella cheese and shredded chicken over tortillas. Season with a slight bit of cayenne pepper. Fold and cut into quarters. Cook over medium heat in skillet until filling is heated and cheese starts to melt. You can also microwave these for 20 seconds, or until cheese has just melted (times will very depending on microwave). Makes 32 mini size quesadillas.

RUSH HOUR TIP
Great for snacking and a great "starter recipe" for kids, these quesadilla bites are easy to assemble, easy to cook up in the microwave, and easy to eat. Kids can think up other combos of meats and cheeses, and even vegetables, for a variety of tasty combinations. (Check out all the 'flavored tortillas' available today too!)

A Thought for Today
"No one else's plan will fit you as well as the plan you put together for yourself!" ~Carrie Myers Smith, author and personalized wellness coach www.womeninwellness.com

Weekly Challenge

MAKING A PLAN…

A few weeks ago I took the words of Carrie Myers Smith to heart and made an appointment for my whole family with a local nutritionist. I felt we all needed just a little "tweaking" with our eating skills and a nutritionist could point us all in the right direction. Here are a few very simple pointers that she used to get my family back on track.

1. Always eat at the dining table. This includes all meals, snacks, desserts. If it is edible, it shall be eaten at the KITCHEN or DINING ROOM table… no exceptions. (This one simple rule will drastically change the eating patterns of most families.)

2. Never eat directly out of the package, box, bag, etc., that the food comes in. Put a portion on a plate or in a bowl and sit down at the table to eat it. If you want more, make the decision to get another helping, rather than automatically and absentmindedly reaching into the box or bag until you've finished its total contents all by yourself.

3. Learn your food groups, and always incorporate at least two at a time.

4. Eat smaller meals more frequently, rather than over eating at one or two meals, with long periods of getting hungry in between. Your body runs best on a consistent amount of fuel and you will eat more consistently, rather than over stuffing yourself, then starving, then stuffing again.

5. Eat slowly and enjoy your food. Add good family conversation during the meal. Regard your meal times as treasured time with your family … not interruptions in your personal schedule.

MAY 8

Cal-Zoned Out
A KID FRIENDLY RECIPE
1 to 2 pieces per person
(And a shout out of Happy Birthday to my daughter, Sammy!)

INGREDIENTS
1 tube refrigerated crescent-style rolls
¼ cup pizza sauce
½ teaspoon crushed garlic
¼ teaspoon crushed basil
½ teaspoon crushed oregano
1 (8 ounce) package mozzarella cheese
2 tablespoons melted butter
Parmesan cheese, grated
Fillings, according to taste:
   Pepperoni
   Pre-cooked Italian sausage
   Chopped onion
   Green pepper, chopped
   Black Olives
   Pineapple
   Anchovies
   Canadian Bacon
   Mushrooms
   You name it…

Open can of crescent-style rolls and separate. Fill with desired items. Fold into triangles and pinch edges shut, to form pouches. Arrange on cookie sheet and bake for 12 to 15 minutes at 375 degrees. When done immediately brush with melted butter and sprinkle with the grated Parmesan cheese. Can serve with extra pizza sauce for dipping!

RUSH HOUR WISDOM
This is a great dish to make ahead and freeze in individual Ziploc® bags for snacks or party food!

MAY 9

Rush Hour Cinnamon Donuts in a Jiffy
A KID FRIENDLY RECIPE TO EAT—BUT NOT TO COOK!

(I would strongly advise keeping young children away from such amounts of hot oil and make sure appliance is securely stationed on a quiet kitchen counter, away from elbows, turning bodies, inquiring minds, and cords to trip over.)

INGREDIENTS
1 tube of refrigerated buttermilk biscuits (not the flaky kind0
Cinnamon sugar
Canola oil for "deep frying"

Cut "donut holes" out of biscuits by using a 1 –inch biscuit cutter. Heat canola oil in deep fryer, or electric fry pan, to 375 degrees. Fry 2 to 3 donuts at a time till browned, turning once in the deep oil. Fry donut holes separately. As done remove from oil with long-handled tongs or slotted spoon. Drain on paper towels and roll in cinnamon sugar while still warm.

RUSH HOUR WISDOM
Kids can help with the cutting out of the donut holes and then work on rolling in cinnamon sugar or thinking up other decorations.

A Thought for Today

"If you are not enjoying what's on the end of your fork then drop it, put your hands in the air, and slowly step away from the table!"~Carrie Myers Smith, *Squeezing Your Size 14 Self into a Size 6 World, A Real Woman's Guide to Food, Fitness and Self-Acceptance,* ISBN 1891400304, published by Champion Press, Ltd.

MAY 10
Thelma's Rhubarb Pie (submitted by Judy B.)
1 double crust pie

"This pie was made by my mother, Thelma, ever since I was a young girl. I always looked forward to spring, and the rhubarb, and my mother's pie." ~ Judy B.

INGREDIENTS
Pie crust, for 1 (9–inch) double crust pie
4 cups garden fresh rhubarb
1 2/3 cups sugar
1/3 cups all purpose flour
Dash of salt
2 tablespoons butter

INGREDIENTS
Combine 4 cups rhubarb with 1 2/3 cups sugar, 1/3 cup all purpose flour and a dash of salt. Let stand 15 minutes. Meanwhile, prepare pastry for double-crust 9-inch pie. Line a 9-inch pie pan with bottom pastry. Fill with rhubarb mixture. Dot with 2 tablespoons butter. Adjust top crust over filling, cutting slits for escape of steam. Seal and crimp around edge. Bake at 400 degrees for 45 minutes, or until browned well.

A Thought for Today
"Happiness is not a destination. It is a way of life…"
~Burton Hills

MAY 11

Mikey's Mac
A KID FRIENDLY RECIPE
6 servings

INGREDIENTS
¼ cup butter
¼ cup flour
½ teaspoon salt
Dash of white pepper
Dash of nutmeg
1 ½ cups milk
¼ cup grated Parmesan cheese
1 (12 ounce) package macaroni or penne pasta, or similar pasta of your choice
¼ cup of the starchy water, reserved from the pasta cooking pot

While pasta is cooking to al dente in its large pot of boiling water, make a basic white sauce (to which you are going to add Parmesan cheese). To make sauce, in a sauce pan, melt butter and stir in flour with a wire whisk, cooking and stirring till a blended roux is formed. Season with salt and pepper and a dash of nutmeg. Slowly stir and blend in milk, continuing to heat and stir with a whisk until sauce becomes smooth and thickened. Lastly stir in the Parmesan cheese. Drain pasta of choice (saving a little of the starchy water). Toss warm pasta with warm sauce to coat. Add a little bit of starch water to help the coating process if needed. Serve with additional Parmesan cheese to pass.

RUSH HOUR TIP
Try Mike's recipe with a spinach flavored pasta or a sun-dried tomato pasta to add a subtle background taste. Or you might want to try gourmet pasta from the specialty section of your market Fresh, handmade pasta has a "tooth" (texture) all its own which is fabulous for showing off a subtle sauce. Turn that kid friendly recipe into a sophisticated dinner with subtle flavors for all to enjoy.

.

MAY 12

Pizza Dippers

4 to 6 servings

INGREDIENTS

1 (4 ounce) can tomato paste
1 (8 ounce) can tomato sauce
1 tablespoon oregano, crushed between fingers
½ tablespoon minced garlic
12 chopped olives
¼ teaspoon pepper
1 cup mozzarella cheese
1 loaf French bread, cut in slices

Mix all ingredients in a saucepan except the cheese and bread, and cook over low heat. Simmer for 10 minutes. Add cheese and stir constantly until cheese is melted. Serve hot with bread for dipping.

A Thought for Today

"My house, filled with happiness....that is my destination. To be a part of the laughter and joy of all who live here... that is my way of life." ~Brook NoⅡl, the Rush Hour Cook

MAY 13

Julie's Texas (or is it 'Jersey) Hash

This recipe comes via Julie's Mother-in-law. Since Julie lives in New Jersey, I really think we need to rename the recipe "Julie's 'Jersey Hash"…but I'll continue as written… Julie says that her Texas Hash is a real favorite with her kids and she makes it often for the whole family to enjoy.

INGREDIENTS
2 large onions (white or Spanish)
Olive oil
2 pounds lean ground chuck
A little salt to taste
1 (8 ounce) can Contadina® tomato sauce
1 can (2 cups) Del Monte® stewed tomatoes with juice
1 (8 ounce) package curly noodles

Slice and brown onions (really brown) in smallest amount possible of olive oil. Remove from pan. Brown ground chuck and salt to taste. Combine fried onions with browned ground beef. Add the tomato sauce and stewed tomatoes. Stir in curly noodles (uncooked). Pour mixture into 13 X 9-inch greased casserole dish. Cover and bake at 350 degrees for 45 minutes. Remove cover and bake for 15 minutes more.

RUSH HOUR TIPS
Upon first read 2 large onions sounds like a lot doesn't it? …However the caramelization that goes on when those onions brown is what makes this recipe great.

A Tomato Tidbit
Did you know that when storing leftover tomato-sauced dishes—if you pre-spray your plastic containers with non-stick spray before filling, you can eliminate the stubborn tomato stains that usually get absorbed into the containers? This spray-technique can also be used on your rubberized spatulas—to avoid tomato stains there as well. *Bonus tip: Pre-spraying your rubber spatula with non-stick cooking spray also helps when working with thick, sticky ingredients, such as molasses, honey, and frostings!

MAY 14

Friendship Cookies
A KIDS IN THE KITCHEN RECIPE

YOU WILL NEED::
A mixing bowl and a large spoon, or an electric mixer
Measuring cups and measuring spoons
A sifter, if you have one
Plastic wrap and construction paper
A pencil or marker, and a pair of craft scissors
Waxed paper and a rolling pin
Table knife, spatula, cooking spray, cookie sheet, and pot holders
And one adult to help you

INGREDIENTS for the Dough:
1 ½ sticks butter, slightly softened
¾ cup powdered sugar, sifted
1 large egg
1 ½ cups all-purpose flour, sifted
Pinch of salt

INGREDIENTS for the Decorations:
Assorted tube-style icing
Assorted sprinkles and jimmies

Cream butter in a mixing bowl with a spoon or an electric mixer. Add sugar and beat until smooth. Stir in egg, flour, and salt. Mix together until thoroughly combined. Shape the dough into a ball and wrap with plastic wrap. Chill dough until firm (about 1 hour).

While dough is chilling, have your children trace their hand print on construction paper. Using a pair of scissors, cut out each hand print to form a pattern (to be used for their hand shaped cookie). Set aside.

Once chilled, roll out dough on waxed paper to a thickness of ¼-inch. (Dust your rolling pin with flour to prevent sticking.) Place the hand patterns on the dough and carefully cut around each pattern with a table knife. Using a non-stick sprayed spatula, carefully transfer the hand-shaped, cut-out cookies to a cookie sheet. Bake for 10 to 12 minutes in a 350-degree oven, just until golden brown and set.

Once cookies have cooled, "decorate" each hand-shaped cookie with tube-icings of various colors.—You can use red-icing for "nail polish;" different colors, along with sprinkles and jimmies, to make finger rings, watches and "friendship" bracelets. See if every body can figure out who's hand is who's from the "personality" of the decorations you have created.

Weekly Challenge

ARE YOU…?

Are you continuing to make May your "Makeover-Month?" You only have a couple more weeks to go. Memorial Day will be here before we know it! Just remember the words of Zig Ziegler who once said, "A goal properly set is halfway reached."…and according to the date we should be halfway there! Are you?

MAY 15
Soft Pretzels
A KID FRIENDLY RECIPE
1 pretzel per serving

INGREDIENTS
1 (11 ounce) package of refrigerated breadsticks
1 beaten egg white
1 tablespoon water
Coarse salt
Mustard (optional) at serving time

Unroll and separate breadsticks. Gently stretch each dough into a 16–inch "rope." Shape rope into a pretzel by crossing one end over the other to form a single "bow" with two 4–inch "tails." Where the dough crosses, twist it once to secure the circle. Bend each tail into a second and then a third circle, tucking their ends underneath the main circle. You should now have a pretzel shape. Moisten tail-ends and pinch slightly to secure. Place on greased baking sheet. Mix together beaten egg white and water and brush over pretzels. This will give them a nice glaze, that we so love with pretzels. Sprinkle with coarse salt. Bake at 375 degrees for 12 to 15 minutes, or until golden brown. Eat as is or serve with your favorite mustard for dipping.

Kitchen Tips

Family Favorite Collection: When mom is gone or working late, providing family members with easy access to favorite recipes helps avoid costly and unhealthy drive-thru runs. Place your family's 10 favorite recipes in a clearly marked folder for easy reference.

3, 4, and 5-Ingredient Standbys: Have quick and easy recipes on standby for busy nights. Use your Whirlpool g2® or Velos® or microwave to have dinner on the table in 15 minutes or less, from start to finish. Print out my favorite "5-Day Weekly Menu" along with shopping list at www.rushhourcook.com/menu5.htm

---

MAY 16

Chicken Filled Croissants
6 servings

INGREDIENTS
1 pound cooked chicken, thinly sliced into strips
4 tablespoons honey
1 teaspoon prepared mustard of your choice
1 small red onion, thinly sliced
6 large bakery croissants

In a skillet, over medium heat combine honey, mustard, and onion to make a warm sauce. Fold in chicken to glaze and heat through. Do not let mixture boil. Meanwhile split and lightly toast croissants. Fill with warm chicken mixture and serve.

RUSH HOUR TIP
When slicing breads and pastries use a serrated knife and a "sawing" motion so you don't crush the bread.

The Perfect Pantry
Has anyone seen my tomato paste? While having other family members help with the shopping and unpacking seems like a great benefit, it loses its charm when ingredients are hard to find. Label your pantry shelves to avoid the "missing ingredient game." (This also makes it easier for other family members to navigate the kitchen.)

MAY 17
Ultra-Quick Chicken and Rice

Looking for a quick, tasty dinner cooked-up and served all in one pan? This is it!

INGREDIENTS
4 boneless chicken breasts
1 (10.75 ounce) can cream of chicken soup
1 2/3 cups water
½ teaspoon pepper
½ cup instant white rice, uncooked
2 cups broccoli florets (fresh or frozen)

Brown chicken breasts in a skillet over medium heat. Remove from pan and set aside. Pour soup, water, and seasoning into pan and heat to boiling. Stir in the instant rice and broccoli. Place chicken on top of mixture. Cover and cook over low heat for 5 to 10 minutes, or until rice is tender and chicken is cooked through. Add fresh fruit or a salad of your choice to complete the meal.

RUSH HOUR TIP
You can also prepare this recipe with any other cream soup of your choice, such as cream of mushroom, cream of broccoli, etc., Instant brown rice may be exchanged for the white rice.

Make a Must-Have List

Using a magnet, place a large blank sheet of paper on your fridge. Throughout the week, write down all the must-have items in your household. Include everything from toiletries to kitchen items. Make photocopies of this list. When you go shopping, use this list as an "inventory" to figure out what items you need. This is also a great way to "prompt" your memory for other items to pick up when you make an impromptu grocery store stop. Keep a copy in each of your car's glove boxes for quick and handy reference.

MAY 18

Hammy Noodles in a Flash

Rich, creamy, cheesy and all of 10 minutes cooking time for a very kid- friendly dinner. Slice up some fruit while the pasta is cooking and you have a complete meal.

INGREDIENTS
3/4 pound cooked ham, diced
1 ½ cups shredded cheese (you choose the type: Parmesan, Mozzarella, Swiss or Cheddar)
1 ½ cups light cream
1¼ pound linguini pasta
Salt and pepper to taste

Cook pasta according to package directions. Rinse, drain, and set aside. Warm cream over low heat. Once hot, add diced ham and cook till heated through, stirring frequently. Do not let cream boil. Add cheese. Continue cooking (but do not boil) until cheese is thoroughly melted, continuing to stir constantly over low heat. Season with salt and pepper to taste. Cooking time will be about 10 minutes. Mix sauce with pasta in large serving bowl and serve family style. Tada!

RUSH HOUR TIP
When heating milk and/or cream—do so over low to moderate heat, and do not let them come to a boil. You want to heat the milk to just before boiling, to a point where bubbles are beginning to form on the side of the pan—this is called "scalding." Hot milk can foam up quickly and spill over the top of the pan, creating both a fire hazard and a mess if left unattended or carelessly cooked.

MAY 19

Split-Second Burritos
4 to 6 servings
How quick is this (and easy too)!

INGREDIENTS
1 pound ground beef
1 onion, chopped
2 tablespoons chili powder (or to taste)
1 can refried beans
6 large flour tortillas
1 (8 ounce) can enchilada sauce
2 cups shredded Cheddar cheese
Salsa
Sour cream
Black olives

Brown ground beef and onion in skillet. Mix in chili powder. Microwave tortillas for 30 seconds just to soften. Divide beans and meat onto the 6 tortillas. Fold tortillas over meat/bean mixture and place in microwave dish, seam side down. Top with enchilada sauce and cheese. Microwave 2 to 4 minutes (cooking time will vary with different microwaves), until cheese is melted and burritos are heated through. Top according to taste with salsa, sour cream and black olives.

A Thought for Today

"Nobody gets to live life backward. Look ahead--that is where your future lies." ~Ann Landers, American Advice Columnist

That is not to say we can't learn from our past, but it is to say we shouldn't waste our valuable energies dwelling on things that are no longer changeable. Turn your positive energy toward the future and make change happen before it's happened without you! Or, if I may use a culinary metaphor, take the salvageable leftovers and the lessons learned from yesterday's burnt dinner, to create a gourmet masterpiece for a future menu.

MAY 20

Poor Man's Casserole

4+ servings

INGREDIENTS

2 cups ground round, browned
1 pound frozen vegetables, thawed
3 cups mashed potatoes
1 cup "yellow" cheese, grated (a.k.a. Cheddar, American, etc.)
Seasonings to taste

Mix meat with vegetables and place in 9 x 13–inch casserole dish. Spread mashed potatoes over top of meat and vegetable mixture. Sprinkle grated cheese over top of potatoes. Bake, uncovered, in 350-degree oven for 20 to 30 minutes, or until heated through.

RUSH HOUR WISDOM

Today's tip applies to the versatility you can find in a recipe. Although Poor Man's Casserole is a tasty treat when made with sautéed ground beef, this recipe can also be a great way to use up leftover meats and leftover mashed potatoes, assorted leftover vegetables, and even a variety of cheeses. The next time you have a beef roast and mashed potatoes—make extra and serve this recipe the following night. Leftover turkey and chicken would work well too with a little of their gravy mixed in with the veggies and then topped with the mashed potatoes and baked. Taco meat and a spicy cheese would add yet another flavor to the dish. Even leftover lamb roast, the inclusion of some wine, and the selection of a different vegetable combo, would make an excellent potato topped casserole. And if you find yourself with leftover meat and no potatoes—use boxed-instant ... I'll never tell. Taking a recipe and "making it your own" can be a fun way to expand your culinary efforts...especially when you are "experimenting" with budget leftovers.

MAY 21

Kids-Love-It-Casserole
A KIDS IN THE KITCHEN DAY RECIPE

Kids love this pizza-style casserole and it is so easy and quick to make…a great starter dish for you to use as a teaching lesson! Have them press the dough into the baking dish while you brown the meat. Let them sprinkle on the cheese, and be responsible for watching the cooking time on a timer. The fact that they helped you make this 'specialty' dinner will make it taste even better!

INGREDIENTS
1 pound ground beef
1 (15 ounce) can chunky tomato sauce
1 can refrigerated pizza crust dough
1 ½ cups mozzarella cheese, shredded

Cook meat until browned. Add sauce and cook until heated through. Meanwhile, press pizza dough into a 9 x 13–inch dish. Sprinkle ½ cup cheese over dough. Add meat mixture. Bake in a 425-degree oven for 10 to 15 minutes. Sprinkle on remaining cup of cheese and bake an additional 5 minutes, or until cheese is melted.

A Thought for Today
DON'T WASTE A DAY

"Great opportunities to help others seldom come, but small ones surround us daily." ~Sally Koch, American Writer

—And just so too, are we surrounded with daily opportunities to teach our children to cook and be comfortable in the kitchen. So today, take a little bit of "family time" to "family cook" this "family dinner." ~Brook Noel, the Rush Hour Cook

MAY 22

Beer-Batter for Fried Fish

Makes enough for 1 fish fry

INGREDIENTS
2 cups self-rising flour
½ teaspoon each: salt and pepper
1 (12 ounce) can of beer

Mix flour and seasonings together. Divide out a few tablespoons and set aside. Add the beer to remaining flour and stir until combined. Batter will be thick. Before dipping fish fillets in batter, dust them with the separated-seasoned flour. Then dip them into the batter, coating well. Fry coated fish in a deep amount of hot oil. Drain fish on paper towels before serving.

RUSH HOUR TIP
Use any firm white fish fillets in this recipe—such as cod, whitefish, and walleye.

Weekly Challenge

ALWAYS LEAVE…

the gas tank at least a quarter full. How many times have you dashed out to the car late, frazzled, behind schedule, only to find you are "running on fumes?" With no time to do so, you have to stop and fill up! This is especially common when more than one person in the family shares a car. One of the most endearing things about my husband is, he always leaves the tank filled … my knight in shining armor!

MAY 23

Colorful Shrimp and Scallop Kabobs
4 servings

INGREDIENTS
12 premium, large shrimp
12 large sea scallops
3/4 cup bottled Italian salad dressing, divided
1 each: green, red, orange, and yellow bell peppers
Wooden skewers that have been soaked in water

Thaw (if frozen), rinse, and pat dry the seafood. Put in plastic bag with ½ cup salad dressing. Place in refrigerator to marinate ½ hour. While shrimp and scallops are marinating soak at least 18 (10–inch) skewers in water. Meanwhile rib and seed peppers, and cut into 1½–inch "square-ish" pieces. Remove seafood from fridge, drain and discard used marinade. Using 2 sewers (side by side) thread on the shrimp, scallops, and peppers alternately to make colorful kabobs. Grill over medium hot coals for about 12 minutes, or until seafood is opaque. Turn once halfway through and marinate with reserved salad dressing. When ready to serve, brush again with remaining reserved dressing.

MAY 24

Picken Chicken
4 to 6 servings

INGREDIENTS
1 pound pre-cut chicken breast strips
1 onion, chopped
1 green pepper, seeded and chopped
1 teaspoon chili powder
1 teaspoon red pepper flakes (optional)
1 teaspoon freshly minced garlic (or garlic powder)
¾ cup store bought salsa (your choice)
1 package flour tortillas cut in half

Sauté onion and green pepper until soft. Set aside. Using the same pan, stir-fry chicken strips until no longer pink. Add chili powder, red pepper flakes, and garlic. Add back onion and green pepper. Simmer to blend. Just before serving, add salsa. Serve warm with tortillas and your favorite condiments.

MAY 25

Make Your Own BBQ Rub

INGREDIENTS
2 tablespoons barbecue seasoning
1 tablespoon garlic powder
1 teaspoon onion salt
1 teaspoon mixed steak seasoning
1 teaspoon lemon pepper
A pinch of crushed red pepper flakes

Mix well and rub into meat on all sides before broiling or grilling.

RUSH HOUR WISDOM

Let meat rest for about 10 minutes after applying the rub (before cooking). Never return cooked meat to original platter after cooking. Always serve on a fresh platter!

MAY 26

Roasted Garlic

INGREDIENTS
Choice, large heads of garlic
Olive oil
Foil for wrapping

To roast your own garlic—cut top off of head of garlic. Drizzle with olive oil. Wrap with foil. Bake in a 375-degree oven until soft. Individual cloves squeeze right out of the skins when done—adds a sweet flavor to your recipes; great when making garlic bread too.

A Thought for Today
NOT JUST FOR COOKING

"Wear a head of garlic on a string around your neck when you are gardening. It will keep the mosquitoes away!" ~Mary B. Goode, organic gardener

MAY 27
Infusing Garlic #1

This is absolutely delicious when cooking leg of lamb, but is great for beef and pork roasts as well.

INGREDIENTS
Fresh garlic
Roast of choice

Divide a head of garlic into cloves and peel. Pierce slits into the roast and insert garlic cloves down into the slits using as many or as few as you want.

Infusing Garlic #2

INGREDIENTS
Garlic powder
Butter
Steaks of your choice

In a little dish make a paste of butter and a liberal amount of garlic powder to taste, by mashing together with a fork. Just before you serve your grilled steaks, spread and melt the butter over the surface of the steak, finishing it off with a wonderful melt-y, garlicky glaze. Hmmm. Hmmm. Hmmm.

MAY 28

Taco Pizza

6 to 8 servings

INGREDIENTS
1 loaf Rhodes™ bread dough, thawed
1 cup taco sauce
Left over taco meat and leftover toppings
Crushed tortilla chips or hard shelled tacos

Preheat oven to 375 degrees. Grease cookie sheet and roll out bread dough to fit sheet. Cover dough with taco sauce or you can substitute salsa. Add taco meat, black olives, onions, tomatoes, cheese—any leftovers you have. Bake for 20 to 25 minutes, or until bubbly and crust is golden brown. Garnish with crushed tortilla chips (or crushed taco shells) and sour cream. For those adventuresome types add jalapeno peppers and hot sauce!

A Thought for Today

"He who plants a garden plants happiness."
~Chinese proverb

Quick Snack Recipe Bonus

Broiled Melbas
1 cup light mayonnaise
1 cup freshly grated
Parmesan cheese
1 teaspoon parsley
30 melba round crackers
Combine mayonnaise and Parmesan cheese. Add parsley and stir. Spread a teaspoon onto each melba round and broil on a cookie sheet until golden brown (1-2 minutes). There is plenty of room for variation in this recipe. Be creative when choosing your toppings. Makes 30 melba treats.

Weekly Challenge

GARDENING FOR THE SOUL

"When the root is planted deep, there is no reason to fear the wind."~Chinese proverb

This is traditionally the time that gardeners all across the land start their planting. Summer gardens can be such a fun and aesthetic hobby. Just think how great you'll feel when you pick that first ripe patio tomato, or when you pick fresh chives and parsley to garnish your meal. Maybe you want to make pickles with those little cucumbers, or pick pole beans with your granddaughter. What ever your pleasure, plant a little space and make it your place to honor this great, rich land of ours. I believe years ago they called those "Victory Gardens."

Champion Press Ltd. has just released a fabulous book for those interested in both gardening and cooking with their results, be it a patio garden, a little herb garden, or a more ambitious endeavor. *Basil to Thyme: Culinary Endeavors From The Garden To The Kitchen*, by authors Tom Haas and Jan Beane (ISBN 1932783113). Log on to www.championpress.com to learn more.

MAY 29

Red White and Blue Cake for Memorial Day
A KIDS IN THE KITCHEN RECIPE
8 servings

Here's an easy dessert your kids will enjoy decorating. I'd definitely repeat this one for the 4th of July.

INGREDIENTS
1 boxed cake mix (your choice)
White frosting or whipped topping
Blueberries, left whole
Strawberries, halved

Bake cake according to package instructions, in a 9 x 13-inch pan. Cool. Frost with either white frosting or white crème topping. With the blueberries and the strawberries make a flag design on top of the cake. Use the blueberries for the star portion and the strawberries, cut side down, to make the red stripes. Serve proudly.

A Thought for Today
DON'T FORGET TO REMEMBER...

Memorial Day…what a great day to have a picnic, join with friends and family, celebrate our good fortune to live in this great country of ours, and kick-off the summer season. Let's all take a moment to remember and honor those who have fought for our freedoms and have given with their most precious gift of all…their lives.

MAY 30

Julie Gulling's "1/3rds Marinade"
For a Memorial Day BBQ

Yield 1 cup marinade

Julie Gullings, of Moorhead, Minnesota says this marinade recipe is one of the first things she learned to "cook." She used to make it for her boyfriend, and now he's her husband—so it must be good! So get out the grill everybody and give this a try for your Memorial Day barbecue.

INGREDIENTS
1/3 cup water
1/3 cup soy sauce
1/3 cup honey

Mix ingredients thoroughly in proportions given. Pour over chicken or pork and marinate covered overnight, or all day. While baking or grilling meats, bring marinade to low boil for 5 minutes or so (can be used as additional sauce while cooking or as a dipping sauce if thoroughly cooked).

BBQ Safety

A tip on barbecue-safety: Always marinate raw meats, covered in the refrigerator. After transporting the meat to the grill, discard left-over marinades if not using during cooking. Never re-use marinades in a raw state. When the meat is done, be sure to use a fresh platter for serving (not the original platter used to transport the raw meat).

MAY 31
Grandad's BBQ Sauce

In keeping with our barbecue theme here is a recipe my grandfather used to use:

INGREDIENTS
1 cup ketchup
¼ cup water
¼ cup vinegar
2 tablespoons butter or margarine, melted
1 teaspoon onion powder
1 tablespoon brown sugar
1 tablespoon soy sauce
A dash of Worcestershire sauce
Freshly cracked pepper to taste

Mix all and simmer gently to blend. Use on chicken or ribs.

JUNE 1
Andy's Steak Marinade

INGREDIENTS
3 tablespoons Worcestershire sauce
2 tablespoons steak sauce
1 teaspoon garlic powder
1 teaspoon salt
1/8 teaspoon black pepper
1 teaspoon onion powder
¼ cup water
Individual Black Angus T-bone steaks at grilling time

Combine all ingredients in small sauce pan and bring to simmer. Baste the individual steaks with marinade and let set for at least 30 minutes. Baste again when putting steaks on the grill and continue to baste frequently. Cook steaks to your liking—cooking time will depend on hotness of coals, thickness of steaks, and your personal preference.

JUNE 2
East Meets West Curry Rub

Today's recipe is a rub to add a different taste to your everyday chicken. Apply this rub before cooking up your favorite fowl (this is also good on turkey).

INGREDIENTS
1/3 cup sugar
1 tablespoon paprika
1 teaspoon curry powder
1 teaspoon black pepper
½ teaspoon salt

Rub onto surface of chicken or turkey and let "marinate" for 30 minutes before cooking.

A Thought for Today
STARS AND STRIPES

With Memorial Day still on my mind, let's keep our flags proudly flying high, their stars and stripes back-dropped by that marvelously blue summer sky of this great country that we are all fortunate to live in.

JUNE 3
Charlotte's Tex-Mex Madness
4 to 6 servngs

INGREDIENTS
1 pound lean beef, diced
1 cup shredded taco cheese, divided
5 cups chopped fresh tomatoes
1 cup salsa
3 cloves garlic
1 tablespoon chili powder
5 cups instant white rice, cooked separately and set aside
Sour cream for garnish

Sauté beef for 2 to 3 minutes over medium-high heat. Add ½ cup of cheese and the rest of the ingredients, except rice. Simmer until vegetables are tender—about 5 minutes. Spoon over cooked rice and top with remaining cheese. Garnish with sour cream.

Food and Family Tips

Take the Sugar Challenge: According to the USDA, Americans consume an average of 158 pounds of added sugars per year! Challenge each family member (including yourself) to trade in 3 sugar-filled snacks for healthy alternatives. Have a contest to see who can go the longest!

Throw a snack together (literally): For a healthy after school energy-booster, toss pretzels, nuts, crackers, dried fruit, coconut, granola, and a few Nestle Chocolate Chips into a plastic bag and shake. Children love to create their own concoctions!

Mama-Made TV Dinners: When cooking a lasagna or casserole, undercook just a bit and place in single-serving microwave-safe dishes. Cover with foil, write re-heating instructions on top, and freeze. When mom is gone, pull out one of the pre-made servings, and with just a few minutes in your Velos or microwave, dinner is on!

JUNE 4
"Miss Kim's" BBQ's
8 to 10 servings

Tired of barbecuing on the grill—why not "barbecue" in the slow cooker! Your dinner can be cooking away (un-tended) while you are enjoying the outdoors, taking a walk, or maybe playing a soft-ball game with the kids. This delicious recipe hales from the busy household of Kim Meiloch, Port Washington, Wisconsin.

INGREDIENTS
2 to 3 pounds round steak, trimmed of fat and cut into cubes
3 to 4 tablespoons brown sugar
2 teaspoons salt
3 tablespoons Worcestershire sauce
1 tablespoon vinegar
$\frac{1}{4}$ teaspoon each: dill, chives, parsley, sweet basil, dry mustard
1 cup water
1 tablespoon grape jelly
2 tablespoons cornstarch, dissolved in $\frac{1}{2}$ water
Good sandwich buns at serving time

Place cubed meat in slow cooker. Mix rest of ingredients, stirring well and pour over meat. Stir again to coat all. Cover with lid and cook on low setting 6 to 8 hours, or until meat is very tender. Serve meat and sauce on good buns. (Can shred meat if desired.)

The Raw Rule
Try to serve a raw fruit or vegetable with every meal. I guarantee you will pack in a load of extra vitamins if you add this rule to your repertoire.

JUNE 5

Rob's Buffalo-Style Chicken Wings
Served with Blue Cheese Dressing

INGREDIENTS

3 pounds chicken wings, jointed, cut into thirds, and wing tips discarded

1 stick butter, melted

½ teaspoon cayenne

¼ teaspoon cumin

¼ teaspoon chili powder

1 tablespoon Louisiana-style Hot Sauce (or can substitute 1 teaspoon Tabasco® sauce)

A dash of salt

Blue cheese or Ranch dressing, for dipping at serving time

Melt butter and mix in seasonings to make a hot-spicy-marinade-baste. Arrange wing pieces in single layer on a cookie sheet. Baste with seasoned butter and broil under preheated broiler for about 6 to 7 minutes per side, turning halfway through to baste again. Cooking time should be about 12 minutes. Keep warm in 300-degree oven until serving time. Serve with blue cheese dressing or ranch dressing on the side for dipping. Pass the bottle of Hot Sauce for those who like it extra hot.

Awesome Appetizers

One of the best ways to naturally reduce how much food you eat at each meal is to have a nice salad 20 minutes prior to the main course. Salad is quite filling! A glass of water is another way to naturally reduce hunger. Try a salad and a glass of water prior to your meals. I know you'll see the difference. This is a great habit for kids to learn. If your kids aren't salad-eaters, try a glass of water with fresh vegetables, like carrots, broccoli, celery, etc., with ranch dressing. By prioritizing our vegetables before our meals, we don't run the risk of becoming so full of the "main course" we forget to leave room for the all important side dish.

Weekly Challenge

I remember reading somewhere that a gift can be as little as something you do for a person that they can easily do for themselves…for example opening the car door for someone, grabbing and carrying a heavy package for someone who is struggling, making a fresh pot of coffee when you take the last cup, throwing in a load of laundry or transferring one to the dryer as you are passing by, taking out the garbage and retrieving the container when you get home (without being asked). The list could be endless; little common-caring gifts of courtesy that don't go unnoticed by the recipient, who could have done it themselves, but didn't have to.

JUNE 6

Pudding Popsicles
A KIDS IN THE KITCHEN RECIPE

Pick a hot summer day and let your kids have fun in the kitchen with this easy Popsicle recipe. Who wants vanilla? Who wants chocolate?

INGREDIENTS
Wooden Popsicle sticks
Popsicle molds or ice cube trays
Instant pudding (your favorite flavor), prepared according to instruction on package

Simply prepare pudding and freeze in molds, such as ice cube trays until solid. When Popsicles start to set up, insert Popsicle sticks.

JUNE 7

Blue Cheese Chicken

4 servings

INGREDIENTS
4 boneless, skinless chicken breasts
1 pound Blue cheese, crumbled
2 cups sour cream
4 pressed cloves of garlic
1 cup Italian seasoned bread crumbs, in pie plate
1 beaten egg
½ cup flour, in pie plate
Canola oil

Mix together blue cheese, sour cream, and garlic and set aside. Wash chicken and pat dry. Dip first in flour to coat; then in egg to coat; then in bread crumbs to coat. Brown chicken breast on both sides in Canola oil in a skillet. Transfer to baking dish. Pour on sour cream mixture. Cover with foil and bake at 350 degrees for 40 to 45 minutes, until chicken is thoroughly cooked and mixture is bubbly.

Garlic Tip

Heating your garlic cloves for about 10 seconds in the microwave softens them and makes them easier to peel or press.

A Thought for Today

INTERESTING THOUGHT…
"Do good with what you have, or
it will do you no good." ~Anonymous

JUNE 8
Mom's Ham and Broccoli Roll-Ups
6 servings

INGREDIENTS
6 slices deli ham
6 slices deli Swiss cheese
6 trimmed stalks of broccoli, cooked al dente
1 tablespoon butter
2 tablespoons flour
2 teaspoons dry mustard
1½ cups milk
Salt and pepper to taste
Paprika to taste
Additional 1 tablespoon butter
Grated parmesan cheese, to taste

Place slice of cheese on slice of ham, then broccoli in center. Roll up jelly-roll fashion and arrange side by side in a buttered baking dish. Over moderate heat melt the butter, mix in the flour, and cook to make a roux. Slowly mix in milk, stirring all the while, to make a smooth sauce. Add in spices. Pour over roll-ups. Dot with additional butter. Sprinkle with Parmesan. Bake in 450–degree oven until hot and bubbly, about 15 minutes.

It's Not Enough to Eat Your Veggies...

You have to eat them right! Avoid these common mistakes in order to maximize nutrient intake.

Do not place vegetables in water until after it is boiling. The greater the time spent in the water, the less the nutrient retention.

When possible, leave skins on while cooking. More nutrients are lost via the exposed surface.

Steaming is still the best cooking method for preparing your vegetables.

JUNE 9

Refreshing Melon Dessert

6 servings per melon

INGREDIENTS
Honeydew or Cantaloupe melon
Vanilla ice cream
Fresh grated coconut

Cut melon into portion-size wedges and place on individual dessert plates. Top each wedge with a scoop of rich vanilla ice cream and a sprinkling of fresh coconut. So definitely simple, yet so divinely good—especially after a BBQ dinner.

JUNE 10

Pecan Pie Bars

2 dozen

INGREDIENTS
1 box yellow cake mix, divided
4 eggs
½ cup butter, melted
1 firmly-packed cup brown sugar
1 ½ cups dark corn syrup
1 teaspoon vanilla
1 cup chopped pecans

Combine ½ of the cake mix with 1 egg and the butter in a bowl. Mix well. Press mixture into a greased 9 x 13-inch cake pan. Bake at 350 for 15 minutes. Combine remaining cake mix, 3 eggs, brown sugar, corn syrup, and vanilla in a bowl. Beat for 2 minutes with electric mixer at medium speed. Pour over crust. Sprinkle with chopped pecans. Return pan to oven and continue to bake 30 to 35 minutes longer, or until light brown and set. Cool before cutting into bars.

RUSH HOUR TIP

Sweets for the sweet—the next time your child gets a case of the hiccups, try having them swallow a teaspoon of sugar—without drinking anything with it. Their hiccups should go away!

JUNE 11
Creative Picture-Frames
A KIDS IN THE KITCHEN CRAFT-PROJECT

MATERIALS FOR BASIC PROJECT
Colorful puzzle pieces (pick an old puzzle that has some pieces missing)
Children's tacky craft glue
A 5 x 7 or 8 x10 flat picture frame
A craft cloth or newspaper to protect your table top.

Simply glue the puzzle pieces, making an interesting design or pattern, onto the picture frame. Use enough pieces to cover the entire frame. When the frame has dried you can opt to further decorate with sequins and beads, or acrylic paints. Put in a favorite photograph and display for all to see.

MATERIALS FOR ADVANCED PROJECT
Postage stamps
Buttons
Small sea shells
Smooth beach wood or small stones
Pinecones
Cut up postcards or maps
Inexpensive small charms or trinkets

Take these "souvenirs" and create a theme-picture frame using the same method as before. Put in a picture taken on a favorite vacation from where you collected these "treasures."

Weekly Challenge

SPREAD THE WEALTH...
"It is by 'spending' oneself that one becomes rich."
~Sarah Bernhardt

I cannot imagine truer words. "Being rich" is not a matter of having money. It's a matter of experiencing life, enjoying the moment, involving yourself with your children, family and friends; it's committing to a cause of great importance to you, learning new ideas, keeping an involved and educated mind, feeling with all your heart--those are the riches that are measured by a full life--not the ones you" take to the bank."

JUNE 12
Walnut Chicken Salad with Tarragon
6 servings

INGREDIENTS
3 cups cooked chicken breast, cut into bite-size pieces
½ cup low-fat sour cream
½ cup low-fat mayonnaise
1 cup chopped celery
½ cup toasted walnuts (heat in dry pan on stove top to release flavor)
1 tablespoon dried tarragon
Salt and pepper to taste
Leaf lettuce for serving
Fresh fruit of choice, sliced to garnish plate

In medium bowl combine first 6 ingredients to make a salad. Season with salt and pepper to taste. Mound salads on individual lettuce leaves and surround with seasonal, fresh fruit.

JUNE 13
Four "Faster than a Speeding Bullet" Appetizers

#1 Fruit Wraps
Wrap bite-size pieces of fresh Cantaloupe or Honey dew melon with thin slices of Prosciutto (specialty-cured European ham from Spain. Find in specialty section of your meat market). Secure with tooth pick.

#2 Cherry Tomatoes
Halve cherry tomatoes and very gently squeeze out a little of the juice and seeds. Fill halves with herb-cream cheese. Top with freshly snipped chives.

#3 Ritzy Crackers
Simply spread strawberry-cream cheese on good buttery crackers.

#4 Ritzy Spuds
Boil small new potatoes until tender. Cool. Cut in half and scoop out centers. Fill halves with sour cream and top with caviar.

JUNE 14
MaryAnn's Chocolate Mint Brownies
2 dozen

1ST LAYER
½ cup butter or margarine, melted
1 cup sugar
4 eggs
½ teaspoon baking powder
1 cup flour
1 (16 ounce) can Hershey® Syrup

In a large bowl combine above ingredients. Beat until smooth. Pour into a greased and floured jelly roll pan. Bake at 350 degrees for 20 minutes. Remove from oven and cool on counter for 10 minutes before proceeding with second layer.

2ND LAYER
½ cup butter or margarine
2 cups powdered sugar
2 tablespoons milk
1 teaspoon peppermint extract

Mix all ingredients and spread over cooled brownies. Put into refrigerator for 20 minutes to set before proceeding with third layer.

3RD LAYER
½ cup butter or margarine
1 cup chocolate chips

Melt butter or margarine and chocolate chips in a small pan over low heat, stirring till blended. Spread mixture over brownies and return to refrigerator for 5 minutes more. Cut into bars and serve. Yum!

JUNE 15

MaryAnn's Krispy Kookies
Makes 2 dozen

INGREDIENTS
1 cup white sugar
1 cup brown sugar
2 sticks butter, softened
1 egg
1 teaspoon vanilla
1 cup oil
3 ½ cups flour
1 teaspoon each: salt, baking soda, cream of tartar
1 cup Rice Krispies®
1 cup oatmeal
½ cup chopped nuts

Cream together the butter and sugars. Add the egg and vanilla and mix well. Add oil and mix. Mix together flour, salt, baking soda, and cream of tartar. Then mix into cookie mixture. Fold in Rice Krispies®, oatmeal, and nuts. Mix well. Make balls as if you were making peanut butter cookies, place on cookie sheet, and flatten with a glass-bottom dipped in sugar. Dip glass in sugar between pressings of each cookie. Bake at 350 degrees for 10 minutes.

Melting Chocolate
Here is a great tip for melting chocolate and making smooth sauces. When low heat or gentle heat is involved, and you don't have a double boiler, set your small pot in a larger skillet filled with an inch or so of simmering water. Melt the chocolate slowly in this make-shift "water bath" and you will have the same affect as using a double boiler.

JUNE 16

Gram's Summertime Pie

8 servings

INGREDIENTS

1 pie shell, blind-baked and cooled

Whipping cream, beaten stiff with a little sugar

Fresh strawberries (whole or halved), or blueberries, or raspberries,
   choose one fruit for this recipe

¼ to ½ cup or so of currant jelly

1 to 2 tablespoons water

Bake and cool a standard pie shell. Fill with whipped cream. Arrange your fruit selection on top of the whipped cream, close together and covering all the cream. Gently melt together the currant jelly and water to make a glaze. Drizzle glaze over berries to coat. Chill in refrigerator until serving time.

RUSH HOUR TIP

When whipping cream, make sure to pre-chill your bowl and beaters, for easier whipping.

A Thought for Today

CHANGE

The other day as I was parking my car I noticed a bumper sticker that read: "Change is inevitable. Growth is optional." What wisdom packed into 6 little words! So the next time you face a challenging change, remember what an opportunity you have to grow.

JUNE 17
Wendy Louise's Berry Desserts

This recipe is just a reminder of how easy and delectable a dessert can be!

INGREDIENTS #1
Choice fresh strawberries, hulled, cleaned and left whole
Brown sugar
Sour cream

On your prettiest dessert plates arrange a few choice strawberries, a side of brown sugar, and a generous dollop of sour cream. To eat, dredge strawberry in brown sugar and then dip into sour cream.

INGREDIENTS #2
Choice fresh blueberries
Brown sugar
Sour cream

Place blueberries in individual dessert cups or stemmed glasses. Sprinkle generously with brown sugar. Garnish with sour cream and a touch more brown sugar. Serve with dessert spoons.

Eat Your Vegetables
Research shows that only 43% of meals served in the US include vegetables. If all else fails, try to encourage your child to celebrate today, National Eat Your Vegetables Day on June 17th.

JUNE 18

"Easy as Pie" Strawberry Pie
A KIDS IN THE KITCHEN RECIPE
8 servings

INGREDIENTS
1 standard pie shell, baked and cooled
1 package strawberry Jell-O®
1 cup hot water (you can heat in microwave)
1 package frozen, sweetened-sliced strawberries, not thawed
Whipped cream or whipped topping

Bake and cool pie shell. Dissolve the gelatin with 1 cup of hot water. Stir in the frozen strawberries, breaking them up with a fork as they thaw and gelatin chills and begins to set. When partially set, pour filling into pie shell. Chill pie in refrigerator until thoroughly set. At serving time top each piece of pie with whipped topping.

RUSH HOUR VARIATION
Think about other fruit and gelatin combinations you would like to try!
Some other combinations might be:
Raspberry Jell-O® with frozen raspberries, not thawed
Orange Jell-O® with a chilled can of mandarin orange-slices (and their juice)
Lemon Jell-O® with chilled canned peach-slices (and their juice), etc., etc.

Weekly Challenge

THE POWER OF A SINGLE GLANCE...

"Our workday lives are filled with opportunities to bless others. The power of a single glance or an encouraging smile must never be underestimated." ~G. Richard Rieger

I'll never forget one day I went into the grocery-bakery department to pick up a birthday cake for my daughter. I was in such a hurry, but I took the time to stop and talk to the woman behind the counter. It was such a beautiful cake, that I just had to compliment her on her cake-decorating skills. My positive gesture just "made her day" and I felt all the better for taking a little time to make someone happy. So often we hear criticism when something goes wrong, but how rarely we hear compliments when things go right! Who can you make happier today or tomorrow with an unexpected compliment?

JUNE 19
Barb's Green Bean Casserole
6 to 8 servings

INGREDIENTS
2 (10 ounce) packages frozen green beans (I like French Cut), thawed
1 standard can cream of mushroom soup, undiluted
½ cup white wine
¼ cup Parmesan cheese, divided
Butter
Canned Onion rings

Mix beans, soup, wine, and half of the Parmesan and put in buttered casserole. Top with dots of butter and remaining Parmesan. Arrange onion rings on top. Bake in 350 to 400 degree oven for 20 minutes, alongside other foods, such as baking chicken or a roast.

Green Bean Basics (for fresh green beans)

Serving Size: Allow ¼ cup of beans per serving.

Storage: Store green beans in a plastic bag in your refrigerator. Beans last about 5 days when stored this way.

Preparation: Always rinse and drain beans. If there are strings, remove them. Snap off the ends of the beans before cooking.

JUNE 20
4-Way Chicken Salad
2 servings

INGREDIENTS
1 cup chopped, cooked chicken
¼ cup mayonnaise
1 stalk celery, ribbed and diced
¼ cup diced onion
Salt and pepper to taste
   ADDITION #1: curry powder to taste and drained pineapple chunks
   ADDITION #2: halved green grapes or chopped apple and walnuts
   ADDITION #3: thinly sliced water chestnuts and halved grapes
   ADDITION #4: green peas and diced Cheddar cheese

Mix first 5 ingredients to make a salad and then fold in one of the additions. Mound on leaf lettuce or serve on toast points.

JUNE 21
Marilyn Brinkley's "Mom's Steak and Gravy"
6 to 8 servings

INGREDIENTS
2 to 3 pounds round steak
4 cans cream of mushroom soup
1 envelope Lipton® onion soup mix

Cut all fat from steak. Cut into 4 x 4–inch pieces. Place meat in crockery pot on high setting. Pour in the dry onion soup mix and then cover with all 4 cans of soup. Cook on high for 7 to 8 hours. Serve over mashed potatoes or rice. Add some summer fruit and a glass of iced tea to complete your summer meal. Put dinner on in the morning, and voila—it's ready when you get home from work in the evening.

JUNE 22
Matt's Delicious Burgers

This delicious recipe was sent to us by Cathie Rosemann, way back when snow was still on the ground here in Wisconsin. Of course Cathie lives in Dallas/Ft. Worth—so she probably grills year 'round!

INGREDIENTS
1 pound lean ground beef
1 tablespoon Lawry's® Seasoning Salt
1 tablespoon dry minced onion
¼ cup Teriyaki Marinade (not baste)

Thoroughly mix meat with seasonings and Teriyaki Marinade. Form mixture into hamburger patties. Grill as preferred.

JUNE 23

You know what…We're going out to eat tonight…I'm taking a holiday! Reservations for 3 at 6:00 pm at my family's favorite little Mexican restaurant.

JUNE 24
Summertime Tips for the Slow Cooker

You know what they say… "Crockery-pot cooking keeps both the cook and the heat out of the kitchen." So many times we think about crockery cooking just in the winter, with soups and stews to warm us up! But how about in the summer to cool us off! Here are some Rush Hour Ideas:

#1. Keep those BBQ'd brats warm in a crockery-bath of beer and onions. Or simmer them first in the beer and then finish them on the grill. Either way, adding the slow-cooking method, along with the barbecue method makes for tasty brats.

#2. Pre-cook chicken in slow cooker, simmering on low setting all day long, while you're away at work. Finish the chicken off on the grill with your favorite BBQ sauce, just long enough to glaze and crisp the sauce to your liking. This is, by the way, a great way to have thoroughly done chicken, without burning the BBQ sauce in the process.

#3. Pre-simmer ribs (cut into 3 to 4-rib serving-size pieces) in crockery-pot, till meat is thoroughly done and tender. Finish off on the grill with your favorite "dry-rub" or grilling-sauce to get that special outdoor taste—again without burning the ribs, while trying to get them done enough on the grill!

#4. In the summer serve slow-cooker cooked dishes with rice pilaf or noodles, instead of heavy mashed potatoes. Add a plate of sliced-fresh garden tomatoes or a platter of summer fruit as a non-cook side dish. Serve with iced tea or iced water with lemon wedges. Eat outside—dining "al fresco" always makes food taste sooooo good.

A Thought for Today
"Time will not be hurried." ~ Anonymous
"Nor will the slow cooker." ~ Wendy Louise

JUNE 25

"Mud-Pies"
A KIDS IN THE KITCHEN RECIPE
Makes 1 pie or 12 mini-tarts

INGREDIENTS
1 standard single-crust pie shell, baked by your mom (either
   as single pie or as small, individual tarts) and cooled
1 package chocolate pudding, prepared according to package
   instructions
Chocolate Syrup, optional
Whipped topping, optional
Oreo® cookies, crushed and crumbled fine, not optional
Gummy® worms

Bake and cool pie crust. (If making tarts, you can bake the pie shells by forming the dough into muffin tins, to make individual tartlets.) Fill pie(s) with your favorite chocolate pudding and chill until set. Top with chocolate syrup and whipped cream or whipped topping. Cover with a top-layer of crushed Oreos® until the dessert looks like black-earth. Top with creepy-crawly Gummy® earth worms. Devour!

"Mud-Slides"
Use all the ingredients listed above, except omit pie crust. In parfait glasses or dessert bowls, layer pudding and toppings to taste—ending with an "earthy" covering of chocolate cookie crumbles. Dangle a tangle of Gummy® worms crawling on the top.

Weekly Challenge

TEAM WORK

"Never give up, for that is just the place and time that the tide will turn." ~Harriet Beecher Stowe

Have you ever been at a point where you just want to "throw in the towel"…you are "tearing your hair out"… you "just can't seem to get your point across"…or your wishes met… Who can you show an extra little bit of patience to today? What can you do to have better communications among your family members? How can you better organize to: get the laundry done, the garbage out to the curb, the lawn mowed, the weeds pulled, the house dusted, the groceries bought, the dog walked, the cat's litter changed, the hamster fed, the dishes done, the leak in the faucet fixed, the garage organized, your car washed etc.etc… so you can ALL have more time to enjoy the outdoors, a relaxed summer night on the patio, or a night of family games and fun. Start thinking about how you can delegate different "chores" to different age-levels. This summer try and RELAX more. You just don't have to be Wonder Woman or Wonder Dad. Delegate. Rotate chores. Make them fun. Give out awards or rewards for jobs well done. Use a buddy system or team work to lessen everyone's load and make summer more fun for all.

JUNE 26

Annelle's Quick Vegetarian Meal in a Tortilla
1 serinvg

Simple as 1-2-3-4-5-6 and you have a light refreshing snack or meal.

INGREDIENTS
1. Take a flour tortilla and sprinkle with a little cheese.
2. Heat under broiler until cheese is melted.
3. Top with thin slices of tomato, avocado, and red onion.
4. Add optional fresh spinach, black olives, and bell pepper.
5. Add garlic powder and picante sauce to suit your taste.
6. Roll up and eat.

RUSH HOUR WISDOM
For step 5 in Annelle's recipe try one of the great fresh salsa recipes from this book in place of the store bought picante sauce called for.

JUNE 27

Jane V's California Vegetable Deluxe
8 to 10 servings

INGREDIENTS
1 (20 ounce) package frozen California vegetables
½ pound Velveeta® cheese, cubed
1 stick butter, melted
1 tube crushed Ritz® crackers

Cook vegetables according to package directions. Drain liquid from vegetables and add cheese cut into small cubes. Stir gently. Put mixture into 2 quart casserole dish. Mix melted butter with crushed crackers and put over top casserole. Bake in conventional oven at 350 degrees for 20 minutes.

JUNE 28
Vickie's Oven Parmesan Chips
4 to 6 Servings

INGREDIENTS
4 medium baking potatoes, scrubbed but peel left on
¼ cup butter or margarine, melted
1 tablespoon finely minced onion
½ teaspoon salt
1/8 teaspoon pepper
Dash of paprika
2 tablespoons grated Parmesan cheese

Cut potatoes into ¼-inch thick slices. Place on greased baking sheet in single layer. Mix melted butter, onion, salt, pepper, and paprika together. Brush mixture on one side of potatoes, then turn and brush other side. Bake at 425 degrees for 15 to 20 minutes, until potatoes are tender and golden. Sprinkle with Parmesan cheese and serve immediately. Serve as a great alternative to French fries.

Conquering Crinkly-Wrinkly Potatoes
To avoid cracked and wrinkled skins on your baked potatoes spread a small amount of oil on the outside of the potato before baking.

JUNE 29
Patricia Kuhn's Fresno Peach Pie
8 servings

INGREDIENTS
1 (9-inch) pie shell, baked and cooled
5 to 6 fresh peaches, peeled and sliced, to be divided
1 cup sugar
3 tablespoons cornstarch
½ cup water
2 tablespoons butter
¼ teaspoon almond extract
Freshly whipped cream at time of serving, (Patricia says "real" whipped
   cream is a must for this recipe.)

In a saucepan, combine cornstarch, water, sugar, and 1 cup crushed peaches (from the 5 to 6 peaches). Cook on medium heat until thick, stirring constantly. Remove from heat and stir in butter and almond extract. Set aside to cool. Place the remaining sliced peaches in the baked and cooled pie shell. Pour the cooled glaze over the top, covering all the peaches thoroughly. Chill and serve with freshly whipped cream. Oooh la la!

JUNE 30
Joyce's Peanut Butter Oatmeal
I serving

This recipe was sent-in, back when the weather was still chilly…but I think it would make a great camping breakfast or hiker's meal, before setting out on a summer's-day adventure. Here is Joyce Gearhart's recipe for Peanut Butter Oatmeal. Joyce hales from Mount Wolf, Pennsylvania, where she enjoys this breakfast dish not only for its flavor, but for its beneficial affects on lowering cholesterol and helping with weight loss.

INGREDIENTS
½ cup regular oatmeal
½ cup water
½ cup fat-free milk
I tablespoon peanut butter
1/8 teaspoon salt
I teaspoon brown sugar

Mix ingredients in glass bowl. Microwave 3 minutes until creamy, stopping to stir several times. Eat warm, with your favorite accompaniments.

A Thought for Today
TRUE VALUES

"When we neglect the most important priorities, our final reward will be all the unhappiness money can buy."
~Richard A. Swenson, M.D.

JULY 1

Josie-Lynn's Peanut Colada Muffins

Makes 1 dozen

Here's a great snack recipe for camping and hiking, or just to tuck in a picnic basket. Josie-Lynn Belmont, from Woodbine, Georgia, sends in this delectable recipe.

INGREDIENTS
1 cup chunky style peanut butter
1 cup sugar
2 eggs, beaten
½ cup milk
1 teaspoon coconut extract
1 cup, flaked, sweetened coconut
2 cups all-purpose flour
2 teaspoons baking powder

Cream together peanut butter and sugar. Beat in eggs, milk, extract, and coconut. In separate bowl, mix flour and baking powder together, then add to the peanut butter mixture. Don't overwork batter. Fill muffin tins, lined with cupcake papers. Bake at 375 degrees for 20 to 25 minutes, or until muffins test done. Serve plain or warm with butter.

A Thought for Today

TEN-MINUTE TIDY

Boy, that list of chores I was talking about the other day kept getting longer and longer and longer. Take a tip from Deborah Taylor-Hough, author of *A Simple Choice.* Deborah uses what she calls "The Ten Minute Tidy." She sets a kitchen timer and everyone drops what they are doing and picks up, straightens up and helps to organize main rooms, such as the living area, great room, or family room. Just 10 minutes, when everybody pitches in, gets the job done! Then everyone can go out and play. I think it would be a great idea to do a "ten minute tidy" at least every other day and maybe a "twenty minute tidy" on Sundays!

JULY 2

Bubbles
A KIDS IN THE KITCHEN CRAFT PROJECT

Remember the magic of bubbles, when you were a kid? So many specialty shops offer giant bubble wands now, so here is a recipe for homemade bubbles. Make a couple gallons and have a ball!

INGREDIENTS
5 cups water
½ cup liquid Joy® dishwashing detergent
2 tablespoons glycerin (found at the pharmacy)

Add dish soap and glycerin to pan of water. Stir gently to mix—trying not to make suds! Dip in dippers and blow, as for store-bought bubbles. Or, mix bubbles in bucket and dip in larger wands and wave in the air to make giant bubbles.

Weekly Challenge
SHOW HOW PROUD YOU ARE…

to be an American. Display your flag with flying colors. Or if you don't have one, go out to your local hardware store and buy one! Take your family to see the local display of fireworks … and for heavens sakes, if you are setting off your own, do so with care! (I speak from experience because my husband is a maniac when it comes to this.)

JULY 3

Americana Cake
A KIDS IN THE KITCHEN RECIPE
See Memorial Day entry (May 29) for Red, White and Blue cake.
By any name it's a great cake!

JULY 4
Caleb's Brat's and Beer
2 per person

INGREDIENTS
At least 2 bratwurst per person
A corresponding number of good buns
Beer
Water (optional)
A pinch of whole pepper corns
A pinch of red pepper flakes

Pierce brats through casing with a fork one or two times. Place in slow-cooker crockery pot. Pour on beer and add water to cover brats. Throw in the seasonings. Cook all day on low setting, or 4 to 5 hours on high setting. Finish off on grill over hot coals. Toast buns alongside the brats. Serve with ice cold beers and fresh corn on the cob.

JULY 5
The Rush Hour Cook's Poupon Potatoes
4 servings

INGREDIENTS
1 pound cubed potatoes
1/3 cup Dijon-style mustard
¼ cup olive oil
1 small onion, chopped

Mix mustard and oil together. Add potatoes and onion, and toss to mix. Spread in baking pan and cook for 45 to 50 minutes in a 400-degree oven. Serve with grilled meats.

RUSH HOUR WISDOM
Man cannot live on barbecued meat alone…thus, the perfected potato.

JULY 6
Cheesy Scalloped Spuds
A KID FRIENDLY RECIPE
6 to 8 servings

INGREDIENTS
6 potatoes, peeled and sliced
3 tablespoons butter, melted
½ teaspoon salt
¼ teaspoon pepper
1 cup shredded Swiss or Cheddar cheese, divided
1 cup milk

Preheat oven to 425 degrees. Arrange ½ potato slices in an 11 x 7–inch casserole dish, coated with cooking spray. Drizzle 2 tablespoons melted butter over potatoes. Sprinkle with half the salt and pepper and 1/3 cup of cheese. Repeat layers. Drizzle with remaining tablespoon of butter. Bring milk to a low boil in a small sauce pan and pour over the layered mixture. Top with final 1/3 cup of cheese. Bake for 40 to 45 minutes, or until potatoes are tender.

The One-Bite Rule
In our house we practice the "one-bite" rule. My daughter isn't forced to eat an entire meal she loathes, although she is required to try one bite of each new food. A friend suggested this to my husband and I, and we were pleased to discover this added many new foods to her "edible repertoire." In taking that first bite, she discovered she really did like cheesy spuds after all.

JULY 7
Ranch Potatoes
8 to 10 servings

INGREDIENTS
6 medium potatoes
2 tablespoons olive oil
1 teaspoon each: paprika, parsley, pepper, garlic powder
1 packet dry ranch-style dressing mix

Preheat oven to 425 degrees. Cut potatoes into quarters and then into thirds (you should end up with 72 potato pieces). Mix all dry seasonings together. Place oil, spices, and potatoes into a zipper-top bag and shake to coat. Place in a single layer on baking sheet. Bake for 40 to 45 minutes or until tender and golden brown.

JULY 8
The Rush Hour Cook's Dijon Potatoes
4 to 6 servings

INGREDIENTS
4 medium potatoes, sliced thin
3 tablespoons flour and 2 tablespoons butter
1½ cups milk
½ cup Dijon-style mustard
½ cup shredded Swiss cheese

Mix flour and butter and heat in saucepan over medium heat, stirring to make a roux. Add milk, stirring and cooking until sauce thickens. Stir in mustard. In a greased casserole dish, layer potatoes and sauce-mixture. Top with shredded cheese. Bake in 350-degree oven until cheese has melted, sauce is bubbly, and potatoes are tender and warmed through, approximately 35 to 45 minute

JULY 9
How to Become a Certified Potato-Head
A KIDS IN THE KITCHEN BOREDOM-BUSTER

Is your child in love with the potato? Now he or she can join the "Spuddy Buddy Club." They can enjoy a free membership and download fun activities through Spuddy's Fan Club. To become a member log on to: www.idahopotato.com and click on Spuddy Buddy.

Weekly Challenge
VOLUNTERING

Nothing beats the satisfaction of giving back ... of giving of yourself, your time, and your talent. It could be "candy striping" at a hospital, working on a political campaign, teaching Sunday school at your church, taking in a foreign exchange student, working on a crisis hot line or helping at a shelter. What can you give back to enrich your life while enriching others? Check out www.volunteering.org for ideas.

JULY 10
Lucile's Coleslaw
Written to make 1/2 cup of coleslaw dressing

INGREDIENTS
Cream (half-and-half)
Cider vinegar
Sugar
Salt
Pepper
Shredded cabbage and Shredded carrots (or use a pre-packaged Coleslaw mix)
Paprika

Make a cream dressing by mixing about ½ cup cream and 1 to 2 tablespoons cider vinegar together. The cream will automatically thicken. Add the sugar, pepper, and salt to taste. Toss with shredded cabbage and carrots. Garnish with a sprinkling of paprika for color. Store in fridge until serving time. Stir again to mix just before serving.

JULY 11

Lucile's Pea-Nutty Salad
8 servings

INGREDIENTS
2 (10 ounce) packages of frozen green peas, thawed and drained
2 cups honey roasted peanuts
½ cup sour cream
½ cup mayonnaise
1 teaspoon sugar

Mix all together until well incorporated. Store in refrigerator until serving time.

JULY 12

Kristi Clayman's Strawberry Pretzel Salad

Our neighbor from Wauwatosa, Wisconsin, Kristi Clayman says she inherited this childhood favorite from her uncle, who often brought it to family gatherings. Now Kristi's husband asks her to make it all the time. Kristi you can make this for us any day!

INGREDIENTS
2 cups crushed pretzels, divided
¾ cup melted butter
3 tablespoons sugar
8 ounces cream cheese, at room temperature
1 cup additional sugar
9 ounces Cool whip® (or similar whipped topping)
6 ounce package strawberry jell-O®
2 (10 ounce) packages frozen strawberries, sliced into thirds

Spray a 9 x 13–inch pan with cooking spray. Mix 1 ¾ cups crushed pretzels with melted butter and 3 tablespoons sugar. Spread in pan and bake at 400 degrees for 8-10 minutes. Cool in refrigerator for approximately 1 hour, or until chilled. Blend together cream cheese, the 1 cup of sugar, and the whipped topping. Spread mixture over the chilled pretzel layer and chill 1 hour. Meanwhile dissolve gelatin in boiling water, according to package instructions. Stir in the frozen strawberries and refrigerate mixture until begins to set. Spread thickened gelatin mixture over cream cheese layer and top with remaining ¼ cup pretzels. Refrigerate for 1 more hour to completely set the salad.

JULY 13

Cathie Roseman's Stained Glass Dessert

INGREDIENTS
1 can peach pie filling
1 can pineapple chunks, including juice
1 can mandarin orange sections, drained
1 package frozen sweetened strawberries
2 bananas, sliced
Vanilla ice cream

Combine fruits and mix well. Chill for several hours and then pour over vanilla ice cream.

JULY 14

Linda Saframek's Southwest Chicken Wraps
4 servings

INGREDIENTS
4 breaded chicken patties, baked (you choose the brand and spice)
1 cucumber, peeled and diced
1 tomato, diced
1½ cups shredded lettuce
½ cup ranch dressing
¼ cup salsa (you choose the brand and the heat)
4 flour, or sun-dried tomato, tortillas

Dice cooked chicken patties and divide among the four tortillas. Layer on cucumber, tomato, and lettuce. Combine ranch dressing and salsa, then pour over all. Roll up and enjoy. (Linda says you can add shredded cheese too, before you roll up your wrap. She also points out this is a great way to use up dibs and dabs from your refrigerator.)

JULY 15

Judy Ring's Pizza Salad
10+ servings

INGREDIENTS
1 pound spiral macaroni, cooked and cooled
½ to 1 whole green bell pepper, chopped (can use other colors too)
¼ cup chopped sweet onion
1 cucumber, seeded, quartered and sliced
1 can garbanzo beans, drained and rinsed
8 ounces of mozzarella cheese, cubed small
3 to 4 pieces of pepperoni, from a stick of it, sliced and cubed small
½ bottle of Salad Supreme®
1 small bottle of a good, zesty Italian dressing, for best taste

Mix all ingredients together in a glass bowl and let marinate at least 2 hours (refrigerated) before serving.

RUSH HOUR TIP
This recipe tastes even better if left to marinate longer. Leftovers are great the next day.

JULY 16

Dad's Chili Dogs
A KIDS IN THE KITCHEN RECIPE

INGREDIENTS
Hot dog buns, split open
Hot dogs, steamed or heated in micro-wave
Leftover or canned chili, warmed (again can use microwave)
Shredded Cheddar cheese, for sprinkling on top
Chopped onion, for garnish for adults

Split open hotdog bun and place on plate. Fill with ingredients in order listed. Serve with plenty of napkins and a knife, fork, and spoon for spills.

Weekly Challenge

"CHRISTMAS IN JULY"

You've heard that old saying let's have "Christmas in July?" Well, let's do it; let's celebrate (as the Victorians did) with mid-summer food and festivals with our families. The origins of this holiday started in Victorian times when most gifts were made by hand, and people had to start early to get everything done by Christmas. Well, certainly that is no longer the case in our modern world, however any excuse for a holiday or a party is good enough for me! What can we do to "chill" and celebrate with our families while the temperatures rise. What "summer gifts" can we think up to surprise those we love?

Think about the "gifts" of time and attention you can give to those special people that surround you every day--your spouse, your children, your pets, your "extended-family" of friends and distant relatives, people at the office, or the guy that comes to fix the air conditioner when it "konks-out" on a hot mid-summer afternoon. How delightful to present them with a cool drink and a plate of home-made cookies. Or maybe it's a handmade card (or a handwritten, yes I said handwritten, letter) to a distant relative, just to say hello.

JULY 17
Simply Refreshing Sorbet-Berry Dessert Salad

We'll start our Christmas in July theme, by "chilling out" with this simple to make, refreshing dessert salad.

INGREDIENTS
Your favorite fruit-flavored Sorbet (from the ice cream section of your
  supermarket)
Leaf lettuce leaves/ and or sprigs of mint
Fresh blueberries
Fresh strawberries
Fresh red raspberries or blackberries
A sprinkling of powdered sugar

Arrange a generous scoop of your chosen sorbet on a lettuce leaf if serving as a salad. Sprinkle with fresh berries. Dust the berries with a slight amount of powdered sugar. Serve as a salad. For dessert, arrange sorbet and berries in pretty chilled dessert cups or stemmed glasses. Sprinkle with a dusting of powdered sugar and add a sprig of mint.

RUSH HOUR TIP
Substitute orange, pineapple, or coconut sherbet in place of the sorbet for more refreshing combinations.

JULY 18
Audra's Ambrosia Spread
makes 2 cups

Audra says, "A friend of mine served this with hot almond muffins and it was love at first bite. I had to have the recipe. I fix it more in the winter when I bake more. It will keep for a month really well."

However this would make a great treat for our Christmas in July theme.

INGREDIENTS:
1 (8 ounce) package cream cheese, softened
1 (8 ounce) can crushed pineapple, drained
¼ cup toasted coconut
¼ cup finely chopped almonds
¼ cup finely chopped pecans
1 teaspoon grated orange peel
1 tablespoon granulated sugar

Combine all ingredients in a mixing bowl and beat until smooth. Serve with breads, muffins, crackers, or fruit. Store in airtight container in the refrigerator.

A Thought for Today
LET'S HAVE A PARTY...

Organize a BLOCK PARTY for the whole neighborhood or a neighborhood cookout in your back yard. Or maybe it's a "Garden Party" for a Sunday afternoon. My mother organized a Patio Walk for her apartment complex, to share the beauty of seven exquisite gardens, all patio planted. Classical music was played and lemonade and tea sandwiches were served, as people strolled the grounds, stopping by each garden. Mom made little maps, and each garden-hostess got a little garden gift and a balloon to signify their garden. Everyone loved it! More great reasons to have a party might be a neighborhood soft ball tournament, croquet or horse shoe tournament, or a little bocce ball with appetizers and drinks afterward. What ever the reason, 'tis the season to get out there and PARTY.

JULY 19
Your 1st Annual Potluck BBQ Cook-Out

INGREDIENTS
You gather the grill or grills, and the charcoal.
The men bring their favorite marinated meats and cook them.
The women each bring a favorite pot-luck side dish and serve them.
You provide the beverages…annnnd trophies for the best dish and side dish.
For dessert July 23rd's recipe might be in order!

A Thought for Today

"The more 'serendipity' you allow in your life, the 'funner' your world will be."~Brook Noel

JULY 20
"**B**e **L**ight and **T**rim" Sandwiches for Dinner

INGREDIENTS
Make your favorite BLT sandwiches. Skip the mayo and add a layer of ripe, smooth avocado slices to each sandwich. Sprinkle with just a tad of salt and freshly cracked pepper. You'll be amazed at how good the addition of the avocado tastes, while foregoing the mayo.

RUSH HOUR WISDOM
Make your dinner in the kitchen, but serve it out on the patio, or in the shade of your garden. Use decorative paper plates and cups for a quick festive look with minimal clean-up.

> Did you know that you can dice onions and peppers in advance and store them in your freezer for up to one month? This is a great way to make dinner prep a breeze!

JULY 21

Here are two sauces to turn wonderful fresh summer fruits into sensational desserts.

Quick Crème Fraiche Sauce
(for elegant fruit desserts)

INGREDIENTS
¼ cup sour cream
½ cup heavy cream
1 tablespoon brown sugar

Mix all till smooth. Cover and refrigerate in glass container for at least 1 hour before using. Use as a topping on fresh berries and summer fruits (such as peaches and nectarines). Garnish servings with a little more brown sugar.

Banana Crème Sauce
(for elegant fruit desserts)

INGREDIENTS
1 banana, sliced
½ cup sour cream or traditional yogurt

Combine banana and sour cream (or yogurt) in a blender and process until smooth. Serve as a topping-sauce on fresh berries or fresh peaches. Top dessert with a sprinkling of fresh coconut or crumbled macaroon.

JULY 22

Five-Bean Summer Salad

Cousin of the 3 bean salad—the longer it marinates the better it gets.

INGREDIENTS
1 can green beans, drained
1 can wax beans, drained
1 can kidney beans, drained
1 can, black beans, drained
1 can garbanzo beans, drained
2 green onions (with tops) diced or
1 small red onion, diced, or to taste
3 cloves garlic, smashed
1 tablespoon sugar
1 cup of your favorite bottled Italian dressing

Drain all beans well and mix together in a glass bowl. Add onions, garlic, and dressing. Toss to coat. Cover and refrigerate until serving time. Best if marinated several hours before serving. Stir once in a while to redistribute marinade.

RUSH HOUR WISDOM

Start your "to-do list" for the holidays now. Mark your calendar with various deadlines and goals. Get a head start, since December will be here before you know it!

Bread Basics

I am a big fan of French or special breads with dinner. If a loaf is too large for your family or you have leftovers, bread can be reheated successfully. Wrap bread in a dampened towel and bake for several minutes in a 350-degree oven to help retain moisture. After bread has been reheated once, it usually won't survive another heating. In that case, slice bread, butter, and season with your choice of seasonings. Broil until lightly browned. Store these in airtight containers as snacks; use as croutons in salads; or garnish for soups and stews.

JULY 23
Double-Fudge Brownie and Ice Cream Sandwiches
A KIDS IN THE KITCHEN RECIPE
Makes 16 to 18

What kid, or adult for that matter, doesn't like ice cream sandwiches? Here's a doubly delicious homemade version of that well-loved summertime treat.

INGREDIENTS

2 boxed Fudge Brownie Mixes (use whatever brand you like)

½ gallon of ice cream, slightly softened (use vanilla, or chocolate, or chocolate swirl ice cream; mint chip would be good too—and coffee ice cream would be good for an adult version)

Butter for greasing 2 brownie-baking pans (use size recommended on box)

Waxed paper for lining the bottom of each pan (this makes for easy removal)

Grease your baking pans and then cut out waxed paper to fit in the bottom of each pan. Mix both batches of brownie mix and divide between the two pans. Bake according to package instructions and then cool. Once cooled, turn out one pan of baked brownie onto a cookie sheet. Spread a generous layer of slightly softened ice cream over the entire brownie layer. Remove second baked brownie and place on top of the ice cream layer, pressing down slightly. Place in freezer to firm up and set (approximately 2 hours). Cut into sandwich size pieces at serving time. Or, after whole cake is firm, cut into serving size portions and freeze in individual baggies for instant summer snacks and desserts.

Weekly Challenge

"IN KEEPING WITH THE SEASON…"

Are your kids bored? Restless? Can't think of a thing to do? Start them on a Christmas Craft Project, while they actually have the time to do it! Start now (as the Victorians did) to make gifts for relatives, handmade picture frames, ready-mix stepping stones with bits of mosaic, decorative-painting on glasses, decoupage on glass plates. Make a quaint bird house, weave a basket, bead a necklace. Sew a sampler. Knit a scarf. Pick berries and make jam. Go to your local craft supply store and see what all they have to offer. Pick out a project and get started! Come December the recipients of your "handmade gifts" will be awesomely appreciative. This is also a great boredom buster for summer. One of my favorite craft resources is The Oriental Trading Company. They have many ready-made craft kits at economical prices.

JULY 24

Mamma's Homemade Jams and Jellies

INGREDIENTS
Sure-jell®
Your favorite summer fruit, per Sure-jell® directions
Sugar, perSure-jell® directions

My mom makes the best Strawberry Jam and the most wonderful Blackberry and Red Raspberry Jellies. There is nothing more wonderful than opening a fresh jar of summer-made jelly or jam in the middle of winter to spread on toast or English muffins. Her secret? Sure-jell®. So when your favorite fruit is in season, buy yourself a packet of Sure-jell® and just follow the directions inside the box. Inside the box will be a long list of recipes—Jams on one side, Jellies on the other. Come winter, you'll be so glad you did!

JULY 25
Green and Gold Cornbread Casserole
9 servings

INGREDIENTS
1 (8.5 ounce) package corn muffin mix
3 eggs
2 cups shredded Cheddar cheese
1 (10 ounce) package of chopped broccoli, thawed and squeezed dry
1 shallot, minced (or 1 or 2 green onions chopped)

Stir bread mix and eggs together. Stir in remaining ingredients. Pour into a greased 9 x 9 x 2–inch square baking pan. Bake in 350–degree oven for 30 minutes, or until knife inserted in center comes out clean. Cut into 12 squares and serve warm.

JULY 26
Brenda West's Ham and Cheese Corn Muffins
9 Muffins

INGREDIENTS
1 (8.5-ounce) package corn muffin mix
½ cup deli ham, chopped
½ cup shredded Swiss cheese
1/3 cup milk
1 egg, slightly beaten
1 tablespoon Dijon mustard

Preheat oven to 400 degrees. Combine muffin mix, ham, and cheese in medium bowl. Combine milk, egg and mustard in 1-cup glass measurer. Stir milk mixture into dry mixture. Mix until just moistened. Fill nine paper cup lined muffin cups 2/3 full with batter. Bake 18 to 20 minutes or until golden brown. Serve warm.

RUSH HOUR WISDOM
Make up a batch of these muffins alongside your favorite salad and you have a great combo for a ladies' luncheon or a light dinner.

JULY 27
Loretta's Chicken-Macaroni Salad

Loretta Poxleitner, from Cottonwood, Idaho sends in this super-easy, pasta-salad recipe that she makes for her husband Glenn.

INGREDIENTS
¾ cup cooked chicken breast, cubed (or 1 can chicken meat)
2 cucumbers chopped
2 tomatoes, seeded and chopped
12 ounces cooked macaroni (or pasta of choice)
1 cup Ranch-style dressing (or more as needed)

Combine all ingredients and add enough dressing to thoroughly moisten. Loretta also suggests that tuna could be substituted for the chicken.

RUSH HOUR WISDOM
Here's a great tip for when you are "dressing" a salad. Hold out a cup or two of the salad greens, pasta, or whatever. Dress the primary bowl of salad first—that way if you over-dressed your salad, you can just mix in the remaining greens, pasta, etc., to balance it out. Remember that when it comes to salad dressing "less is more." You want to be able to taste all the ingredients—not just the dressing!

Pasta Hints and Tips
- For soups, always choose tiny pasta so it "scoops" easily with a spoon. Orzo and farfelle are two good examples. Like wise for casseroles that contain pasta, stick with smaller noodles like penne or elbow macaroni. If making a layered casserole, try lasagna or another wide flat noodle.
- To avoid sticky-pasta masses, add 2 tablespoons of oil per gallon of water.
- For even cooking, make sure that the pasta is completely immersed in the water.
- Stir pasta immediately after immersing in water to help eliminate clumping.
- If you will be using the pasta in a casserole, slightly undercook on the stove. It will complete its cooking process during baking.
- To reheat pasta, drop it into boiling water and let stand for 2 minutes. Drain and serve.

JULY 28
My Aunt Joan's Turkey (or Chicken) Salad

This recipe has been in my family for many years. It is a great way to use up leftover turkey around the holidays, but also tastes great as a refreshing chicken-salad in the summer time.

INGREDIENTS
4 cups cooked diced turkey (or chicken)
1 can water chestnuts, rinsed, drained, and sliced thin
¾ pound seedless green grapes (halved if you like)
¾ cup diced celery
1 small can pineapple chunks, drained
1/3 cup sliced or slivered almonds
1 ½ cups mayonnaise (can use lite-mayo if you wish)
1 ½ teaspoons curry powder
1 tablespoon soy sauce

Combine first 6 ingredients in salad bowl. Mix mayonnaise, curry powder and soy sauce to make smooth dressing. Toss all to combine. Chill until serving time.

A Thought for Today

My brother lovvvvvved broccoli. Every summer he used to go into 'training' for his barefoot-water-skiing tournaments and he attributed his strength and endurance to his broccoli (and broasted chicken) diet. One of the last conversations we had was of trading recipes and talking about the benefits of broccoli…what a funny conversation for a brother and his little sister (the Rush Hour Cook) to be having. That was eight years ago. Today would have been his 35th birthday, Happy Birthday, Caleb!

JULY 29

Judy Brown's Broccoli Supreme
6 servings

INGREDIENTS
2 (10-ounce) packages chopped broccoli, cooked and drained (or can use fresh—
   chopped, cooked and drained)
1 cup mayonnaise
2 eggs, well beaten
1 can cream of mushroom soup
1 medium onion, chopped
1 cup grated Cheddar cheese
1½ cups herb-seasoned stuffing crumbs
¼ cup butter, melted

Combine mayo, eggs, soup, and onion with the cooked broccoli. Pour into a buttered 9 x 13–inch baking dish. Sprinkle with the grated cheese. Toss the stuffing crumbs with the melted butter to moisten. Sprinkle on top of the casserole. Bake in 350–degree oven for 30 to 45 minutes, until bubbling and done.

A "Kid" Thought for Today
"Never underestimate the value of a vegetable!"

Okay kids, today I am going to talk to you about the dreaded "V-word"…yes…vegetables…I know, I know…but they are so good for you. This week I have blended them into casseroles and salads, adding cheese, and fruit, and bread crumbs, chicken, and even macaroni. So the next time your Mom says, "Try just a bite" I hope you will, because a daily serving of vegetables (beyond French fries) is very important for a kid (and adults too)!

JULY 30
Judy Brown's Easy Zucchini Casserole
A KID FRIENDLY RECIPE
6 to 8 servings

Today's recipe is yet another way to get everyone to eat their veggies. This would be an easy 'beginner' recipe for your child to help you make. I'm going on the philosophy here that "if they help make it…they will help eat it."

INGREDIENTS
2 medium zucchini, sliced and unpeeled
2 green peppers, seeded, ribbed and diced
1 large onion, diced
2 ripe tomatoes, seeded and diced
1 cup macaroni, cooked
Velveeta® cheese (must use Velveeta®)

Butter and lightly flour a 9 x 13–inch baking dish. Mix all vegetables together and divide in half. Layer half of mixed vegetables in bottom of dish. Top with cheese. Layer on the cooked macaroni and top with more cheese. Finish with a top layer of remaining vegetables and then more cheese. Bake at 375 degrees for 45 to 60 minutes.

RUSH HOUR WISDOM: *Judy Brown says, "This recipe is so easy that you can use whatever amounts you want. You can't mess this one up!"*

Weekly Challenge
YOU DON'T HAVE TO BE EINSTEIN…

"Out of clutter find simplicity.
From discord find harmony.
In the middle of difficulty lies opportunity."
~Albert Einstein

Although written years ago, I think these words offer inspiration and stress-releasers for today's contemporary family. Why don't you try to implement at least one of Einstein's ideas into your household this week…to chase away those mid-summer-stressors.

JULY 31
Lori's Almost Vegetarian Zucchini Alfonse
6 servings

INGREDIENTS
4 medium to large zucchini
½ pie plate flour
Salt and pepper
Olive oil for cooking, plus 2 tablespoons more
1 package spaghetti sauce mix, to taste
1 (8 ounce) can tomato sauce
1 cup shredded mozzarella cheese
3 tablespoons grated Parmesan
1 ripe avocado, peeled, pitted, and sliced at time of serving
Bacon, cooked crisp and broken into bite-size pieces (*see suggested microwave cooking method that follows)

Cut zucchini in half length-wise and then each half into 3 flat slices, ending with 6 long slices per zucchini. Lightly season flour with salt and pepper. Dredge slices in seasoned flour, shaking off any excess. In skillet, using a medium to high heat setting and olive oil to cover bottom of pan, fry zucchini in 4 batches until golden brown and tender. Add more olive oil as needed. Do not over crowd pan. Set batches aside on paper towels. Turn down heat setting. Add 2 more tablespoons olive oil, tomato sauce, and spaghetti sauce mix to pan. Stir together and simmer 1 or 2 minutes to make sauce. Add back the zucchini slices into the sauce. Top with shredded mozzarella cheese. Cover and cook gently until cheese melts and all is heated through. Do not over cook. Uncover and arrange avocado slices onto the sauce-y zucchini. Top with crisped bacon and serve. Add a tossed salad and French bread to complete the meal.

Microwave Bacon
Standard-cut bacon (not too thick, not too thin)
Paper toweling
Microwave-safe plate or paper plate

A convenient way to make crisp, rendered bacon is to cook it in the microwave on paper toweling. Place bacon strips on several layers of paper toweling, on a paper plate. 4 strips of bacon usually need to cook about 4 minutes on high; 6 pieces for 6 minutes on high. (Cooking time is approximate due to variances in microwaves and thickness of bacon.) When bacon has crisped to your liking remove from microwave. Throw away the paper towels! Throw away the paper plate! Throw away the grease! Your bacon is now ready to crumble and use in a recipe.

RUSH HOUR WISDOM
This dish is meant to be delicately seasoned, subtle in flavor and not drowning in sauce. The zucchini slices should be golden and tender but still hold their shape. Vegetarian Note: You will see that, this dish could very easily be turned into a vegetarian dish, by leaving out the bacon

AUGUST 1
Smooth Avocado Sauce

INGREDIENTS
1 large or 2 medium ripe avocados, peeled and pitted
½ cup water
1 to 2 tablespoons juice from a fresh lemon or lime
1 garlic clove, mashed
Sea salt and white pepper, to taste

Blend all on high speed in blender or food processor until very smooth. Adjust seasonings to taste and serve immediately. Makes a great alternative for any recipe calling for Guacamole sauce.

AUGUST 2
Judy B's Iowa-Garden Cucumbers and Onions

INGREDIENTS
Quart jar
Cucumbers, peeled and sliced
1 medium onion, peeled and sliced
2 teaspoons salt
¼ teaspoon pepper
2 cloves garlic, sliced
1/3 cup sugar
1/3 cup vinegar

Slice cucumbers and onions into the quart jar. Add the rest of the ingredients. Fill to top of jar with cold water. Let stand 1 to 2 hours in the refrigerator. (Judy says you can add more cucumbers when needed.)

AUGUST 3
Judy Brown's Squash Casserole

INGREDIENTS
2 pound yellow squash, cooked and mashed
1 small onion, grated
1 can cream of chicken soup
½ cup sour cream
2 small raw carrots, grated
1 small jar pimentos
2/3 to 1 stick oleo, margarine or butter, melted
1 cup corn bread stuffing mix

Mix cooked and mashed squash with next 5 ingredients and put in greased 9 x 13–inch baking dish. Melt oleo, margarine, or butter and toss with corn bread stuffing mix. Sprinkle over top of casserole and bake in 350–degree oven for 30 minutes.

RUSH HOUR TIP
If you don't have your own garden take advantage of all the farmer's markets that should be springing up around your part of the country right about now. There is nothing better than garden grown produce for taste and texture!

A Thought for Today
"Dreams come a size too big so that we can grow into them."
~Josie Bissett

AUGUST 4

Judy B's Seasoned and Simmered Beef Dish for a Crowd

INGREDIENTS
2 pounds ground beef
1 can corned beef
1 medium-size bottle ketchup
2 tablespoons instant onion
¼ cup brown sugar
¼ teaspoon chili powder
½ teaspoon vinegar
1 tablespoon flour
¼ cup water, add if needed during simmering

Brown ground beef, add onion. Drain off any excess fats. Add rest of ingredients and simmer 30 minutes. Or transfer to slow cooker and simmer 6 hours. Or simmer in an electric roaster. Recipe may be doubled, tripled, and so on as needed.

A Thought for Today
"However high a bird may soar, it seeks its food on earth."
~Danish Proverb

However far men may roam, during half-time, they don't seem to make it past the snack table! With football season just around the corner, I thought I'd throw in this recipe from Judy B. in Iowa. It sounds like a perfect dish for those hearty-snacking football-watchers. Besides, hasn't pre-season started?

AUGUST 5
Refreshing Orange Fluff Drink
A KID FRIENDLY RECIPE
2 servings

INGREDIENTS

1 can orange juice concentrate, still frozen
1 teaspoon vanilla
1 emptied orange juice can of milk
1 teaspoon instant protein
8 ice cubes
Fresh mint from your herb garden

Blend all in blender until fluffy. Serve in tall glasses over ice cubes. Garnish with a sprig of fresh mint.

AUGUST 6

KID-FRIENDLY SIDE DISHES

Sauté a Side Dish

Get out of the grind of rice and potatoes with some of these alternate side dishes. Although not in most people's typical repertoire, they are delicious, feature fruit and veggies—and kids love them! (HONEST!)

Buttered Bananas

INGREDIENTS
1 banana per person
Brown sugar
Butter

Gently sauté whole firm bananas in butter. Cook uncovered until tender—not mushy. Melt brown sugar into the bananas at the end.

Caramelized Apples

INGREDIENTS
1 apple per person
Brown sugar
Butter

On stovetop, melt butter in a Pyrex style baking dish. Add peeled and sliced apples in a single layer, turning to coat. Sprinkle with a few tablespoons of brown sugar. Cover and gently simmer until fork tender and glazed with melted sugar, being careful not to overcook. 10 minutes should be the maximum.

Glazed Carrots

INGREDIENTS
1 large package fresh carrots
3 to 4 tablespoons butter
2 tablespoons brown sugar

Cut fresh, peeled carrots into julienne strips. Simmer in pan of water till fork tender. Drain off water. Melt in butter and brown sugar to coat the carrots, continuing to cook until glazed.)

Weekly Challenge

LAUGHTER AND KINDNESS

The other day I came across an old English proverb in a garden book: "Tickle it with a hoe and it will laugh into a harvest." Those words just made me smile and then I equated that same concept with our children. "Tickle a child with laughter and kindness, and he/she will grow into a beautifully happy adult." Who can you "tickle" this week?

AUGUST 7

Mary W's Chicken Lasagna
8 to 10 servings

INGREDIENTS
1 tablespoon olive oil
2 chicken breasts, cut into bite-size pieces
1 sweet onion, chopped
½ green pepper, chopped
1 (10 ounce) package chopped broccoli (an optional variation)
8 ounces lasagna noodles, un-cooked
2 cans Cream of Chicken soup, use reduced-fat
½ to 1 cup skim milk
1 (4 ounce) can mushrooms pieces, drained
1 (8 to 12 ounce) package low-fat, shredded cheese of your choice

Sauté chicken breast pieces in 1 tablespoon olive oil, along with sweet onion and green pepper, until chicken is opaque and vegetables are tender. (Sometimes I also add chopped broccoli to this mixture.) Set aside. In a 9 x 13–inch pan layer ingredients beginning with soup, then noodles, then chicken mixture, followed by mushrooms, cheese, and soup. Repeat layers till all is used. Cover with foil and bake 45 to 50 minutes in a 350–degree oven. Remove foil and bake about 10 more minutes till everything is a nice golden color. Cool 5 to 10 minutes before cutting into serving-size squares.

AUGUST 8

Homemade Stickers
A KIDS IN THE KITCHEN CRAFT PROJECT

INGREDIENTS
Assorted paper pictures (cut from magazines)
Scissors
Small bowl
White glue
White vinegar
Paintbrush or cotton swabs
Waxed paper

Combine two parts glue and one part vinegar in bowl. Stir well. Brush a thin layer of glue mixture onto the back of each cut out with a paint brush or cotton swab, making sure to cover all the edges. Place the stickers on a sheet of wax paper and allow to air dry completely, (about an hour). Any flavor of powdered gelatin dessert, mixed with a small amount of water can also be used for the "glue" to paint on the back of the stickers. (Tastes great for licking the stickers!)

AUGUST 9

Arroz Mexicano (Mexican Rice)
"It can be a lot of fun to let your travels and vacations influence your cooking."
~Wendy Louise

INGREDIENTS
1 cup long grain rice
1 tomato chopped (or 3 tablespoons tomato sauce)
2 teaspoons minced onion
2 cups chicken broth
¼ teaspoon salt
¼ teaspoon cumin
2 tablespoons canola oil
Sliced banana at serving time

In a skillet, brown rice in hot oil. Add rest of ingredients and bring to a boil. Cover, reduce heat, and simmer until tender and fluffy. Do not stir. Cooking time will be about 25 minutes. Serve with sliced banana on top (this is called Tampico style). Great side dish with chicken.

AUGUST 10
Souped-Up Spaghetti

Spaghetti has to be one of our family's all-time favorites for a quick, fall-back dinner straight out of the pantry. However, prepared sauces can get boring quickly! I usually try to make my favorite sauce and then freeze extra batches. But when I'm out of sauce or forget to defrost, I take a prepared sauce and "dress it up." Try dressing up your own spaghetti sauce with the following tips.

INGREDIENTS
Your favorite jarred sauce
Sliced olives
Diced mushrooms
Bell peppers
Red pepper flakes
Jalapeno slices
Parmesan cheese
Minced garlic
Minced onion
Italian sausage
Ground beef or turkey

Add ingredients to a prepared sauce (pick and choose which you like). Make sure to allow at least 10 minutes of simmer time for flavors to meld a little. If using meat, brown the meat and then add the sauce to the meat mixture. All other ingredients can be added directly to the sauce.

AUGUST 11

Chicken and Vegetable Skillet
4 servings

INGREDIENTS
2 tablespoons olive oil
4 skinless boneless chicken breast halves, cut in 1-inch cubes
1 carrot, sliced 1/4-inch thick
10 ounces frozen broccoli, thawed
4 cloves garlic, minced
16 ounces angel hair pasta
2/3 cup chicken broth
1 teaspoon dried basil
¼ cup Parmesan cheese

Cook pasta according to package directions. Chop chicken into strips and brown in oiled skillet over medium heat. Remove chicken. Place carrots in skillet, allowing to cook a couple minutes before adding broccoli and garlic. Let mixture cook for 2 minutes. Add broth, basic and cheese and stir to combine. Heat through and then add chicken. Reduce heat and simmer for several minutes. Serve over pasta.

RUSH HOUR TIP
An easy way to chop or snip food (especially sticky food) is to coat a pair of shears (or your chef knife) with cooking spray and chop or snip away.

Spice Primer
Stuck on which spice to choose?
Here are a few simple guidelines...

Beef: Rosemary, basil, garlic, onion powder
Pork: sage, garlic, chives, basil, marjoram, oregano
Chicken: sage, basil, marjoram, thyme
Fish: sage, fennel, dill, basil and parsley

AUGUST 12

Sara's Blue Cheese Chicken
4 servings

INGREDIENTS
4 boneless chicken breasts
½ cup flour
1 beaten egg
1 cup breadcrumbs
2 cups sour cream
4 pressed cloves of garlic
¾ pound Blue Cheese, crumbled
4 pressed cloves of garlic
Cooking oil

Dip chicken in flour and then beaten egg mixture. Then dredge in breadcrumbs. Brown chicken on both sides over medium heat in an oiled skillet. Place browned chicken breasts in a baking dish. Mix Blue Cheese, sour cream, and garlic. Pour mixture over chicken. Cover and bake in a 350-degree oven for 40 to 50 minutes or until heated through, chicken is done and mixture is bubbly.

RUSH HOUR WISDOM
Remember to prepare your kitchen before you start to cook. Read through your recipe, making sure you have all your needed ingredients. Get out the tools you will need. Having everything ready and on-hand makes the timing of cooking so much easier.

A Thought for Today
"The more light you allow within you, the brighter the world you live in will be." ~Shakti Gawain

AUGUST 13

Taco Beef with Rice

4 to 6 servings

INGREDIENTS

1 pound ground beef

1 (1.25 ounce) package taco seasoning mix

1 (15 ounce) can tomato soup

1½ cups water

1½ cups uncooked white rice

1 jar chunky Salsa

*Shredded Cheddar cheese *Lettuce * Onions *Sour cream

*These are optional ingredients—feel free to choose any "taco toppings"
   that your family enjoys

Tortilla chips (or tortillas)

Cook beef and taco seasoning in skillet until browned. Drain fat. Add soup, water, and rice and heat to a boil. Cover and cook over low heat for five minutes or until done. Top with toppings of choice. Serve with tortilla chips for dipping or with tortillas.

RUSH HOUR TIP

To avoid chewy tortillas mist them with water and then sauté quickly on both sides in a greased skillet over medium heat.

Weekly Challenge

CAN YOU BELIEVE?

Summer is coming to an ebb already and school is about to start. Don't wait till the last minute to get a head start on new clothes, shoes, and school supplies. Get your kids off to a relaxed start to the new school year. Let them help pick out fashions (with in reason) and backpacks, lunch bags, etc. A trip to Cost Cutters® might be in order too!

AUGUST 14

Summer Cubes
A KIDS IN THE KITCHEN RECIPE

Let kids toy around with making flavored ice cubes with punch, Kool-Aid® and soft-drinks. If you use the ice cube flavor that matches your drink, you can also avoid a watered down drink.

AUGUST 15

B-L-Turkey Roll-Ups
6 servings

INGREDIENTS
½ head iceberg lettuce, shredded
2 large tomatoes, chopped
12 turkey bacon slices
1/3 cup fat-free mayonnaise
¼ teaspoon black pepper
6 flour tortillas

Cook bacon in a large skillet over medium heat until crisp. Drain and cool, pressing between paper towels to remove maximum fat. Combine lettuce, tomatoes, pepper, and mayonnaise in a large bowl and mix well. Spread lettuce mixture evenly down each tortilla and then top with 2 strips of bacon. Roll up each tortilla and serve.

RUSH HOUR TIP
To make this recipe a bit quicker, microwave your bacon. Simply place bacon between two paper towels on a microwave-safe plate. Cook for 2 to 4 minutes (depending on your microwave.) This tastes just as good as pan fried and helps to remove fat into the paper toweling.

AUGUST 16
Turkey Meat Loaves
6 to 8 Servings

INGREDIENTS FOR LOAVES

2 pounds turkey
½ teaspoon salt
½ teaspoon pepper
3 tablespoons dehydrated onion flakes
1 large egg
1 ¼ cups soft bread crumbs
1 (8 ounce) can tomato sauce

INGREDIENTS FOR SAUCE

1 (8 ounce) can tomato sauce
2 ½ tablespoons brown sugar
3 tablespoons parsley flakes
2 tablespoons Worcestershire sauce

Combine all ingredients for meat loaf; shape into 8 oval patties. Bake at 450 degrees for 15 minutes or until cooked through. Spoon off any excess fat or grease. Combine sauce ingredients and pour over patties. Return to oven for 5 more minutes. Serve.

Conquer Kitchen Clutter

*Use caddies to round up like items such as condiments, cooking utensils, cleaning supplies, etc.

*Assign each family member a drawer. Teach them that if they want to have something in the kitchen it should go in their drawer—not on your counter!

*Take stock of your cabinets. Do you have dishes you hardly ever use taking up valuable space? Consider transferring these dishes to another closet or store carefully in crates.

*Twice a year, go through all your cabinets and take out any non-perishables you haven't eaten during the past six months. Donate these items to a food drive.

AUGUST 17
Summer Green Beans Supreme

INGREDIENTS

1 to 1 ½ pounds freshly picked green beans, trimmed of ends and vein,
   or 2 (10 ounce) packages French cut, frozen green beans, thawed
2 tablespoons butter
1 finely minced shallot
2 cloves of garlic minced
4 slices of bacon, cooked and crumbled, 2 tablespoons of drippings retained
¼ to ½ cup crumbled blue cheese or Feta cheese

In a skillet brown and cook bacon until crisp (about 8 to 10 minutes). Remove from skillet, drain on paper toweling, crumble, and set aside. Save 2 tablespoons of bacon drippings in the skillet. Add butter, shallot, garlic, and beans to the skillet. Cook and stir until beans become just tender. Transfer skillet contents to serving bowl and garnish with crumbled bacon and crumbled cheese.

AUGUST 18
Cozumel Turkey or Chicken Quesadillas
2 to 4 servings depending how hungry you are

INGREDIENTS

4 (8 inch) flour tortillas
4 tablespoons Ranch-style salad dressing
8 ounces cooked turkey meat or cooked chicken meat, sliced bite-size
1 avocado peeled and sliced
1 cup shredded Colby-Jack cheese
Salsa, optional at serving time

Spread each tortilla with 1 tablespoon ranch-style dressing. Divide up turkey or chicken between the tortillas, and place on one half-side of each tortilla. Top the meat with avocado slices, then sprinkle each with ¼ cup cheese. Fold in half to form quesadillas. In a large non stick skillet, or griddle, sauté tortillas for 2 minutes per side, turning once. Serve warm and melt-y. Pass salsa on the side.

AUGUST 19

Oven Roasted Cornish Hens

I hen per serving

INGREDIENTS
Fresh lemon, halved
Poultry seasoning
Paprika
Rice pilaf at serving time

Rub hens with lemon, sprinkle with seasonings. Roast whole, un-stuffed, for 50 minutes in a 450–degree oven. As juices form in pan, baste the birds often. Serve with a boxed-mix rice pilaf, made according to instructions on box (I like one that includes wild rice) and baked acorn squash. (See recipe below.)

AUGUST 20

Summer Squash

INGREDIENTS
Farmer's market acorn squash
Butter
Brown sugar

Cut squash in halves, then quarters and remove any fibers and seeds. Dot cavity with butter and sprinkle with brown sugar (about I tablespoon each). Wrap in foil and bake in same oven with Cornish hens.

FIVE-A-Day Contest

If you want to try to encourage fruit and veggie consumption in your home, try a five-a-day contest. Put each person's name on a chart on the fridge. Tack up a list of "serving" sizes (i.e. ½ banana = 1 fruit, 1 small apple = 1 fruit, ½ cup carrots = 1 vegetable) see who can eat themost each day and let the winner of the week choose a special meal. (You can do this same style competition with water consumption.) Of course, it's not the competition that we're after, but the habit of observing how much of the good-raw-stuff we actually eat in a day!

Weekly Challenge

THE POWER TO LISTEN

"One of the greatest forces we can have is the power to listen to others. It provides us with the power to be listened to by others..."~excerpted from *A Thousand Paths to Tranquility*

One of the best things I remember about growing up with my Mom, is that she always had the power to listen to both me and my brother, before she "made final judgment" on an issue we were considering. This open line of communication and respect developed into a great bond of trust between the three of us, with each of us being able to talk frankly, honestly, and comfortably with each other. This is a quality that my Mom had with her Mother, and that I now share with my Daughter. How are you with listening, really listening, to others and do they in return listen to you?

AUGUST 21

Terrific Teriyaki Burgers

It's burger and corn on the cob weather. Here's a few of our favorite burger recipes.

INGREDIENTS
Lean ground beef hamburger patties
Bottled teriyaki sauce

As you grill your favorite style of hamburger patties, baste their surface (both sides) with teriyaki sauce (straight out of the bottle) while they are cooking. P.S. Happy Birthday Mom!

A Thought for Today
BEING A VISIONARY
"The road to success is always under construction."
~Arnold Palmer, Pro Golfer

AUGUST 22
Mom's Blue Cheese Burgers
4 servings

INGREDIENTS
1 (plus) pound of lean ground beef
Salt and Pepper to taste
¼ cup finely diced onion
1 package crumbled blue cheese
Good hamburger buns, toasted on the grill

Lightly salt and pepper the ground beef and mix in the diced onion. Gently shape the meat mixture into 8 thin patties. Place crumbled blue cheese in center of 4 patties. Place the remaining 4 patties on top and seal the patty-edges together (sealing in the filling). Gently form the doubled patties into a uniform-size burger. Grill patties 6 to 10 minutes per side (or to your liking) over prepared barbecue coals. While burgers are grilling toast the buns on the grill.

RUSH HOUR TIP
Toasting the lightly-buttered buns, right next to the burgers on the grill, just adds that extra added touch. Remove the buns to your serving platter and have them waiting for your perfectly grilled burgers.

AUGUST 23

MaryAnn's Cedarburgers
8 burgers

MaryAnn Koopmann, presently from Belgium, Wisconsin (and previously from Cedarburg) shares this recipe for delicious hamburgers.

INGREDIENTS
1 ½ pounds ground chuck
¼ cup chopped onion
2 tablespoons French dressing
1 egg
¼ cup beer
½ cup saltine crackers, crushed
2 tablespoons grated Parmesan cheese
¼ teaspoon salt
Another ¼ cup beer
4 tablespoons French dressing

Gently mix all but last 2 ingredients together in a glass bowl. Form meat mixture into 8 burgers. Do not overwork mixture. Mix last 2 ingredients together for a basting sauce to use while grilling. Grill burgers on an outdoor grill for 8 to 10 minutes, each side, or until done to your liking. Baste the burgers throughout the grilling process. Serve burgers on good buns.

RUSH HOUR TIP
Thanks MaryAnn, for this delicious recipe. I'm thinking it might make a wonderful meatloaf come winter time, when it's too cold to barbecue in Wisconsin.

AUGUST 24
The Best Burgers Ever, Plain and Simple

INGREDIENTS
Ground beef (calculate 1/3 pound per person)
Salt and Pepper to taste
Minced onion
Hickory bark, chipped and soaked in water to moisten

Mix beef, salt and pepper, and onion together and form into patties. Break up hickory bark into chips (or use commercial chips) and soak in water, while you are preparing your coals and forming your hamburger patties. When you start to grill your hamburgers, throw some wet chips onto the coals. Grill the burgers to your liking, with the barbecue lid closed—this will add a nice smoky-hickory flavor to the burgers.

RUSH HOUR TIP
Mixing diced onion directly into your ground beef when forming hamburger patties, helps keep the meat from drying out while cooking. The hickory chips add wonderful taste.

AUGUST 25
"California" Burgers

INGREDIENTS
Bottom of bun
Burger
Leaf lettuce
French onion dip
Sliced garden tomato
Avocado slices
Salt and pepper
Top of bun

Stack in order given. Close up bun and enjoy.

AUGUST 26

Grilled Corn on the Cob

1 to 2 cobs per person

INGREDIENTS

Fresh farmer's market corn on the cob (I like the mixed yellow and white
   kind. In Wisconsin we call that "candy corn" because it is so sweet and
   tender.)
Water, for soaking corn
Foil
Melted butter, at serving time
Salt and pepper, if desired

Pull back husk on corn and remove silk. Soak corn in water and pull husk back
up around cob. Wrap in cooking foil and place on grill alongside burgers. Turn
occasionally. To serve remove foil, pull back husks, and roll cob in melted butter.
(Use husk as handle.) Salt to taste, if you wish. Cooking time about 15 minutes.

AUGUST 27

The "Bestest-Ever" Way to Eat a Hamburger...

A KID FRIENDLY RECIPE:

For the kids:
Have you ever had a good lean-beef hamburger on buttered toast—rather than
a bun? There is just something about meat on buttered toast! Try it without
ketchup and see what you think.

For the Grown-ups:
Serve the burgers, "open-faced," on one piece of buttered toast. Pile on sautéed
mushrooms and jarred brown gravy.

Weekly Challenge

Do more than exist: live.
Do more than touch: feel
Do more than look: observe
Do more than hear: listen
Do more than listen: understand
Do more than think: reflect
Do more that just talk: say something
~ Author unknown

AUGUST 28
"A Recipe for Family"

INGREDIENTS
Pizza
Cold, frosty root beer
Family "Jam Session"

Today rather than "food for the body" we are going to work on "food for the soul." Order in your favorite pizza and soft drinks, and have a good, family "jam session." Talk about the summer and "summer-rize" all the great things you experienced. Talk about the upcoming school year and summarize the goals you might have for this brand new grade and brand new school year. Air out your hopes; air out your fears. Get everybody on the "same page" before the school-year gets into full swing.

KITCHEN STRATEGIES

Make sure your dishwasher is empty before you start dinner preparations. This way you can transfer used dishes to the dishwasher as you go and avoid a pile to clean up later! Also fill your sink with hot, soapy water. Wipe down countertops as you go to avoid dried and crusty foods that need to be scrubbed off. Cooking becomes a lot easier when we get the "clean-up" under control. You can also try my favorite method—whoever cooks, doesn't clean. Let those who enjoy the meal share in the clean-up, too.

AUGUST 29

Greek Spaghetti
4 servings

INGREDIENTS
Olive oil
5 cloves of garlic, smashed and peeled
Red pepper flakes (optional)
Fresh parsley chopped
1 pound cooked spaghetti noodles
Shavings of fresh Parmesan cheese

Cook pasta in boiling salted water until al dente. Drain and set aside. In skillet sauté garlic cloves in olive oil until just golden (do not burn). Remove garlic cloves and add pepper flakes and fresh parsley. Sauté 1 minute more. Pour over pasta and toss to coat. Garnish with Parmesan shavings Serve with a good garlic bread or tomato bread.

AUGUST 30

Mushroom Pasta
4 servings

INGREDIENTS
Olive oil
2 tablespoons butter
5 cloves garlic smashed and peeled
1 package sliced mushrooms
1 tablespoon Sherry or Madeira wine
1 pound angel hair pasta, cooked al dente
¼ to ½ cup starchy cooking water from the pasta pot
Shaved Parmesan cheese for garnish
Chives, chopped for garnish

Cook up pasta and keep warm in a serving bowl. Sauté garlic in olive oil and butter until golden. Remove garlic. Add mushrooms and sauté until browned. Add wine and starchy water to blend. Pour mushroom sauce over pasta and toss to mix. Garnish with shaved Parmesan and freshly snipped chives. Serve with tomato bread and a nice salad.

AUGUST 31

Mom's North Woods Fruit Grunt

6 servings

Looking for a dessert that can be prepared in a jiffy? Try this Fruit Grunt recipe featuring Jiffy® cake mix and whipped cream. Mom used to send us out to pick berries for this dessert. We had blueberries in the front yard, and blackberries and red raspberries in the back yard. (Of course, if you don't have a cabin, fruit from your market will do).

INGREDIENTS
A loaf-size baking pan
Butter
1 cup (or so) fresh fruit
Any flavor Jiffy™- boxed cake mix (we like yellow)
Sugar
Whipped cream, at serving time

Generously butter a bread-loaf pan. Place fruit in the bottom. Sprinkle with sugar. Prepare cake mix as directed and then pour over fruit in bread pan. Bake as directed on the box. Let cool and then invert to un-mold. Serve warm with whipped cream. Hmmm, I can taste the summer vacations I experienced as a child!

Rush Hour Back to School Season Tips

Chart Your Way to Success: Create a checklist for each family member and tuck into a plastic sleeve. List out **everything** that needs to be done before school i.e., eat breakfast, lunch money, pack homework. Let children enjoy the feeling of success that comes with marking each item done with a dry-erase marker.

Wake-Up Call: Don't wait for that first Monday to begin getting up early! Adapt your new wake up time for the whole family one week prior to school starting.

SEPTEMBER 1
BBQ Meatloaf Sandwiches
4 servings

INGREDIENTS
1 pound ground beef
¼ cup dry bread crumbs
¼ cup diced onion
1 egg
¾ cup BBQ sauce, divided
Hamburger buns

Mix ground beef, bread crumbs, egg, onion, and ¼ cup BBQ sauce together lightly to form a loaf. Put half of loaf in a greased, rectangular bread pan. Pour on ¼ cup BBQ sauce. Place second half of loaf in the pan and seal sides. Bake for 40 to 45 minutes. Top with remaining ¼ cup BBQ Sauce and bake 5 minutes more. Slice and serve on hamburger buns.

More Rush Hour Back to School Season Tips

Satisfying Smoothies: There may not be a better breakfast option. What else is healthy, quick, and tastes like a milkshake? For my 10 favorite smoothies recipes, visit www.rushhourcook.com/smoothie.htm

Gooooood Morning Family!: Start each day like Ty from *Extreme Home Makeover*. Wish a sincere "good morning" to all (even if family members look at you funny). Just as breakfast is the most important meal for our physical needs, a sincere good morning is the best emotional breakfast.

Don't be a stranger: It's no secret that when a parent and teacher work together, the results benefit the child. Take a moment to stop by the school and introduce yourself to your child's new teacher. Share any special considerations from the summer (a divorce, etc.) that may affect your child.

SEPTEMBER 2

Karl's Alsace Lorraine Pie

6 to 8 servings

INGREDIENTS
1 single-pie pie crust
½ of a sweet onion, chopped
4 ounces slab bacon (rind removed), coarsely chopped
2/3 cup whipping cream, chilled
2 tablespoons sour cream, chilled
1/3 cup sharp Cheddar cheese
Pepper to taste

In skillet, brown bacon, and remove excess fat. Add onion and sauté until translucent. Set aside to cool. (This will be the topping for your pie.) Meanwhile in food processor, electric beater, or with whisk, beat whipping cream and sour cream until soft peaks form. Fold in Cheddar cheese and season with pepper. Set aside. Place pie crust on a cookie sheet and crimp edges to about ½ -inch height. Pour in cream filling and spread evenly. Sprinkle on the bacon-onion topping. Bake at 425 for 10 to 15 minutes, or until topping just begins to brown. Slice in wedges and serve warm.

A Family Challenge

DETERMINING A COMMON GOAL

Families work and play so much better together when they have a common goal, a direction, and a future toward which they are all growing. One of our Champion Press authors, Deborah Taylor-Hough writes about developing a family philosophy specifically for family purpose and unity in her book *A Simple Choice*, ISBN 1891400495. I have a friend who stenciled her family's Mission Statement around the border of her kitchen walls, making a decorative and inspirational reminder for all to see on a daily basis. She used beautiful colors and stenciling (instead of a wall paper border) to decorate her kitchen with the inspirations that meant the most to her family. Take some time to think about your goals, before starting your stenciling project.

SEPTEMBER 3

Family Mission Statement
A KID AND ADULT FRIENDLY "RECIPE" FOR A FAMILY CRAFT PROJECT

INGREDIENTS
Paint
Stencils
Creativity
An inspirational phrase or design voted on by the family
A setting where it can be seen and enjoyed daily

SEPTEMBER 4

Baked Eggs in Bacon Cups
estimate 1 to 2 eggs per serving

Here's a great recipe to try for Labor Day Weekend. Why not have a nice family brunch, starring the recipe below? Use nice place settings; add some champagne or sparkling juice. After brunch, enjoy a game together or a walk with your family.

INGREDIENTS
1 or 2 large eggs per person
Equal amount of Canadian style bacon rounds
Parsley and pepper
Spray a standard muffin tin with cooking spray. Press a Canadian bacon slice into each muffin well, forming a little cup shape. Sprinkle with a little pepper and parsley. Carefully break one egg into each bacon-cup.

Sprinkle a dash more pepper on top. Bake in a 350-degree oven for approximately 12 minutes (or until eggs are done to your liking). Un-mold and serve hot, with a garnish of fresh parsley. Add a selection of your favorite sweet rolls and pastries and you have an instant breakfast buffet.

OPTIONAL VARIATION
Melt your favorite shredded cheese over the eggs, at last minute of cooking and garnish with a little dusting of paprika for color.

SEPTEMBER 5

Friday is always "Kids in the Kitchen" day at the DAILY RUSH. With football season starting, here is a great snack kids can help make for all to enjoy during the game.

Packer Party Mix
use any amounts to taste

Combine your favorite oat and wheat cereals, nuts, small crackers, mini pretzels, and oyster crackers and toss with a little melted butter. Sprinkle with your seasonings of choice. Crisp in a 350-degree oven for about 10 minutes. Serve warm or at room temperature. Once cooled, mix can be stored in an airtight container to keep crisp.

SEPTEMBER 6

Brussels Sprouts with Water Chestnuts
8 servings

INGREDIENTS
¼ cup chopped onion
1 (8 ounce) can water chestnuts, drained and slivered
½ stick butter
8 cups Brussels sprouts, halved and steamed to tender
Salt and pepper to taste
Toasted pine nuts (optional)

Sauté onions, water chestnuts, and butter. Pour over steamed Brussels sprouts. Salt and pepper to taste. Top with toasted pine nuts.

A Thought for Today
ENTHUSIASM

"Success is waking up in the morning, whoever you are, wherever you are, however old or young, and bounding out of bed because there's something out there that you love to do, that you believe in, that you're good at something that's bigger than you are, and you can hardly wait to get at it again today." ~Whit Hobbs

SEPTEMBER 7
Zucchini Puree for Steamed Vegetables
4 to 6 servings of sauce

For this recipe put away the cheese, the au gratin, the creamed soup mixed with veggies, the batter-coated and fried, the casserole, the calories. We are focusing on a veggie plain and simple, lean and steamed, healthy and end-of-summer good—straight from the farmer's market.

INGREDIENTS
1 to 2 zucchini, peeled
Salt and pepper to taste
Garlic salt to taste

Cut zucchini and steam until soft. Place in food processor and puree. Season to taste. Serve over steamed vegetables, such as broccoli or green beans.

A Few More Back-to-School Tips

Homework Helpers: So much for counting oranges and apples, today's kids are learning information we often never heard of. Use these Internet source for homework help: www.britannica.com www.askjeeves.com Type in any homework questions and watch for results. Or go to www.google.com and type in "Homework Help" and you'll find millions of options only a click away.

Helpful habits: Start developing healthy homework habits from day one. After a healthy snack have children do their homework prior to play.

Mom... my back hurts: Instead of letting children realize the pain you once faced carrying them in the womb, find a backpack that works. Many children are hauling 10-20 pounds of books a day. Try a roller-pack to help save the back.

SEPTEMBER 8

Tomato Bruschetta

24 slices

With the end of summer on its way, here's a great recipe for using up those last garden fresh tomatoes.

INGREDIENTS

1 large garlic clove, peeled and smashed
24 (½ -inch thick) slices of French baguette bread
1½ cups of diced, vine ripened, garden tomatoes
2 to 3 tablespoons minced red onion
1 tablespoon extra-virgin olive oil (I like the infused garlic olive oil)
Snipped fresh basil, parsley, or chives

Rub the smashed garlic clove over each side of the bread slices, to infuse a garlic flavor. Place the bread slices on a cookie sheet and toast in a 350-degree oven for about 10 minutes, or until lightly browned and crisp, turning once. Watch carefully so the bread doesn't burn. While the bread is toasting combine the diced tomatoes, red onion, and olive oil in a small bowl. Spoon the tomato mixture onto the toasted bread slices and garnish with snipped basil, parsley, or chives. Serve immediately.

RUSH HOUR TIP

Always use a serrated knife and literally "saw" the bread, with a back and forth motion. This way you avoid crushing and squashing the bread by pushing down with a dull or plain-edged knife.

School Isn't Just for Kids!

School isn't just for kids: Adult students are the fastest growing educational demographic in the United States. If you have a passion you want to follow, today's online learning opportunity offer flexibility unavailable in the past. Check out www.classesonlineusa.com or www.educationforadults.com for an overview of today's options.

SEPTEMBER 9

Here are two quick, easy, and summery desserts for these last days of summer.

Fruit Cup Ambrosia

Arrange fresh orange and grapefruit sections in your fanciest stem ware. Sprinkle with freshly grated coconut. Garnish with a stemmed maraschino cherry.

RUSH HOUR TIP

You can also use canned mandarin oranges and canned grapefruit sections, both drained, if fresh fruit is not available.

Summer Melon Dessert Variation

Serve generous wedges of fresh cantaloupe or honeydew melon, dollop-ed with a scoop of contrasting sorbet or sherbet in the center. Top with toasted coconut.

Variety is the Spice of Life

The best meals are those that contain variety. Check your meals against the list below for maximum affect...

Variety in nutrition: Mix carbos and veggies. Despite all the fad diets, research still shows that the majority of our calories should come from carbs (about 55-60% percent) and 30-35% should come from protein.

Variety in texture: Pair crunchy foods with soft foods and crispier foods with tender foods. The contrast in texture helps accentuate each food more.

Variety in taste: Try serving the spicy with bland, or sweet foods with sour foods. Combinations of flavors enhance one another.

Variety in temperature: Serve a hot dish with a cold dish for maximum contrast and flavor.

SEPTEMBER 10
Wendy Louise's Grilled Garden Tomatoes
1/2 tomato per serving

INGREDIENTS
Garden ripe tomatoes
Butter
Bread crumbs
Grated Parmesan
Snipped chives

Halve each tomato and gently squeeze out some of the juice and seeds. Place tomato halves in a foil-lined pan. Dot each with butter, bread crumbs, Parmesan and snipped chives. Grill briefly under broiler (approximately 5 to 10 minutes) to warm through and melt topping. Be careful not to overcook! Serve warm as a side vegetable. These are great with grilled meats and make a pretty garnish on the plate.

RUSH HOUR WISDOM
Take the time to keep your kitchen knives very sharp. You'll be less likely to cut yourself with a sharp knife than a dull one. Ever try to slice a tomato with a dull knife? Before you know it you've squashed the tomato and cut your finger in the process. Or how about carving that holiday roast…that you've 'pushed' off the platter, right onto Grandma's heirloom table cloth, or into her lap. Your good knives should be kept sharp, washed and dried by hand, and stored in their own designated place…away from children, and away from fumbling fingers in mixed-utensil drawers. And since today's featured recipe is nice and easy—there is plenty of time to go and sharpen those knives!

Weekly Challenge

BEING REALISTIC

"Stop chasing the unattainable dream. Take action today by picking a realistic goal!" ~Carrie Myers Smith, author and wellness-coach

Take Carrie's words to heart and pick a truly attainable goal to work on. Pick it today. Once you have reached that goal, you can move onto another, and then another. Pretty soon what was first thought to be unattainable has now been set behind you, "in a cloud of dust." For example, say I want to lose 40 pounds ASAP. How about I set my sights on 10 pounds; then 10 more pounds; and so on. Start with an attainable, realistic step, and keep attaining as you move forward one step at a time.

SEPTEMBER 11

Potato Pile

4 to 6 servings

INGREDIENTS
¼ cup melted butter
¼ cup water
½ package dry onion soup mix
5 medium potatoes (unpeeled)

Preheat oven to 350 degrees. Cut scrubbed potatoes into ¼-inch thick slices. Mix all other ingredients together. Spread a layer of 1/3 of the potatoes in bottom of 2 -quart casserole. Top with 1/3 of butter/soup packet mixture. Repeat layers twice more. Bake for 50 to 60 minutes, or until fork tender.

SEPTEMBER 12

Carla's Raspberry Vinaigrette Salad

8 servings

INGREDIENTS

8 cups torn Romaine lettuce
1 cup fresh raspberries
½ sliced almonds, toasted
½ cup seedless raspberry jam
¼ cup cider or white wine vinegar
¼ cup honey
2 tablespoons plus 2 teaspoons vegetable oil

Place torn Romaine in salad bowl. Top with raspberries and toasted almonds. In a blender, combine remaining ingredients and blend until smooth. Pour dressing over salad just before serving and toss lightly.

SEPTEMBER 13

Donna Wood's South of the Border Meatloaf

4 to 6 servings

INGREDIENTS

1 ½ cups finely crushed corn chips
1 cup milk
1 ½ pounds ground chuck/beef (I use half and half)
2 cups salsa (your favorite brand), divided
2 eggs beaten
2 tablespoons chives, divided

Preheat oven to 350 degrees. Soak the corn chips in the milk until soft and then add remaining ingredients keeping 1/2 the salsa and chives on the side. Firmly pack mixture into loaf pan. Mix remaining salsa and chives and spoon over the top of meatloaf. Bake for 1 hour, or until done. Serve with additional salsa and sour cream if desired.

SEPTEMBER 14

Tasty Potato Skins
A KID FRIENDLY RECIPE
8 servings

INGREDIENTS
4 large potatoes, baked
2 to 3 tablespoons melted butter
1 cup mixed Colby-Jack cheese
Sprinkling of paprika
Sour cream
Diced green onion
Salsa

Cut potatoes lengthwise into quarters. Scoop out pulp down to ¼-inch shells. (Save the baked potato pulp for another recipe.)Arrange potato shells on a broiler pan. Brush with melted butter, sprinkle with paprika, and broil for approximately 8 to 10 minutes, or until crisp. Sprinkle on cheese last 30 seconds of broiling to melt. Serve warm and garnish with sour cream, diced onion and salsa.

Speaking of Potatoes...
How to Make the Perfect Mashed

In order to have the right end result, you need to start with the right potato. For a light and fluffy potato use a Russet, for a smooth and creamy texture try Yukon Gold.

While you peel your potatoes, get that water boiling! Instead of placing whole potatoes into the water, cut them into uniform 1-inch squares for more even cooking.

Contrary to popular belief, you don't want a rolling boil--but a strong simmer. Let your potatoes cook for 15 minutes.

Mash your potoatoes while they are nice and hot. Once mashed to your desired consistency, mix in any salt, cream or other ingredients.

SEPTEMBER 15

Cappuccino Parfaits
6 servings

INGREDIENTS
1 tablespoon plus 1 teaspoon instant coffee (regular or decaff)
1 tablespoon hot water
1½ cups cold milk
1 (4 serving size) package instant vanilla pudding
¼ teaspoon cinnamon
1½ cups whipped topping
6 chocolate wafer cookies, crumbled

Dissolve coffee crystals in hot water. Add milk, pudding, and cinnamon. Beat mixture for 1 or 2 minutes to blend. Let stand a few minutes to thicken. Gently fold in the whipped topping.

Divide ½ of mixture into 6 stemmed glasses. Layer in ½ of crushed cookies. Spoon in remaining pudding mixture. Top with remaining cookies. Garnish with additional whipped topping. Dust with additional cinnamon. Refrigerate until serving time.

5 Steps to a Perfect Cup of Coffee

Make sure to buy the correct grind for your coffeemaker. For the best flavor, buy beans and a coffee grinder that can grind to your coffeemaker's specifications.

If you do not grind your own beans, buy only a week's supply at a time. Keep all coffee (and beans) in a tightly sealed container in your refrigerator.

Use a measuring cup or coffee spoon to determine the amount of grounds. This is not the time for guessing games!

Always use cold water when brewing.

Clean your coffeemaker once a week with vinegar and water, then cycle through one empty pot of water.

SEPTEMBER 16
Tomato Provolone Casserole
6 servings

INGREDIENTS
2 to 3 large garden ripe tomatoes
¼ cup flour, seasoned with salt and pepper
2 tablespoons butter
2 green onions, minced, including tops
½ cup sliced black olives, drained
4 slices Provolone cheese
2 eggs, lightly beaten
1 cup milk
1 cup shredded Cheddar cheese
Chopped chives

Cut tomatoes into ½-inch thick slices. Dredge in seasoned flour to coat. Sauté quickly in the 2 tablespoons butter. Set aside. In a buttered 8–inch casserole dish arrange the green onions and black olives. Top with tomato slices, cheese slices, then more tomato slices. Combine eggs, milk, and Cheddar cheese. Pour over layers in casserole. Sprinkle with fresh chives. Bake at 350 degrees for 1 hour, or until set and firm. Remove from oven and let sit for 5 minutes before cutting into 6 wedges to serve. Serve as a brunch, luncheon, or light supper dish.

You Don't Have to Cry About It: Cures for Onion Eyes

I confess, I have not tried all of these, but I rounded them up in my research for "onion eyes." Give them a whirl and let me know what works best for you! (See how to contact me at the back of this book.)

* Place onions in freezer for 20 minutes prior to cutting
* Cut onions under cold running water
* My favorite (which I have done)—Go ahead and cry while cutting a ton of onions at one time. Then freeze in ½ cup increments in airtight freezer containers. Pull out as needed. Frozen onions will keep for 2 months.

SEPTEMBER 17
Fiesta Confetti Beef Bake
6 servings

INGREDIENTS
2 tablespoons butter
3 cloves minced garlic
½ cup chopped onion
1 ½ pounds lean ground beef
¼ cup diced fresh green bell pepper
3 tablespoons flour
2 cups preferably fresh corn, cut off the cob (or can use canned)
2 cups diced preferably fresh tomatoes (or can use canned)
¼ cup chopped pimiento
1 teaspoon salt
1 ½ teaspoons chili powder
¼ teaspoon cumin
Dash cayenne
Slight dash cinnamon
6 slices buttered bread, crusts removed

Melt butter in skillet. Add garlic and onion and cook until limp. Add meat and green bell pepper and sauté until browned. Blend in flour. Add corn, tomatoes, and seasonings. Cook until heated through (about 5 minutes) stirring to mix all. Turn mixture into a 10 x 6 x 2–inch buttered casserole dish. Arrange buttered bread slices on top. Bake at 350 degrees for 25 to 30 minutes, or until bread topping is golden.

Cures for Onion Eyes Continued...

* My second favorite—Have any child over 12 cut them as a punishment for misbehavior.

* Ask for a food processor for Christmas! You can also find a much less expensive solution at most cookware stores in the form of small gadgets that hand dice onions, mushrooms, and more. The Pampered Chef makes a handy and inexpensive gadget for dicing mushrooms and onions quickly.

Weekly Challenge

THE IMPORTANCE OF A GOOD NIGHT'S SLEEP

Is your family getting enough sleep? (Especially your kids, now that they are back in school?) It is said that millions of Americans suffer from chronic sleep deprivation, which inhibits functioning at our maximum. Our immune systems also suffer when we don't get enough sleep. Are your beds comfy? Are your mattresses up to par, pillows fluffy, blankets a comfortable weight, sheets a nice thread count (don't settle for anything less than 230 count per inch). If you can afford them, look for Egyptian cotton, high count sheets, they are ever so luxurious. (I found an incredible deal on the America Online Home Outlet.) Next to food and water, good sound sleep is very important. Do you awake rested and ready to tackle the new day? If not, consider sprucing up your mattress and bedding ASAP.

SEPTEMBER 18

Joyce Gearhart's Angel Delights
A KID FRIENDLY RECIPE
5 dozen bite-size cookies

INGREDIENTS
6 ounces chocolate bits
6 ounces butterscotch bits
1 small jar peanut butter
4 cups mini marshmallows
1 (3 ounce) can chow mein noodles

Melt bits and peanut butter in double boiler. Add marshmallows. When almost dissolved, stir in noodles until thoroughly mixed. Drop by teaspoons-full onto wax paper. Makes 60 teaspoon sized cookies.

RUSH HOUR WISDOM

Forty years ago, a group of Christmas crafters had a cookie exchange, and Joyce says she's been making these cookies ever since. Just goes to show you how good recipes never go out of style!

SEPTEMBER 19

Lorraine's Swiss Steak
6 servings

INGREDIENTS
1½ to 2 pounds round steak, ½-inch thick, cut into serving size pieces
2 to 3 tablespoons cooking oil
1 to 2 tablespoons butter
1 onion, sliced thin or chopped
1 to 2 green bell peppers, sliced into strips or chopped
1 to 2 (16 ounce) cans stewed tomatoes, un-drained
Salt and pepper to taste

Preheat electric skillet to 350 degrees with cooking oil and butter to cover bottom of pan. Cut round steak into serving-size pieces. Brown meat on both sides, then remove from pan. Sauté/fry onion and bell peppers in pan till slightly limp and glazed. Add meat back to pan. Pour on first can of stewed tomatoes, including liquid. Cover and reduce heat setting to a medium–simmer. Cook until meat is tender and flavors have melded, approximately 30 to 40 minutes. While steak is cooking add more stewed tomatoes if necessary, to arrive at the amount of sauce that you like. Adjust seasoning with salt and pepper to taste. Serve with mashed potatoes and the sauce "as is" from the pan.

RUSH HOUR WISDOM

The secret to Lorraine's recipe is its simplicity. Don't "doctor it up" with extra spices—don't "mess" with the sauce—don't hesitate to have it become a family favorite! The wonderful flavor comes from the initial browning of the meat and then the browning of the onion and peppers before you start the simmering process with the tomatoes.

For more delicious skillet recipes like this one, see Wendy Louise's new book The Sensational Skillet, create spectacular meals with your electric skillet (ISBN1891400258) available through Champion Press Ltd. Learn more at www.championpress.com

A Thought for Today
"FOLLOWING THROUGH"
"Much good work is lost for lack of a little more."
~ Joyce Gearhart

SEPTEMBER 20

Barb's Brownies (submitted by Victoria Beckham)
1 dozen

Need a fast dessert? Vicki says, "These are ingredients we always have on hand in the pantry. These brownies are so easy and taste awesome!"

INGREDIENTS
1 cup sugar
¾ cup all purpose flour
½ cup cocoa
2 eggs
1 teaspoon vanilla
¼ teaspoon cinnamon
1 stick butter, melted

Mix all together. Bake at 300 degrees for 30 minutes in greased 8-inch square pan. Cut and let cool before serving.

SEPTEMBER 21
Victoria Beckham's Pineapple Lush Cake

INGREDIENTS
1 (4 serving size) package jell-O® vanilla pudding (can use sugar free)
1 (20 ounce) can crushed pineapple in juice, un-drained
2 cups thawed Cool Whip® lite-whipped topping
1 angel food cake (ready made from store)
Fresh strawberries, blueberries, blackberries, raspberries to garnish

Mix dry pudding mix and pineapple, with juice, in bowl. Gently stir in Cool Whip. Cut cake horizontally into 3 layers. Place bottom layer - cut side up - on serving plate. Spread 1 1/2 cups of pudding mixture onto cake. Top with middle cake layer. Spread 1 cup of pudding mixture on top. Top with remaining cake layer. Spread with remaining pudding mixture. (It's very pretty if you just frost the top of layers, not sides)Refrigerate at least one hour (overnight is okay if covered well).Garnish with fresh berries.

SEPTEMBER 22

Judy Ring's Corn Salad
8 servings

Get the taste and crunch of summer all year 'round with this veggie-relish-style salad. We can't give all the credit to Judy because this recipe came all the way from France, via her friend and house guest Michelle. Judy you keep good company.

INGREDIENTS
1 (27 ounce) can of corn, drained in colander
5 to 7 ounces of salad olives, the bits and pieces kind
1 cucumber, peeled, cut in half and seeded, then sliced
1 green pepper, ribbed, seeded, and cut into 1/2 to 3/4-inch pieces
4 hard boiled eggs, chopped
½ cup of canola oil
2 tablespoons apple cider vinegar, or more if you want, to taste
1 teaspoon black pepper
2 tablespoons spicy mustard

Put the corn, olives, and veggies in a colander and let drain completely before using. Mix the oil, vinegar, black pepper, and mustard in a cup. Pour over veggies and let marinate a couple of hours, covered in refrigerator.

Corny Things To Do Online

Looking for a corny way to pass the time? Log on to http://www.iowafarmer.com/corncam/corn.html and check out the Corn Cam. The Iowa Farmer's Today website shows a constant corn cam. You can also view crops around the world. They say a watched pot never boils... I don't know the rule about corn!

For a litte more entertainment, stop in at www.cornfieldmaze.com This interesting site displays information, photographs and hours for over 330 member corn mazes! The founder of this site has designed over 840 mazes himself! An interesting place to explore.

SEPTEMBER 23
Marilyn Stonecipher's Tomato Bread

INGREDIENTS
Fresh loaf of foccacia bread
Olive oil
Crushed garlic
Garden fresh tomatoes (I prefer red)
Fresh or dried oregano
Grated Parmesan cheese
Shredded mozzarella

Mix good olive oil and garlic, and lightly coat the bread then sprinkle with Pamesan cheese. Thinly slice tomatoes and place on top of bread, then sprinkle with mozzarella and oregano. (I've used Cheddar before when out of mozzarella and that was good too.) Broil until bubbly and brown. Cut into wedges. Makes a great light dinner with just a fresh salad and a glass of good red wine.

Thought for Today
"It's not what you do once in a while,
it's what you do day in and day out
that makes the differece." ~ Jennry Craig

SEPTEMBER 24

Mom's "Lagniappe" Crescent Rolls

INGREDIENTS
1 tube packaged-refrigerator crescent-style rolls
1 green onion or 1 shallot, diced fine
A few fresh mushrooms, diced
A slight amount of butter
A little season salt, or salt and pepper
Fresh parsley and chives, minced

Preheat oven according to package instructions on the tube of dough. While oven is heating, unroll and separate dough into individual, triangular pieces. Set aside. In a pan, in a slight amount of butter, quickly sauté diced mushroom and onion till softened. Lightly season with seasonings of your choice and the minced parsley and chives. Place a teaspoon or so of sautéed filling at the wide end of each crescent roll piece. Roll up dough to encase filling and place on baking sheet (prepared according to package instructions). Proceed to bake, again according to package instructions, adding just a couple of additional minutes to the baking time called for, because the rolls are now thicker and will take just a little longer to bake. Serve warm. Makes a great addition to any dinner and a nice variation from the usual French bread or regular dinner rolls.

RUSH HOUR WISDOM

"Lagniappe" is a French word meaning an extra added detail, a bonus, a little surprise or gift, a garnish, a "specialty of the house" added to indulge the palate. Usually it means a little culinary gratuity…like a chocolate on turned down bed sheets, or an unexpected appetizer when you sit down at the table. In this case, I like to think it's the little surprise filling waiting for you in these delectable dinner rolls. Next time you have company for dinner serve these and see all the compliments you get!

Weekly Challenge

COUPLE'S JOURNALING
AN IDEA BY VICKI PROCHNOW,
Dr. O'Brien's Office, Bay Shore, WI

While waiting for a doctor's appointment the other day, a random conversation yielded this wonderful idea about a way for couples to communicate with each other. Long-time-married, Vicki Prochnow and her husband Russ have kept a mutual-journal since the beginning of their marriage. "The Book" resides on a desk in their home office at all times, waiting for their individual entries or readings there of. Sometimes the journal is entered into often and at other times there might be as long as a month's passing. Vicki loves to go back into the book and see how she felt 10, 15, even 20 years ago. The book has recorded births, deaths, family spats, family joys, vacations, concerns, personal accomplishments, the weather, household issues and who knows what-all ... maybe even a favorite recipe of the day! A quarter of a century of marriage is preserved in this record-keeping-book about their lives together. What a great idea, Vicki, and what a great way to keep your communication lines open at all times.

Vicki also uses her idea for gift giving, maintaining that this is the perfect wedding present or bridal shower gift. Upon occasion her recipients might have been a little dumb-founded or skeptical (perhaps expecting a more extravagant gift?), but then a "thank you note" will arrive in her mail box from an appreciative couple who has come to realize just how valuable her gift has been. Vicki, thank you for sharing your "recipe" for a couple's marriage-book, a way to communicate, and a way to stay close in a relationship.

SEPTEMBER 25

Judy Brown's Spinach Casserole with Cracker Crumb Topping

4 to 6 servings

INGREDIENTS
1 (10 ounce) box Frozen chopped spinach
5 ounces cream cheese
3 ounces hot pepper cheese
1 can cream of mushroom soup
1 can French fried onion rings
1 roll of Ritz® crackers, crushed
1 stick butter

Prepare spinach per directions; drain and set aside. In sauce pan heat both cheeses with soup until cheese melts and mixture is blended. Add spinach and fried onions and mix well. Pour into greased 9 x 9-inch casserole dish. Melt butter and add enough cracker crumbs to soak up butter. Sprinkle crumbs on top of casserole. Bake for 25 to 30 minutes in 250-degree oven.

The Spinach Source

I have found a great site online for researching healthy foods. The World's Healthiest Foods (www.whfoods.com) details the nutrition data, health benefits, scientific studies, description, safety, store selection tips, history, storage information, recipes, and much more for many healthy foods.) When I logged on, I found out that "researchers have identified at least 13 different flavonoid compounds in spinach that function as antioxidants and as anti-cancer agents. The anticancer properties of these spinach flavonoids have been sufficiently impressive to prompt researchers to create specialized spinach extracts that could be used in controlled studies. These spinach extracts have been shown to slow down cell division in stomach cancer cells..." The site is maintained by The George Mateljan Foundation for the World's Healthiest Foods. It was established by George Mateljan to discover, develop, and share scientifically proven information about the benefits of healthy eating, and to provide the personalized support individuals need to make eating The World's Healthiest Foods enjoyable, easy, quick, and affordable.

SEPTEMBER 26

Marilyn Stonecipher's Shepherd's Pie
A KID FRIENDLY RECIPE
4 to 6 servings

"Years ago, before I had kids, a friend of mine used to make this for her family (husband and three kids). I thought it was the strangest thing I had ever seen but I tried it and liked it. Now, years later, I have three kids of my own. I started longing for this about a year ago -- even though I had only had it one time. I remembered the basic premise of the recipe and asked a few people if they knew how to make it. Of course, everyone had a different version -- some used canned mushroom soup, some used canned peas. I just listened and then made up my own version. I thought my kids would probably HATE it and I would never make it again but, amazingly, everyone in the family likes it. Even Josh, my pickiest eater! Now, I make it when I need comfort food but don't have much time (which is ALWAYS since I work full time)."

It goes like this...

INGREDIENTS
1 pound lean ground beef
1/2 onion, diced
1/2 to 1 green pepper, ribbed, seeded and diced
1 teaspoon minced garlic
Salt and pepper, to taste
1 (15 ounce) can diced tomatoes (or use a can of stewed tomatoes and chop them up)
1 small can sliced mushrooms, drained
1 (15 ounce) can sliced green beans, drained
4 to 5 white potatoes (boiled and mashed with cream, butter, salt and pepper)
Shredded Cheddar or Colby cheese

Brown ground beef with garlic, onion and green pepper. Drain. Salt and pepper to taste. Add tomatoes, green beans, and mushrooms. Spray glass baking dish with canola oil. Add ground beef mixture. Top with a layer of mashed potatoes. Sprinkle with shredded cheese. Bake at 350 for about 30 minutes until hot and bubbly. Enjoy with crusty bread and a nice salad.

SEPTEMBER 27
Don and Mary's Pasta Fagioli
6 servings

We eat this at least once a month, year 'round. It's tasty, filling, inexpensive, easy, and low-fat. Who can ask for more than that?

INGREDIENTS
1 tablespoon olive oil
1 or 2 cloves garlic, crushed
Optional: At this time you can sauté 1/2 pound Italian sausage with the garlic. However, we prefer a meatless version and omit this step.
1 (19 ounce) can of Cannelini Beans, with liquid (or white beans, if you can't find Cannelini Beans)
1½ cups spaghetti sauce
1 cup small pasta (such as small shells)
2 sprigs fresh rosemary (or 1 teaspoon dried rosemary)
Water
Pepper
Parmesan Cheese

Heat olive oil in a medium saucepan over medium heat. Sauté garlic for a minute or so (adding in the Italian sausage if you have elected to do so.) Add beans and the liquid from the bean can. Fill the bean can with water and add the water to the pan. Add spaghetti sauce and rosemary. Let this come to a boil, stirring often. Once this starts to boil, add the pasta. Lower heat to medium-low and let simmer about 12 to 15 minutes, stirring often, until the pasta is cooked. If the mixture gets too thick, add additional water while cooking. The final dish should not be too soupy, but it should have a medium-thick sauce on it. Pour into individual serving bowls. Sprinkle with pepper and grated Parmesan. Serve with crusty bread and a green salad.

A Thought for Today
"Be kind, for everyone you meet is fighting a hard battle."
~Plato, Philosopher

SEPTEMBER 28
Mexican Caldo of Beef Soup
8 Servings

INGREDIENTS

2 to 2½ pounds boneless beef rump or chuck roast, cut into 1-inch
   cubes
2 quarts water
1 large onion, halved
2 to 4 cloves garlic, left whole
8 whole peppercorns
3 carrots, pared and cut into 1-inch lengths
½ pound fresh green beans, trimmed and cut into 1-inch lengths
3 ears of sweet corn, cut into 1-inch rounds
3 zucchini, cut into 1-inch pieces
1 pound head of cabbage, cut into 1-inch chunks
1 tablespoon salt

FOR SERVING TIME:
¼ cup fresh lime juice
½ cup minced onion
¼ cup snipped fresh coriander or parsley,
Lime slices (optional)
Salsa on the side for garnish

Heat meat and water in large Dutch oven to boiling; then reduce heat and
simmer, uncovered for 45 minutes, skimming off any foam. Add the large onion,
garlic cloves and peppercorns. Cover and cook 1½ hours, or until meat is very
tender. Then remove the meat from the broth and reserve. Strain the broth,
skim off any fat, and return the broth to the Dutch oven. Add the carrots and
green beans. Heat back to boiling, then reduce heat and simmer for 10 minutes,
covered. Add back the reserved meat, along with the zucchini, corn, and cabbage. Add the salt. Add additional water, if needed, to just cover the vegetables.
Cook partially covered for an additional 30 minutes, or until all vegetables are
tender. To serve, ladle the soup into individual bowls and sprinkle each serving
with fresh lime juice, minced onion, chopped coriander, and garnish with a lime
slice. Serve a salsa on the side for extra garnish.

SEPTEMBER 29

Mom's Creamy Tomato Soup

6 servings

INGREDIENTS
12 to 16 tomatoes, scalded and slipped out of their skins, and smashed
1 medium sized onion or 1 large leek, chopped fine
3 ounces butter
1 teaspoon crushed, sweet basil
1 pint heavy cream
1 tablespoon brown sugar
Salt and white pepper

Melt butter in large soup pot. Cook the onion or leek in the butter until softened and beginning to brown. Add the smashed tomatoes and 1 teaspoon crushed, sweet basil to the pot. Simmer the soup for half an hour. Force the soup through a sieve, discarding any pulp and seeds, and return to the soup pot. In another pot heat the heavy cream with the brown sugar, whisking all the while. While stirring the soup, quickly add the heated cream, stirring all the while. Do not bring the soup to a boil. Lastly, adjust seasoning to taste with a little salt and white pepper. Serve the soup with toasted cheese sandwiches for a light dinner.

Hot Tomato Tips from the Florida Tomato Committee

www.floridatomatoes.com

Coring: Using a sharp paring knife make several angled cuts through the stem and under the core.

Seeding: Lay the tomato on its side and halve with a sharp serrated knife. Squeeze each half firmly enough to push out the seeds. Discard seeds.

Slicing: First core the tomato and lay it on its side. Using a sharp serrated knife, cut a very thin slice off both ends and discard. Slice the tomato to desired thickness.

Peeling: To eliminate the skin in cooked dishes, gently lower 2 or 3 tomatoes at a time into enough boiling water to cover. Boil for 15 to 30 seconds, lift into a colander with a slotted spoon. Rinse briefly under cold running water. Peel off and discard skins.

SEPTEMBER 30
Rustic Tomato Soup
6 servings

For a smokier, rustic version of yesterday's soup consider roasting the tomatoes along with the onion or leek in a little olive oil, (instead of butter,) and adding a few garlic cloves for extra flavor. Halve the tomatoes, leaving skins on this time. Arrange the vegetables, making sure the tomatoes are skin side up, in a single layer in a roasting pan with a little olive oil. Roast in a 425-dgree oven until tender (about 1 hour). With a tongs, pull off the skins of the tomatoes, and discard. Transfer the roasted vegetables along with a can of chicken broth and a broth-can of water into a soup pot and simmer until everything is heated through. Run the mixture (in batches) through a blender and return to the pot. Add the heavy cream and seasonings as per above recipe. Be sure not to boil soup after cream is added. Sprinkle croutons and browned smoky bacon bits on top of each serving, as a garnish if you like. The soup will not be as smooth and creamy as the above version, but more rustic and country style. Serve with a loaf of warmed French bread and cold, un-salted butter.

More Tomato Tips...

Stuffing Shells: Lay the tomato on its side and cut a very thin slice off the bottom using a sharp serrated knife. Slice off the top 1/4 of the tomato and discard. (The top minus the core may be chopped and added to the filling.) Using a sharp paring knife and spoon, cut and scoop out the flesh, leaving thickish walls. Salt the cavities lightly and invert on a cooling rack for 15 minutes to drain.

Yield: 1 medium tomato, seeded, yields approximately 3/4 cup chopped. 1 large tomato, seeded, yields 1 cup chopped. One pound of tomatoes yields approximately 2-1/2 cups of chopped or 2 cups puréed.

Storage: Tomatoes will ripen to a juicy red on their own when stored at room temperature. Refrigeration kills flavor in fresh tomatoes.

OCTOBER 1

#1: Old Fashioned Berry Shortcake
8 servings

INGREDIENTS
1 pint of fresh strawberries
1 pint of fresh blueberries
1 package of refrigerator-tube-style buttermilk biscuits
Whipping cream
Sugar

Wash, hull, and slice the strawberries, toss with a little sugar and store in refrigerator. Wash the blueberries and sprinkle with sugar and store in the refrigerator. Whip the heavy cream with a little sugar (and vanilla if you like) and store in refrigerator. Bake the biscuits according to package directions. While still warm split the biscuits in half, arranging 2 halves per serving on dessert plates. Pile on the berries (with their sugary juice) and top with the whipped cream. Serve immediately, while the biscuits are still warm, for an old fashioned treat like Grandma used to make. The secrets to this recipe are using warm, freshly baked biscuits and real-whipped-cream. This is one time I would suggest you forego the commercial whipped topping for the real thing!

#2: Old Fashioned Peach Shortcake
8 servings

The berry shortcake recipe also works wonderfully with the substitution of fresh peaches, peeled, sliced, and sugared. (Use brown sugar in this case.) Serve on the warm, freshly baked biscuits with sweetened, whipped cream, just as you did with the berry shortcake.

RUSH HOUR TIP
To peel peaches easily, submerge each peach in boiling water for about 30 seconds. Remove with a slotted spoon or sieve and plunge into a bowl of ice water. The skins will peel right off.

OCTOBER 2
Perfect Potato & Garlic Soup
6 to 8 Servings

INGREDIENTS
8 medium red potatoes
1 large onion, coarsely chopped
2 teaspoons dried rosemary, crushed
1 ½ bulbs garlic
2 tablespoon olive oil
2 (14.5 ounce) can chicken broth
1 teaspoon pepper, divided
2 tablespoons all-purpose flour
2 cups light cream

Peel and cube the potatoes. Place potatoes in a 9x9x2-inch baking pan. Sprinkle onion and rosemary evenly over top. Now, this next part gets a little trick, so take it slow! Peel away the dry outer leaves from the garlic bulbs. So the individual cloves should still have their skins and it's all still one big bunch of garlic. Then snip off the pointed top with scissors, being careful to keep the bulb intact—the goal here is to just expose the cloves. Place the garlic bulbs, cut side up, on top of the potatoes. Drizzle olive oil over all. Bake, covered, in a 400 degree oven about 45 minutes or until garlic cloves feel soft and potatoes are tender. Cool slightly. Squeeze the garlic bulbs into a blender. Add half of the potatoes, half the onion, pepper and half of the chicken broth. Blend to desired soup consistency. Transfer the blender mixture into a medium saucepan. Stir in the remaining potato, onion, and broth. Add the light cream and stir to blend. Cook and stir over medium heat until slightly thickened and bubbly.

Potato Storage
Store potatoes in a cool, dark pantry or closet. Remove potatoes from their original plastic bag and store in a box, basket, or mesh bag that allows ventilation. Potatoes do not have to be refrigerated. Discard any old, sprouting, or shriveled potatoes, or green potatoes that will spoil the rest of the batch. When scrubbing and paring potatoes, cut out any eyes that might be beginning to sprout. Discard any overly-sprouted potatoes.

Weekly Challenge

JUST BECAUSE…

This week carve out 30 minutes to write or call someone you have been thinking about. I am especially mindful this time of year (as it nears the anniversary of my brother's death) of just how thankful I am for all the wonderful people in my life. On the tough days, it is those people that truly make my life wonderful. Think of the people that make your life wonderful, and send one of them a card this week as a thank you!

OCTOBER 3

Pizza Sticks
A KIDS IN THE KITCHEN RECIPE
2 dozen sticks

What kid doesn't love pizza? Encourage your child's inner-chef with this pizza variation.

INGREDIENTS
1 package (10 ounces) refrigerated pizza dough
3 tablespoons butter, melted
½ cup grated Parmesan cheese or mozzarella cheese
½ teaspoon garlic powder
1 (8 ounce) can pizza sauce, warmed

Unroll the pizza dough and place on a lightly greased baking sheet. Press to form a 13x9-inch rectangle. Brush with melted butter. Sprinkle with the cheese and garlic powder. Using a sharp knife, cut the dough lengthwise into strips to form breadsticks. Make a cut in the middle to make about 24 sticks. Bake at 425 degrees for about 10 minutes, or until lightly browned. Serve with the pizza sauce.

RUSH HOUR TIP
Go ahead and play! Try using cookie cutters to make shapes. You can also vary the ingredients by trying different cheeses.

OCTOBER 4

"Pita Soup"

6 servings

No, don't fret—there are not actually pitas in this soup, it's just that pita sandwiches and this soup make a perfect light and healthy meal.

For the soup:
4 cans chicken broth
2 cups cooked chicken, cubed or
   torn
1 cup frozen peas
½ teaspoon salt
¼ teaspoon pepper
1 cup noodles of choice
1 cup sliced carrots,
1 cup chopped celery stalks
1-2 cups cooked instant rice (optional)

Heat all ingredients, excluding noodles in a saucepan. Bring to boiling. Add noodles then reduce heat and simmer 10-15 minutes or until vegetables and noodles are tender. Add 1-2 cups cooked rice at the end of cooking, if desired.

OCTOBER 5

Fiesta Casserole

4 to 6 servings

INGREDIENTS:
1 pound ground beef
1 can condensed tomato soup
1 soup can of water
3 teaspoons chili powder
1 teaspoon onion powder
2 cups shredded Cheddar cheese
1 cup sour cream
½ bunch diced green onions
1½ cups chopped tomato
4 cups broken tortilla chips

Preheat oven to 350 degrees. Brown beef in a skillet over medium heat. Add soup and can of water. Stir in chili powder and onion powder. Let simmer for 10-20 minutes. Place broken chips on the bottom of a casserole dish. Top with beef mixture. Top beef mixture with sour cream, onions, chopped tomato and cheese. Bake for 20 minutes. Serve with a simple salad.

OCTOBER 6

Barbara's Seven Layer Salad

INGREDIENTS
Lettuce, torn
Celery, chopped
Green bell pepper, chopped
Spanish onion, chopped
Mayonnaise (you can use low-fat)
Sugar
Shredded Cheddar cheese
Bacon, cooked crisp and crumbled

Layer ingredients in bowl in order given. Refrigerate covered overnight. Do not toss.

OCTOBER 7

Wendy Louise's Elegant Chicken Divan

4 to 6 servings

This is one of the first "company-coming-to-dinner" recipes that I ever made and it remains one of my favorites yet today. It's just a combination that can't be beat and I get rave reviews every time I serve it.

INGREDIENTS FOR MEAT:
4 to 6 chicken breasts, (1 per person)
1 tablespoon salt
6 peppercorns
1 onion, quartered
Celery leaves
Parsley
Water to cover
Poach 45 minutes, or until chicken is done. Set aside. Save 2 cups broth.

INGREDIENTS FOR SAUCE:
1/3 cup butter, melted
6 tablespoons flour
The reserved chicken broth
¾ cup heavy cream
2 tablespoons Sherry, optional
Salt and pepper to taste

Over medium heat make a roux of the butter and flour. Slowly incorporate the broth and cream. Simmer 2 minutes, stirring all the while. Cool the sauce slightly. Add the Sherry and seasonings. Set aside.

INGREDIENTS FOR VEGETABLE:
1 bunch fresh broccoli, trimmed and cut into floret-spears.
Poach for 10 minutes in salted water. Plunge into cold water to stop cooking. Drain well. Set aside.

TO ASSEMBLE AND COOK:
In a buttered casserole dish arrange the broccoli; pour on half the sauce. Arrange the chicken on top. Add ¼ cup Parmesan cheese to the remaining sauce and pour over chicken. (Can make this all ahead and refrigerate until dinner time.) Bake in 375-degree oven till hot and bubbly. Then put under broiler for 2 minutes to brown.

RUSH HOUR TIPS

The first part of this recipe (the poaching of the chicken) is an excellent guide to follow for preparing chicken for any recipe that calls for cooked chicken.

Storing chicken—If not using right away, remove store bought packaging, wash the chicken (removing the giblets and their packaging) and place in a seal-able plastic bag. Refrigerate or freeze. Wash your hands and any surfaces you used while handling the raw chicken.

A Thought for Today
WHAT GOES AROUND COMES AROUND
"I have found that if you love life, life will love you back."
~Arthur Rubenstein, Musician

OCTOBER 8

Crock Chops & Potatoes
6 servings

Gotta' love that slow cooker! Here's a nice and easy recipe for pork chops.

INGREDIENTS
6 pork chops
2 (14.5 ounce) cans cream of mushroom soup
2 soup cans milk
4 potatoes, quartered
1 pound carrots, whole
½ cup onion, chopped
½ teaspoon black pepper
½ teaspoon dried basil

Brown pork chops over medium heat in a skillet, set aside. Combine soup and milk in skillet; simmer while preparing vegetables. Grab the slow cooker, layer in ingredients as follows: onion, carrots, potatoes, and pork chops. Pour soup mixture over all. Sprinkle with pepper and basil Cover and cook on low 4 to 6 hours.

OCTOBER 9
Brown Sugar Chops
6 servings

INGREDIENTS
6 pork chops, about 1 inch thick
1 cup barbecue sauce
1 pint pineapple juice
2 tablespoons Worcestershire sauce
¼ cup brown sugar

Mix all ingredients together except chops. Place chop in marinade for at least 4 hours (24 hours will result in maximum taste). Grill chops for delicious flavor or bake in oven for 30-40 minutes on 375 degree setting until cooked through.

Proper Preparation
If not using right away, remove meats from their store-bought-container and juice-padding-thing on the bottom. Store the meat in a fresh seal-able bag. If marinating meats, use a plastic, seal-able bag or covered glass container, never use metal.

Weekly Challenge
ARE YOU ALWAYS LATE?

Set your clocks 5 or 10 minutes early and don't tell anybody, just pretend you are on regular time. Giving yourself that little buffer-zone of a couple extra minutes will automatically make you on-time, maybe with a minute to spare! Being late for an appointment or a date is disrespectful of another's time. Make a concerted effort this week to be on time everywhere you go.

OCTOBER 10

Crazy Cotton Candy Cake
A KIDS IN THE KITCHEN RECIPE
8 servings

INGREDIENTS
1 box angel food cake mix
1 box (3.4 ounces) flavored gelatin, any flavor (Turn this into a science-experiment!)
Whipped cream, for serving

Make the cake according to the package directions; also adding the box of gelatin. Stir well. Bake as directed on package directions. Let cool completely. Serve each slice topped with whipped cream.

OCTOBER 11

Refried Bean Dip

INGREDIENTS
Canned refried beans
Sour cream (can use low fat)
Chili powder, to taste
Cumin, to taste
Cayenne pepper, to taste
Chopped chilies, to taste

Mix all to desired taste and dipping consistency. Serve with tortilla chips.

Over Cramming Your Refrigerator

Foods need to breathe. Fresh fruits and vegetables need space and air circulation to stay fresh. Overlooked, old 'leftovers' lurking in the bottom of the bins, can spoil your new purchases. Be sure to keep your fruit and vegetable bins 'up dated' with your freshest purchases. Clean up any spills, leaks or residue left behind. The same goes for meats. Next to a filled and organized pantry (and a new lipstick), a clean and organized refrigerator is a cook's best friend.

OCTOBER 12

Barbara's "New Mexican Dip"

INGREDIENTS
3 vine ripened tomatoes, diced
4 green onions, chopped
Black olive slices
2 green chilies, seeded and minced
Salt and pepper, to taste
2 tablespoons wine vinegar
1 tablespoon olive oil

Mix all to make a salsa. Serve with tortilla chips.

OCTOBER 13

Mom's Rustic Guacamole
1 1/2 cups dip

INGREDIENTS
1 cup coarsely mashed avocado
1/3 cup peeled and chopped vine ripened tomato
2 teaspoons seeded and chopped chilies
1 tablespoon chopped onion
1 clove garlic, minced
2 tablespoons fresh lemon juice
2 teaspoons minced parsley or cilantro
Sea salt and cracked pepper, to taste
¼ cup mayonnaise, optional

Coarsely chop and mix all ingredients together. Immerse the pit in the dip to help keep the guacamole from browning. Store in refrigerator until serving, by putting a cap of plastic wrap right down on the surface of the dip. Serve with tortilla chips.

OCTOBER 14

Mom's Easy as 1-2-3 Pork Roast
4 to 6 servings

1 (2 to 3 pound) pork roast
½ cup water
1 package dry onion soup mix

Rub seasonings from soup packet over roast and place roast in slow-cooker crockery pot. Add the water. Cover and cook all day, or until meat is very tender. Serve with mashed potatoes and the crock juices as gravy.

A Thought for Today
OUR DRIVE FOR SUCCESS
"There comes a moment when you have to stop revving up the car and shove it into gear…" ~David Mahoney

OCTOBER 15

Pork Chop Casserole
4 servings

Chicken and beef normally get all the attention when it comes to casserole cooking. Don't forget your "other white meat." Try this pork chop casserole for a change of flavor and pace.

INGREDIENTS
1 cup uncooked instant rice
4 pork chops
1 can Campbell's® beef broth (bouillon)
1 green or red bell pepper, cut into slices
4 slices of onion
4 slices of tomato

Wash rice and sprinkle in bottom of a 9 x 9 x 2 glass baking dish. Brown pork chops in a skillet and place on top of rice. On top of each pork chop, put a thin slice of tomato, onion, and bell pepper. Pour can of beef broth over all. Cover and bake for 1 hour at 350 degrees or until pork is cooked through and rice is tender.

Fight the Flu
With cold and flu season arriving quickly, why not get in the habit of using paper towels in the kitchen (and the bathroom) for general hand washing? Keep a stack, or roll, handy on the counter, instead of using and re-using terry towels. This just might help cut down on colds and germs during flu-season.

Weekly Challenge

EASTER IN OCTOBER

I had a great "Make a Memory" moment the other night with my eight-year-old daughter. It was 9:00 PM and she got it set in her mind that she wanted to go on an "Easter Egg Hunt." So my husband hid eggs outside on our farm and the two of us went around in the dark with flashlights. We had Fantasia music (from the Disney movie) playing in the background. When we finished our egg hunt, we laid on the trampoline and looked at the stars, making up new constellations. The moment inspired us to buy an astronomy magazine which shows what stars are viewable in the different months of the year. What delights can you partake in no matter what the season? These will be the memories most cherished by adults and children alike!

OCTOBER 16
Cranberry Crock Pork Roast
6 to 8 servings

Two ingredients—too easy—too good.

INGREDIENTS
3 pound pork roast
2 cans whole berry cranberry sauce

Place roast in slow-cooker crockery pot. Break up and add cranberry sauce. Cook all day, until tender. Use crock juices as gravy.

Garbage In, Garbage Out!
Just a reminder that as old or spoiled food will make you sick, it can also make your pet very sick. Try to make your garbage-disposing-routine "pet proof" so your "best friends" don't get into mishaps and mayhem. Not only could your pet be poisoned by bad food, but cut or choked by broken glass, sharp plastic pieces, sharp can lids, pop-tops, etc.

A Thought for Today
"Change your thoughts and you change the world."
~Harold R. McAlindon, Writer

OCTOBER 17
Betty's Easy Cheese-y Soufflé
4 to 6 servings

INGREDIENTS
3 tablespoons butter
3 tablespoons flour
1 cup milk
½ pound shredded cheese
6 egg yolks

Preheat oven to 400 degrees. (We will turn down when soufflé goes in.) In double boiler (or sauce pot in water bath), melt 3 tablespoons butter. Add 3 tablespoons flour, stirring to make a roux. Stir in 1 cup milk, continuing to cook and stir until thick and creamy. Add ½ pound shredded cheese (Cheddar or Swiss), and stir until melted and smooth. Add dash of cayenne pepper for seasoning. Remove from heat and start to cool. Incorporate 6 beaten egg yolks into above mixture and cool 15 minutes more.

Beat 6 egg whites to gleamy-stiff and gently fold into the cheese mixture. (Better to under-fold than to over-mix.) Gently slide the mixture into a buttered soufflé baking dish. Tie an optional 3-inch high collar (made out of foil, heavy waxed paper, or waxed butcher paper) around the dish. As the soufflé puffs while cooking, this removable-cuff will support the soufflé.

Place the soufflé into the 400-degree oven and turn down the heat to 375 degrees. Bake at 375 degrees for 30 to 40 minutes, or until soufflé is puffed and done. Do not open the oven door for 30 minutes or the soufflé might fall. (To check for doneness, nudge the baking dish slightly—if the top jiggles firmly it's done.) If you've used a collar, remove it before serving. Serve the well-puffed soufflé immediately. A nice salad of mixed-greens or fresh fruit salad and French bread would complete the meal.

RUSH HOUR WISDOM
Today's recipe uses a double boiler—if you don't have one try the following: to make a 'make shift' double boiler place a sauté pan on your stove top with about an inch of water in it. Then set a smaller sauce pan (that you'll do your actual cooking in) in the simmering, water-filled pan. This works great for melting chocolate and making delicate sauces that scorch, separate, or curdle easily.

OCTOBER 18
Homemade Hot Sauce

The next time you have a recipe that calls for a hot sauce, serve up this spicy version.

INGREDIENTS
1 cup chopped peeled seeded tomatoes
½ cup chopped onion
1/3 cup fresh lemon juice
1 tablespoon chopped hot red chili pepper
1 tablespoon snipped fresh coriander
1 to 2 garlic cloves, minced
¼ teaspoon salt

Combine all ingredients in a small bowl and let stand covered for 30 minutes to meld flavors before serving.

Fun for Hot Sauce Fanatics
http://www.hotsauce.org/

A very fun place to visit for those "who like it hot!" **The International Society of Hot Sauce Aficionados: (ISHSA) has the motto:** *See the World, Taste the Sauce.* Founded in January of 1998, **ISHSA** is dedicated to the Life Long Quest to Sample All Known Hot Sauces. "Recognizing that only the select few with vision, fortitude and dedication will attempt to accomplish this worthy goal, the **ISHSA** was founded to provide information, encouragement, community and *access* to the more difficult to procure hot sauces of the planet." Their rules are as fun as the rest of the site and include, "Officers: {Anyone who wants a title may have one}Bylaws: {None}Meetings: {None}Dues: {None}Membership Fees: {None}Membership Requirements: Love of, or interest in, Hot Sauces of the world!

OCTOBER 19

Julie's Easy and Delicious Taco Soup
6 servings

I think a little of Julie's Taco Soup just might be right for tonight's dinner. Add a side of Charlotte's Sopapillas (see recipe for November 10) and you have a fun and festive meal.

INGREDIENTS
1 pound ground beef
1 (14 ounce) can corn
1 (15 ounce) can chili beans in zesty sauce
2 (10 ounce) cans chicken broth
1 (16 ounce) jar salsa
Tortilla chips, at serving time
Sour cream, at serving time
Shredded cheese, at serving time
Chopped cilantro, at serving time

In a large soup pot or Dutch oven, brown ground beef and drain. Return beef to pot. Add rest of ingredients. Bring to a boil, then reduce heat and simmer for 5 to 10 minutes. Serve with tortilla chips, sour cream, shredded cheese, and cilantro.

OCTOBER 20

Gramma Lucille's Blue Cheese Salad Dressing

INGREDIENTS
1 (8 ounce) package cream cheese, softened
1 package Blue cheese, crumbled
1 dollop of mayonnaise
Cream, to reach desired consistency
Minced garlic or garlic powder, to taste

Mix all in a blender to reach desired consistency. Serve on mixed salad greens or wedges of Iceberg lettuce. Pass extra crumbled Blue cheese for garnish.

OCTOBER 21

Fresh Fruit Salad

INGREDIENTS
Plain or vanilla yogurt
2 tablespoons honey
Fresh fruit cut into bite size pieces

Mix all just before serving.

Berry Tips

Fruits such as strawberries, blueberries, raspberries, and blackberries store better when allowed to breathe. Sort through the fruit when you first bring it home, discarding any overly ripe fruit. The already perishing fruit, hiding in the center, or on the bottom, will cause the rest to mold. Do not wash at this time. Store the fruit covered (but not air tightly) in a container. Wash at time of serving and drain or blot on paper toweling. If the strawberries are very ripe, you can wash and hull them at time of storage, leaving them whole or slicing them, and sprinkling with sugar to store until time of serving.

A Thought for Today

"A child's life is like a piece of paper on which every person leaves a mark." ~Chinese Proverb

Weekly Challenge

GET YOUR DAY OFF TO A GOOD START

It sounds mundane, but select and set out the children's clothes and socks for the next day, the night before; or have them pre-pick their outfit for the next day. Also locate that "traveling" pair of school shoes and set them by the clothes, or by the door. How many times have you been ready to walk out the door, but "can't find the shoes?" Backpacks, jackets, and homework can also be organized the night before. The less you have to account for in the morning, the more relaxed you can start your day. Get your children in the habit of a "school morning routine" and they will start their day on a stress-free high note and so will you.

The same principle can apply for mom and dad. Always set your car keys, house key, sunglasses, and portable phone in a designated place...purse, wallet, briefcase too. If you get in the habit of doing this religiously, you'll end a lot of extra searching and frustration in the morning, when your time is limited. Try implementing these tactics this week and see how much easier your week flows!

Once you've made this organizational tactic a habit, you will find you have some extra time leftover to have a relaxed casual breakfast, such as an un-gulped bowl of cereal, or a cup of tea and some cinnamon toast. (Beats dashing through the drive-thru for a greasy sausage sandwich!)

OCTOBER 22

Enchilada Pie

6 to 8 servings

INGREDIENTS
10 corn tortillas, quartered
2 pounds ground beef
1 (4 ounce) jar diced green chilies
1 (10.5 ounce) can cream of mushroom soup
1 (16 ounce) can stewed tomatoes
1 pound grated mozzarella cheese (or Mexican cheese mix)
1 onion, chopped

Cook ground beef and onions in skillet, drain. Add chilies, soup, and tomatoes to beef mixture. Layer in 9 x 13-inch pan, ½ each of tortillas, then beef mixture, then cheese. Repeat layers topping with cheese. Cover and bake at 350 degrees for 50 minutes, or until warm, bubbly, and cooked through.

Better Safe than Sorry

When in doubt—pitch it! This applies to any foods you have been storing—canned, boxed, in the fridge, in the pantry, in the cupboards fresh or preserved. Almost all packaged foods have an expiration code printed on the package. A lot of packages also include web sites or 800 numbers for consumer assistance. If you have any doubt about a food item that you've been saving…pitch it! Just think of that old saying "better safe than sorry." Get in the habit of rotating your pantry. When you return from a major shopping spree, store or stack like items together, with new purchases to the back or on the bottom, and older or half-used items in the front or on the top, for immediate use. By always rotating the stored items from back to forward, you will be continually updating your cupboards and pantry.

OCTOBER 23

Festive Halloween Snack Mix
A KIDS IN THE KITCHEN RECIPE

Here is a quick, easy, assembly-required snack for the Halloween season. Kids will love you and will love helping too.

INGREDIENTS
10 cups popcorn (Pop up your own, or use pre-popped bags.)
1 cup Reese's® Pieces
1 cup candy corn
2 cups M&M®'s plain candies
1 cup M&M®s peanut candies

Mix together and serve!

OCTOBER 24

Festive Halloween Punch

INGREDIENTS
1 large can Hi-C® orange drink
1 large can pineapple juice
2 liter bottle of 7-Up®
½ gallon orange sherbet

Mix first 3 ingredients together to make a punch. Serve from a large bowl or punch bowl. Spoon in orange sherbet to float on top of each serving, or float little "sherbet islands" in the bowl.

RUSH HOUR WISDOM
You can store punch in the refrigerator, in large containers, and pull out as needed to fill the bowl and 'refresh' the punch. This way you keep the punch continually cold and attractively served.

OCTOBER 25
Awesome Apple Cobbler Cake
6 to 8 servings

For me, the smell of baking apples is a true sign of fall and the impending winter season. I love the smell drifting through the house. Here is a great bake for a wonderful treat and aroma!

INGREDIENTS
6 cups of sliced apples
¼ cup sugar
2 teaspoons cinnamon
½ teaspoon nutmeg
1 packaged cake mix (yellow or white), divided
1 stick butter
Vanilla ice cream for serving (optional)

Combine apples, sugar, nutmeg, and cinnamon. Add ¼ cup of the cake mix, stir to coat apples. Place apples in a 9 x 13-inch buttered pan, Cover tightly with foil and bake at 350 degrees for 25 minutes. Remove pan from oven and set aside. Mix remaining cake mix with melted butter. Stir with a fork until large crumbs form, and then remove foil on baking pan, and spoon crumb-mixture over apples. Return to oven and continue baking 25 to 30 minutes, or until golden brown and apples are tender. Serve warm with vanilla ice cream.

A Thought for Today
THE IMPORTANCE OF LETTING GO
*"Some think it's holding on that makes one strong;
sometimes it's the letting go!"*
~Sylvia Robinson

OCTOBER 26
Sautéed Spinach
4 servings

INGREDIENTS
1 tablespoon olive oil
2 cloves garlic, minced
1 pound baby spinach
Salt and pepper to taste
Mushrooms, chopped

Heat oil in large non-stick skillet. Add minced garlic and cook until soft. Add chopped mushrooms and cook several minutes. Add spinach and sauté until wilted. Season with salt and pepper to taste and serve immediately.

OCTOBER 27
Slow Cooked Pork Roast
8 to 10 servings

INGREDIENTS
1 (3 pound) pork roast
1 tablespoon cooking oil
Salt and pepper
8 ounces mixed dried fruit
1 onion, cut into wedges
½ teaspoon allspice
8 ounces apples juice (or water)

In skillet cover meat with oil, salt, and pepper, and brown on all sides. Transfer roast to slow-cooker crockery pot. Meanwhile add dried fruit, onion, apple juice, and allspice to sauté pan for 1 or 2 minutes. Then pour over roast in slow cooker. Cover and cook all day (8 to 10 hours on low setting) until very tender.

OCTOBER 28
Wendy Louise's Velvety Smooth Vichyssoise
6 to 8 servings

INGREDIENTS
3 cups peeled, sliced potatoes
3 cups sliced whites of leeks
6 cups chicken broth
Salt to taste
1 cup heavy cream, or at least half-and-half
Salt to taste
White pepper
Chopped fresh chives for garnish

Simmer first 4 ingredients until tender and puree in blender. Then force the blended mixture through a sieve into a glass bowl. Stir in the heavy cream and adjust seasoning with more salt and white pepper. Chill mixture thoroughly in refrigerator. Serve cold, in chilled bowls, with a garnish of minced chives.

RUSH HOUR WISDOM
Save this recipe for an elegant occasion, and you will be sure to impress the most sophisticated of diners.

OCTOBER 29
Easy Chicken Noodle Soup

INGREDIENTS
4 skinless boneless chicken breasts, chopped and uncooked
2 cups small noodles of choice
½ cup rice
¼ cup onion, chopped fine
2 cloves garlic, minced
Black pepper and salt to taste

Boil chicken and onion in 1 quart of water over medium heat for 20 minutes. Add remaining ingredients and cover and simmer for 20 minutes. May need to add more water depending on consistency desired. For a more flavorful soup, begin with a store-bought chicken broth instead of water.

Keeping Dinner Rolls Warm
Serve your baked or warmed bread in a basket, wrapped in a generously sized linen dinner napkin or tea towel. In the bottom of the basket place a warming stone heated in the oven. (These look very much like miniature pizza-stones and can be found at gourmet shops.). This will help to keep your bread warm all through the meal.

Weekly Challenge

With fall in full swing and winter just around the corner, flu and colds are going to be on the rampage soon. Take a simple precautionary step by making sure each member in your family is getting their quota of vitamins and minerals. Most dietary experts agree that a nutritional supplement is needed to reach today's guidelines. Check with your doctor or local health store for help in choosing an appropriate vitamin for each family member (children, men, and women all have different needs). Make sure to put the vitamins somewhere you will remember to take them regularly. I like to keep mine near my toothbrush because I know I'll always have water nearby and will be reminded to take them.

OCTBER 30

Gramma Betty's Candy-Apples
A KID FRIENDLY RECIPE
6 apples

INGREDIENTS
6 Red delicious apples
1 package Kraft® caramel candies
1 tablespoon butter
2 tablespoons milk or water
Chopped peanuts
Wooden sticks, to use as handles

Pierce apples with sticks and set aside. Over a double boiler melt a package of Kraft® caramels with 2 tablespoons water or milk, and 1 tablespoon butter, stirring constantly until smooth. When caramel mixture has fully melted, dip each apple in the caramel. Roll in chopped peanuts and leave to stand (and set) on waxed paper. Once cool, wrap each apple individually in waxed paper.

RUSH HOUR WISDOM

When pulling canned items from your pantry—NEVER use bulging, dented, seeping or leaking, or discolored-topped canned items. Their seal has been broken and the food is no longer safe. Don't even think about it! Pitch the can immediately. Then wash your hands.

OCTOBER 31
Make Your Own Face Paint
A KIDS IN THE KITCHEN CRAFT

Help kids make their own face paint for Halloween, with this easy concoction.

INGREDIENTS
2 teaspoons cornstarch
1 teaspoon water
1 teaspoon cold cream
3 to 4 drops food coloring

Combine all ingredients and mix well

NOVEMBER 1
Fruity Fun Muffins
1 dozen

INGREDIENTS
2 cups self-rising flour
1 pint premium ice cream, use a fruit flavor, softened

Mix flour and flavored ice cream (be sure to use a fruity strawberry, cherry, peach, etc.) together to form a batter. Pour into greased or paper-cup lined muffin tins. Bake for 20 minutes at 350 degrees.

NOVEMBER 2
Little-Red-Potato Salad
8 to 10 servings

INGREDIENTS

5 pound bag of small red potatoes, skins left on, halved or quartered
   depending on size
1 tablespoon salt (for boiling the potatoes)
¾ to 1 cup lite-mayonnaise
½ cup buttermilk (or soured milk, see tip that follows)
¼ cup chopped parsley
2 teaspoons dill
2 tablespoons Dijon-style mustard
The juice from a fresh lemon
Salt and pepper to taste
½ Spanish (red) onion minced
2 stalks celery, diced
1 (10 ounce) package frozen green peas, thawed

Cut potatoes into uniform chunks and boil potatoes in a large pot of salted water for approximately 12 to 15 minutes, or until tender but not mushy. Remove from water and drain in colander at least 15 minutes. While potatoes are draining make a dressing by whisking together the next 7 ingredients in a large serving bowl. Fold the potatoes into the dressing mixing to coat all. Lastly fold in onion, celery, and green peas. Store covered, in refrigerator until serving time. Keep in a cooler on ice if taking on a picnic. Salad can be made up to 24 hours in advance.

RUSH HOUR TIP

To sour milk, such as needed for this recipe, pour 1½ teaspoons lemon juice (or vinegar) into a glass measuring cup. Fill cup to ½ cup mark with milk. Stir to mix. Let sit on kitchen counter until milk "sours" and thickens.

As an extra note, this method can be used as a substitute for buttermilk, when a recipe calls for such, and you don't have it on hand.

NOVEMBER 3

Corn Flake Baked Chicken

6 to 8 servings

INGREDIENTS

6 to 8 boneless chicken breasts (or use already cut up fryer pieces)
1 cup mayonnaise (can use fat free)
1 cup milk (can use low fat)
1 teaspoon Italian seasoning or All-Purpose Seasoning
2 cups traditional corn flakes, crushed
A dash of paprika for color

Preheat your oven to 350-degrees and prepare your baking pan with a vegetable-oil cooking spray. Mix the milk and mayonnaise together in a small bowl. Mix the cornflakes and seasonings together on a flat bottomed plate. Dip chicken pieces in *milk mixture* and then roll to coat in the seasoned corn flakes. Place in a single layer in baking dish and sprinkle with a dash of paprika for color. Bake until tender and meat juices run clear, approximately 35 to 45 minutes.

RUSH HOUR TIP

*For an extra rich treat, you can dip the chicken in *melted butter* like my mom used to do, and then roll in the seasoned corn flakes and proceed with recipe.*

A Thought for Today

SUCCESS
"You may be disappointed if you fail,
but you are doomed if you don't try."
~Beverly Sills, Opera Singer

NOVEMBER 4

Not-a-Soup, Not-a Stew Chicken
6 to 8 hearty servings

INGREDIENTS

2 pounds boneless chicken breasts (see tip at end of recipe), cut into
  bite-size pieces
1 onion, chopped
1 cup chopped celery
4 cloves garlic, minced
3 cans chicken broth
1 cup water
1 to 2 cups frozen mixed vegetables (broccoli, cauliflower, green bean
  combo) thawed
1 to 2 cups each: frozen peas and frozen carrots, thawed
1 (8 ounce) package of egg noodles, partially pre-cooked in a separate
  pot of boiling, salted water
Salt and pepper to taste

In a skillet, in a little olive oil, lightly brown the chicken pieces, along with the onion and garlic for 5 to 8 minutes. Add the celery and cook 2 minutes more. Transfer the mixture to a large soup pot or slow-crockery-cooker and add the remaining vegetables (except for the peas). Add the chicken broth, water, and a little salt and pepper. Simmer 2 to 3 hours on the back of the stove, adding more water if necessary. Or, if using a slow cooker, cover with lid and simmer on low for 8 to 10 hours, or cook on high for 4 to 6 hours. During last hour of cooking add the peas and lastly the partially-pre-cooked noodles. (This avoids the peas becoming mushy and the soup becoming starchy.) Make any adjustments of additional salt and pepper to taste. Serve up steaming in large soup bowls. Accompany your soup with warmed French bread and honey butter or unsalted butter.

RUSH HOUR WISDOM

Many of today's recipes call for boneless, skinless chicken breasts (the most expensive chicken cut you can buy). However, cut up fryers (usually packaged in 'family packs' with extra pieces, or choice of pieces, are much more economical than buying just breast meat. And cutting up whole fryers is even more economical (and easy to do, once you've practiced a couple of times). Invest in a kitchen shears and a sharp chef's knife and you'll recover your savings in no time. It is also very easy to skin the chicken yourself. So the next time a recipe calls for boneless, skinless chicken breasts, why not try substituting the rest of the chicken as well... and saving a little in your pocket book.

NOVEMBER 5

More than Just an Apple Pie
Variations for 1 (8 or 9-inch pie)

The next time you are making your favorite apple pie recipe, try adding one of these delicious variations to your recipe.

INGREDIENTS
Apple-Cranberry Pie
When making your favorite apple pie recipe, mix in a handful (about 1 cup) of fresh cranberries and 1 ½ teaspoons orange zest (finely grated orange peel) and proceed with your recipe. (You can increase your sugar by a small amount if you wish, but I like the slight tartness that the cranberries add, against the sweetness of the traditional apples.)

Apple-Raisin Pie
To your favorite apple pie recipe, mix in a handful or so of raisins and the orange zest and proceed with your recipe.

Apple-Deluxe Pie
For a really rich pie, combine the apples, the cranberries, the raisins, and divide your sugar into half white and half light-brown, for a slightly caramelizing affect. Then proceed with your recipe.

Freshen Up
Need a tip to freshen your garbage disposal? Grind a few left-over lemon or lime wedges through it. Have a couple of 'too-old' apples and/or 'dehydrating' oranges in your fruit bin?--Cut them into wedges and run them through the disposal. Never, never, never pour cooking grease and /or bacon grease down your disposal, or you are inviting a major clog and repair bill.

A Thought for Today

"There are two ways of spreading light:
to be the candle or the mirror that reflects it."
~Edith Wharton

Weekly Challenge

DONATE THE GIFT OF WARMTH

Jack Frost is just around the corner! And the weather is quickly turning cold, so make sure you send everyone off in the morning with proper cold-weather clothing: jackets, warm socks, and well-fitting shoes, boots, scarves, etc. Check to see who has outgrown what, what you can pass down or give away, and what you need to replace for the winter season that is just ahead of us. Clean out the mud-room closet and take a load of warm, no longer usable (for you) clothing to your nearest shelter or Salvation Army. You'll be surprised at how warm you will feel!

NOVEMBER 6
Seasoned Sirloin Tips with Vegetables
6 to 8 servings

INGREDIENTS
2 pounds sirloin tips, cut into 1½-inch slices
Fresh cracked pepper
1 large onion, cut into chunks
2 green bell peppers, ribbed, seeded, and cut into chunks
2 red bell peppers, ribbed, seeded, and cut into chunks
3 tablespoons water, plus ½ cup water
3 tablespoons all purpose seasoning blend (such as Mrs. Dash® or McCormick's®
Season-All)
Olive oil

Turn your electric skillet to a high setting and add a little olive oil. Sprinkle the sirloin tips with a little cracked pepper and sauté in the olive oil for approximately 5 minutes, or to desired doneness, turning the meat to sauté all sides. Remove meat from pan and keep warm. Reduce your heat setting to medium and add the peppers and onions, sautéing for a few minutes in the pan juices. Sprinkle with 3 tablespoons of water and continue to cook for 2 to 3 minutes more. Add back the beef to the vegetables in the electric skillet (by the way, there is no reason you can't make this recipe in a non stick frying pan, on the stove top, if you wish) and sprinkle the mixture with the 3 tablespoons of seasoning blend. Add the half cup of water. Bring back up to a simmer, stirring constantly and loosening up any browned bits from the bottom of the pan. Cook until all is heated through. Serve with rice, or rice pilaf (use a boxed mix and follow directions), or a potato dish of your choice, on the side. The meat and vegetables will be nicely coated and seasoned with the pan juices, but there is no "gravy" with this dish.

RUSH HOUR WISDOM

Like slow cookers, we often overlook the convenience and adaptability of this wonderful kitchen appliance—the electric skillet. Don't want to heat up the kitchen by using your stove? Need more cooking space for an elaborate meal? Turn to your electric skillet. With its temperature dial built right in, it affords an accurate and efficient supplemental cooking method. For one-pot meals, or that extra casserole, it really comes in handy. Plus (like the crockery pot) you can transport the item to a pot luck or party and plug it back in, keeping your dish warm and delicious all through the gathering.

NOVEMBER 7

Applesauce Cone Cakes
A KIDS IN THE KITCHEN RECIPE
10 servings

This recipe calls for a "kitchen helper"...someone to measure, someone to stir, someone to decorate...AND SOMEONE TO EAT the fabulous results!

INGREDIENTS
¼ cup vegetable oil
¾ cup brown sugar
1 cup applesauce
1 teaspoon baking soda
1½ cups flour
1 teaspoon cinnamon
10 flat bottom ice cream cones

Preheat your oven to 375 degrees. Mix the oil and brown sugar together. Add the applesauce, mixing well. Add the flour, baking soda, and cinnamon, stirring until all are mixed well. Fill each cone 3/4 full with batter. (The batter will rise while baking.) Stand each cone upright in a well of a muffin tin and carefully place the muffin tin on a cookie sheet in the oven. Bake for 20 minutes, or until cakes are done. (You can test for doneness by inserting a toothpick into the center of a cake and if it comes out clean, the cakes are done.)

RUSH HOUR TIP
After the cone-cakes have cooled, add a "double dip" of frosting and decorations of your choice. Some ideas for frosting are peanut butter, softened cream cheese, cream cheese frosting, vanilla frosting, vanilla icing, or just a sprinkling of powdered sugar. More decorating choices could be jimmies or sprinkles, little candies, cinnamon sugar, decorator-tube-frosting designs, or a drizzling of caramel sauce and chopped nuts. Let your kids decorate their own, and have a fall-harvest-party.

NOVEMBER 8

Donna's Really Yummy Yam's
8 servings

Every year my mother's friend Donna makes this dish to serve as part of her Thanksgiving dinner. Mom raved so much about Donna's side dish that I had to try it for myself. "Yummy Yams" truly lives up to its name and doesn't require a Thanksgiving feast to eat it—a great winter side dish any night of the week.

INGREDIENTS
4 large yams
Whipping cream
1 (16 ounce) can crushed pineapple
1 cup brown sugar
4 tablespoons butter or margarine
1 bag miniature marshmallows
Salt to taste

Peel, dice, and boil yams until soft. Drain and rinse yams and place in large bowl. Add butter, salt, and heavy cream. Whip with mixer (or run through food processor) until almost completely smooth. Can leave some lumps. Spread whipped yam mixture into a greased glass baking dish and sprinkle with brown sugar and drained pineapple. Top with miniature marshmallows and bake at 350 degrees until marshmallows are browned. For a nice variation add a teaspoon of cinnamon to whipped yams before baking.

A Thought for Today
"Life's an open book and an education
helps you write success stories." ~Joyce A. Myers

How about signing up for an adult education course at your community college; a cooking seminar at your local gourmet shop; or a reading-group in your area; or a class for something you've always wanted to learn more about? I know this idea sounds more like a weekly challenge, but of course our weeks are made up of days ... so get out there today and enroll in something that will continue your success for a fulfilled life.

NOVEMBER 9

Marsha La Porte's 3-Layer Strawberry Mold

An unusually involved rush hour recipe (with several layers and phases) but the outcome and taste are well worth it.

INGREDIENTS
3 packages strawberry jell-O®
2 packages frozen strawberries, still frozen but softened
1 (8 ounce) package cream cheese
½ cup mayonnaise
1 cup whipped cream

1st layer: Dissolve 1 box gelatin and 1 cup hot water. Blend in 1 package of frozen strawberries. This will be bottom layer of mold.

2nd layer: Blend 1 slightly set box of gelatin and softened cream cheese with an electric mixer. Let start to set again. Fold in mayonnaise and whipped cream. This will set up as the middle layer.

3rd layer: Dissolve last box of gelatin with 1 cup hot water and blend in remaining second package of frozen strawberries.

Un-molding Gelatin Molds

Before filling your mold, spray it with just a little bit of non-flavored cooking spray. When the mold has chilled and set, dip the mold into hot water just enough to loosen the mold, then invert onto a serving dish. OR Invert the mold onto the serving dish. Then wrap with a warm, wet towel. You will be able to hear the mold release onto the serving dish. Put the Jell-O mold back into the refrigerator until time of serving. OR Just make the gelatin in a pretty glass serving bowl and forget about the challenge of un-molding altogether.

NOVEMBER 10

Charlotte's Sopapillas (Mexican Fritters)
A KID FRIENDLY RECIPE
10 servings

These fritters are a favorite in my household and we always love when Charlotte (our Nanny, from Texas) makes a Mexican dinner that includes these in the menu! (Hardly low in fat, yet addictive so enjoy sparingly!)

INGREDIENTS
1 tube large Grand Style® refrigerated dinner biscuits (10 per tube)
Canola cooking oil
Honey or powdered sugar, for serving time

Separate the biscuits and with your hands, flatten each biscuit to about the size of a thick pancake. Over medium heat, cover the bottom of a non stick pan with Canola oil. Cook the fritters in the hot oil, turning once to brown both sides. The fritters will get puffy and golden when done. Drain on paper towels, before serving. Serve warm with honey to spread, or a dusting of powdered sugar. (Be careful as the oil spatters easily) and the fritters burn easily. They cook rather quickly, five minutes or so. Serve warm.

NOVEMBER 11
Pat's "EASY AS 1-2-3" (forget about the 3) CAKE

This recipe makes one cake or can be made as muffins if you wish. The recipe requires 2 ingredients and can be made in any variation of flavors.

INGREDIENTS
1 can diet soda
1 boxed cake mix

Simply combine a can of diet soda with a boxed cake mix, and bake per box directions.

Here are some suggestions:
Chocolate Cake with Diet Coke or Pepsi
Yellow Cake with Diet Sprite or diet lemon /lime
Pumpkin or Spice Cake with Diet Dr. Pepper

Cleaning Tip
I keep my favorite scrubbing brush by my sink, and seem to use it constantly for rinsing and prepping dishes for the dishwasher. To keep it clean, every now and then, I just pop my well-used brush right into the dishwasher at the end of the night, along with those dishes! You'll extend the life of your brush and have a nice clean one again the next day.

NOVEMBER 12

Tasty Beef Tenderloin

8 servings

INGREDIENTS

1 (4 to 5 pound) beef tenderloin
Cracked black pepper to taste (be generous, about 4 to 5 tablespoons)
½ teaspoon ground cardamom
1 to 2 tablespoons tomato paste
1 teaspoon paprika
½ teaspoon garlic powder (or more if you like garlic)
1 cup low sodium soy sauce
¾ cup red wine vinegar

Preheat your oven to 425 degrees. Coat the tenderloin first with the tomato paste. Then coat with the cracked pepper and cardamom. Place roast in baking pan. Mix together the paprika, garlic powder, soy sauce, and red wine vinegar and pour over the meat. Roast the meat at 425 degrees, basting frequently, for 35 to 40 minutes, or until desired doneness is reached on a meat thermometer. Slice and serve with baked potatoes and your favorite vegetable. Save leftovers for tomorrow's dinner.

Weekly Challenge

MAKING YOUR KITCHEN HOLIDAY EFFICIENT

With Thanksgiving and the Holidays fast approaching we will be spending more and more time in the kitchen, cooking up our favorite family recipes. Why not spend a day this week organizing and cleaning your kitchen: the cabinets, the shelves, the kitchen drawers, the pantry? Give them all a good going over, up-dating and organizing as you go. Go through your recipe box and organize that too. Then when the mood strikes to start your holiday cooking, you'll know where everything is and what supplies you have on hand, or what you might need to replace or update.

NOVEMBER 13

Casual-Night-Sandwich-Dinner

Make delicious meat sandwiches with the leftovers from last night's Tasty Beef tenderloin. Add pickles and chips and a nice molded salad. Have a light and casual dinner tonight; use paper plates and make cleanup a breeze. Focus on good conversation and enjoy each other's company. Take advantage of the to-gether-time to plan a weekend family activity.

INGREDIENTS
Leftover beef tenderloin for sandwiches
Good quality bread or French style rolls of your choice
Chips, pickles and fixings
Molded Jell-O salad

NOVEMBER 14

Simply Delicious Snack Mix
A KIDS IN THE KITCHEN RECIPE

Kids are always hungry and they love to munch and nibble between meals. They also love to concoct their own recipes. Here is a kid-friendly snack that your child can easily make...To make this Distant Cousin of "Trail Mix," your "little cook" will need a large bowl for mixing, a large spoon for stirring, a measuring cup, and an airtight tin for storage.

INGREDIENTS
2 sweet cereals, of your choice
2 non-sweetened cereals, of your choice
1 cup chocolate chips
1 cup raisins
1 cup pretzels

Make a mixture of your favorite cereals, by measuring out equal portions of the sweet cereals and the non-sweetened cereals. (I like to use a mixture of Trix®, Honey-nut Cheerios®, Wheat Chex®, and regular Cheerios®.) To this mixture add your chocolate chips, raisins, and pretzels. Carefully stir to mix well. Store in an airtight container.

A Thought for Today
THE POWER OF POSITIVE THINKING
"Thoughts are energy. And you can make your world
or break your world by your own thinking."
~Susan L. Taylor, journalist

NOVEMBER 15

BBQ Beef for Sandwiches
A KID FRIENDLY RECIPE

INGREDIENTS
1 (4 to 5 pound) beef chuck roast
1 (1 ounce) packet dry onion soup mix
1 (10.75 ounce) can cream of mushroom soup
1 cup bottled BBQ sauce (our favorite is Sweet Baby Rays)
Good buns at serving time

Put roast in electric slow-cooker crockery pot. Sprinkle with soup mix. Pour on canned soup and bottled barbeque sauce. Cover and cook all day (8 to 10 hours) on low setting, half that time on high setting. When meat is done it should shred with a fork. Serve on Kaiser rolls, hoagie buns, or oversize hamburger buns.

RUSH HOUR WISDOM
If you do not have a slow-cooker crockery pot, you could bake this roast, tightly covered, in a 350–degree oven for about 3 hours; again the meat is ready when you can shred it with a fork. Mix with pan juices and serve as above.

NOVEMBER 16

Donna Wood's Italian Beef for Sandwiches
a.k.a. Corn-Noodle-Beef Night

8 to 10 servings

This recipe is a hands down favorite in our household. No matter who I make it for, they immediately ask for the recipe! This one is an award winner for both ease and taste. I often use it when I do in-store presentations or demos.

INGREDIENTS
1 (3 pound) sirloin tip roast
1 jar mild Giardiniera-style Vegetables, un-drained (An Italian jarred vegetable mixture packed in oil and brine found in the condiment or specialty food section of your market)

Place roast in slow cooker, fat side down, with any butcher strings removed. Simply pour on the jar of vegetables, including the juice. Cover with lid and cook on high setting for 1 hour. Reduce setting and cook for 10 to 12 hours more, until meat is so tender you can shred it with a fork. De-fat any juices in the crockery pot and serve the shredded meat mixed with the juice. Serve on buns. Can use the vegetable chunks to garnish your sandwich if you wish. Or have is Sammy-Style. My 10-year-old calls this "Corn-Noodle-Beef NIght" and we have wide egg noodles and corn.

RUSH HOUR VARIATION
For a delicious treat pile the meat open-faced on garlic-butter-spread, split and toasted hoagie rolls. Top with mozzarella cheese and place under broiler just long enough to melt and bubble the cheese.

NOVEMBER 17

A Perfect Cup of Tea

The perfect cup of tea can be a quiet and calming relaxer in the middle of your hectic day.

INGREDIENTS

Bring your water to a boil in a separate kettle. Meanwhile warm your tea pot with hot water. When the tea pot is warmed, dump out the water and put in your favorite tea leaves or tea bags, then pour on your boiling water from the separate kettle. Put on the cover and let your tea steep to desired strength. This usually takes about 5 minutes, then remove tea leaves or bags to avoid bitterness. Some people like to add a "tea cozy" to keep the tea pot warm while serving. And you may also warm your tea cups with warmed water, before filling with tea.

MORE TEA TIPS

If you happen to be using instant tea, combine it in your cup with boiling water, for a more steeped and clear affect. Do not mix the instant tea into water and bring to a boil. Instead, bring the boiling water to the instant tea directly, just as you would when using tea bags or tea leaves. (This also works for iced tea. Combine the instant tea with boiling water, let it "steep" so to speak, and then add ice cubes to ice it down, remembering to add a little extra tea, as the melting ice will dilute the flavor of the tea.) If you do this you will have a clearer, less cloudy, cup or glass of tea.

NOVEMBER 18

Mother's Marmalade Muffins
12 large muffins

Here's an easy muffin recipe to go along with that favorite cup of tea.

INGREDIENTS
2 cups all-purpose flour
½ cup sugar
1 tablespoon baking powder
½ teaspoon salt
2/3 cup raisins (optional)
1/3 cup crushed nuts (optional)
½ cup of undiluted frozen orange juice concentrate, thawed
1 egg, slightly beaten
½ cup melted butter
¾ cup of good quality orange marmalade

Preheat oven to 400 degrees. In a large bowl, sift together the dry ingredients (flour, sugar, baking powder, and salt). Stir in the optional raisins and nuts if using. In a smaller bowl mix together the wet ingredients (orange juice concentrate, beaten egg, butter, and the orange marmalade). Add the wet mixture to the dry mixture and stir only until moistened. Do not over mix batter. Line muffin cups with paper liners, or spray them with non-stick cooking spray. Fill muffin tins two-thirds to three-quarters full and bake at 400 degrees for approximately 25 minutes, or until toothpick inserted in center comes out clean.

RUSH HOUR VARIATIONS
To heighten the orange flavor of your muffins you can also add a pinch of orange zest (finely grated rind from a fresh orange). You can also fold in 2/3 cup coarsely-chopped fresh cranberries (or Craisins®) instead of the raisins. As odd as it may sound, you can fold-in a cup of grated, sharp Cheddar cheese in place of the nuts for yet another interesting flavor.

Easy Muffin Clean Up
Tired of your muffins overflowing the cups and sticking to the top of the pan. Spray the top of your muffin pan with non-stick spray too!

NOVEMBER 19

Gramma's "Sunday-Best" Roasted Potatoes

INGREDIENTS

Here is a very easy recipe for elegant potatoes. The reason we call them "Sunday Potatoes" is because my grandmother always made a roast on Sunday and religiously served these potatoes alongside it. While roasting your favorite beef roast add the addition of roasting potatoes for a flavorful meal. Using good baking potatoes scrub and peel them, then cut in half lengthwise. Cut the halves (again lengthwise) into thirds. Each potato should yield 6 long wedges. During last hour of cooking (the roast) arrange the potato wedges in the cooking drippings of the roasting pan, alongside and around the roast. The potatoes will take on a deliciously roasted and flavorful quality by cooking in the same pan with the meat. And best of all, your meat and potatoes will be done at the same time.

Oven Roasted Potatoes

INGREDIENTS

A variation of Sunday Roasted Potatoes can also be made without the roast, but truly are not quite as tasty as when done in the meat drippings. In a 350-degree oven, roast the potato wedges for about 1 to 1½ hours in a pan, moistened with water, melted butter, and a slathering of sliced onions. You could also add minced fresh garlic, parsley, and salt and pepper to taste. Turn the potatoes once or twice to coat all sides and bake until golden brown. Serve as a side dish with grilled meats or chicken.

Hide-and-Seek Beaters

Tired of searching and scrambling to find your electric-mixer-beaters? Why not store them right in the accompanying mixing bowl, rather than fighting for them in a jumbled up drawer. Then they are right at hand when you go to make your favorite muffins, cake, or mashed potatoes. Especially now with the holidays coming up— you'll probably be using your mixer more often, and being organized will temper any frustration.

Weekly Challenge

PLANNING FOR THANKSGIVING

We have a very busy week upon us, especially if we are hosting Thanksgiving Dinner. Develop a plan and try to stay organized. Do as much work as you can ahead of time, while keeping your menus simple for Monday through Wednesday. (You'll do enough cooking on Thursday.) Make enough Thanksgiving treats so you can have leftovers on Friday, there is nothing more delicious than a Traditional Turkey Sandwich or a Turkey BLT on Toast, the day after.

One way to keep yourself on track is to simplify and organize your shopping. Take advantage of seasonal sales and don't wait till the last minute to purchase all the necessities. On Monday, over that perfect cup of tea or coffee, make your shopping list and schedule for the week. You might want to have a back-up recipe or two for your side-dishes and salads, just in case you cannot find a needed ingredient for your first-choice-recipe. Include these back-up ingredients (or take the recipes with you) with your shopping list. Instead of spending valuable time, racing all around town in search of a sold-out ingredient, just change to your back-up recipe!

A Thought for Today

NO REGRETS...
"Grab a chance and you won't be sorry for a might-have-been."
~A. Ransome, Writer and Novelist

NOVEMBER 20

Apple Print Table Decorations
A KIDS IN THE KITCHEN CRAFT PROJECT

Today is a day to grab a chance, along with some creative time, to be in the kitchen with your children. With Thanksgiving fast approaching you might want to personally craft invitations, place mattes, or place cards for your family's up-coming gathering. You might even want to try stamping a border and center-piece on a plain white, disposable table cloth! Instead of the traditional Turkey-Hand-Finger Print we are going to use an apple theme.

MATERIALS NEEDED

An apple, cut in half from stem (top) down to stern (bottom), leaving you
   with a perfect cross-section of an apple—you'll need one apple half for
   each color you plan to use.

A fork, to use as a handle

Flat disposable trays or paper plates, to hold each color of paint

Red, yellow, and green paint (finger paints or craft paints)

Markers, crayons, colored pencils, for additional drawing and embellishment

Glitter (optional)

White paper, blank white greeting cards, hand made papers, card board,
   craft paper or water color paper. (You might want to experiment with
   different papers for the affect that pleases you most.)

A disposable table cloth and paper towels (for drips and spills, and little
   messes along the way)

An old shirt (from Dad) or a craft smock or apron

DIRECTIONS

Stab the rounded side of your apple half and using the fork as a handle, dip the flat side of the apple into the colored paint of your choosing. Be sure to have a different apple half for each color.

Scrape off any excess paint, on the side of the tray or plate. You don't want to have too much paint on the apple. Do an experimental print before you begin your project in earnest.

Gently stamp the paint-laden-apple onto the chosen piece of paper, until de-sired design is reached. You may print more than one apple, or apple shape, using more than one color…just remember to use a different apple for each color. When doing multiple printings in one design, stamp down your lighter colors first. Stamp on darker colors over them later. You might want to let the colors dry in-between, before adding another color.

While the paint is still wet, you can add the addition of glitter if you like.

If you are impatient, a hair dryer can be used to help dry the paint!

When the paint is dry you may embellish your stamped-print with hand-drawing and hand-writing, using the markers or crayons, or you can add additional stamping. Try cutting up a sponge or a potato for a background texture or shape. Pears or star fruit could add more fruit shapes. Or perhaps you want to hand write or print, a poem, or phrase on the card.

If you are sending cards or invitations through the mail, make sure your project is thoroughly dry, before you put your artistry in the envelope and mail it off! You don't want your hard work to arrive as a gooey, indecipherable mess.

For those that you give to in person, I would advise having an inexpensive frame on hand, because I am sure your visiting grandparents will want to frame your artwork as a memorable souvenir to display proudly for all to see.

NOVEMBER 22
Gravy 101

Your Thanksgiving dinner is going to need gravy and this is how we do it "Rush-Hour Style."

INGREDIENTS
Pan juices
Thickener (flour or cornstarch)
Liquid (water, broth, wine, etc.)
Seasonings
Butter

Make your gravy from the cooking juices remaining in the pan after you have removed your meat to hold in a warm (200 degree) oven. If you have a lot of juices to work with you might want to reduce (cook them down) a bit and skim off any excess fats floating on the top. Then thicken your gravy to your personal preference. I happen to like my gravy on the thinner side.

When thickening gravy…to insure velvety smooth results (rather than lumpy) first mix your flour or cornstarch (your thickener) with an equal amount of water (using approximately 2 to 3 tablespoons of each), and either blend with a whisk in a small dish or shake until well-mixed in a small covered jar. Slowly blend this mixture into the pan-juices, stirring all the while with a wire whisk, while you drizzle in the thickener. When the gravy has thickened, blend in additional water or broth or wine, stirring all the while, to arrive at your desired consistency. (While stirring be sure to get up all the cooking-bits of flavor from the bottom of the pan for extra added flavor.) Be careful not to over thicken your gravy as it will taste flour-y and artificially thickened. Better to skimp on the thin side. If you need to enrich the color or flavor of your gravy, add a few dashes of Kitchen Bouquet®, Sauce Robert®, or Worcestershire sauce. Adjust seasonings with salt and pepper at end of cooking. Lastly for gloss and finish, swirl in a pat or two of butter just until melted. Gravy is best served hot, so pass at the table in a small dish or "gravy boat" and keep the rest warm on the stove.

RUSH HOUR TIP
Another very easy way to thicken gravy is to blend in a small amount of instant-mashed-potato-flakes, instead of the water/flour or water/cornstarch mixture.

NOVEMBER 23

Utensil Essentials (a must for every kitchen)

It dawned on me while I was reciting gravy instructions, we should review the importance of good kitchen utensils…like a wire whisk for example. Here are a few of my favorite items, outside of the obvious big appliances (like blenders, crockery pots, food processor, coffee bean grinder, Kitchen Aid® counter top mixer, etc.). These are the little things, all tangled up in your kitchen drawer, the everyday "work horses" that make your tasks ever so much easier—the basic necessities a good cook can't live without!

ESSENTIALS
Long handled tongs
Chef quality wire whisk
Assortment of chef knives that are ALWAYS SHARP:
   (one for carving, one for chopping, a serrated one for bread, a small
    paring knife, a flexible fillet knife, and an all-around "chef's" knife, and
    kitchen shears)
Long handled cook's fork, spoon, soup ladle, and strainer-spoon
Meat thermometer
A Swing-A-Way® hand held (non-electric) can opener
Waiter style corkscrew/bottle opener
Set of measuring spoons and measuring cups
A large, handled glass measuring cup (such as two cup or four cup)
Colander and sieve
Sanitary cutting boards (that can be put in dish washer)
An old fashioned four-sided grater
A vegetable scrubbing brush
Large handled potato peeler (the kind that is easy on arthritic hands)
Wooden cooking spoons
Spatulas for serving
Rubber spatulas for mixing and folding
Citrus juice-reamer
Garlic press
A hand dicer for mushrooms and onions
A sieve cover (that can be placed over a pan for straining)
And last but not least a hand-held electric mixer

I thought with the holidays coming up, you just might want to check out your utensil situation, before you get to the mashed potatoes and you've misplaced your potato peeler. Or you go to make Gramma's favorite dressing and your measuring spoons and cups have been long gone to your daughter's last summer "mud pies" in the sand box! And for all you "first timers" just setting up your kitchens (and remember we've all been there, done that) maybe my list will help you along. Just as a painter can't paint without a good brush and canvas, a cook can't cook without the proper utensils.

A Thought for Today

"Great opportunities to help others seldom come, but small ones surround us daily..." ~Sally Koch, American Writer

NOVEMBER 24

Mrs. Murphy's Carrot Cake, submitted by Judy Brown

Thank you Judy, for another great recipe! Wow your guests with the choice of pumpkin pie or carrot cake.

FOR CAKE:
Cream together:
> 1 1/2 cups vegetable oil
> 2 cups white sugar
> 4 eggs, beaten very well

Sift together:
> 2 cups flour
> 2 teaspoons baking powder
> 2 teaspoons soda
> 2 teaspoons cinnamon
> Pinch salt

Stir both together well and add:
> 1/2 cup chopped nuts
> 3 cups grated carrots (I put carrots in the blender and I think because you have to add water to blend them, it makes the cake so moist. I drain and squeeze all the water out, but carrots still remain moist.)

Pour batter into greased and floured 9 x 13-inch baking pan.
Bake at 350-degrees for 1 hour. Cool and frost.

FOR FROSTING:
Cream together:
> 1 stick butter, room temperature
> 1 (8 ounce) package cream cheese, room temperature

Blend in:
> 1 box powdered sugar
> 2 teaspoons vanilla

Mix to desired spreading consistency; if need be with a little milk.

A Thought for Today

IT'S TIME TO "TALK A LITTLE TURKEY"...

Especially about thawing it! Don't forget that big frozen bird takes a lot of time to thaw. Butterball® recommends a day of refrigerator thawing per every four pounds! So 'we best get cooking'...oops, I mean thawing.

Butterball Turkey Talk-Line® (1 800 BUTTERBALL or www.butterball.com), Jennie-O Turkey Hotline® (1 800 887 5397 or www.jennie-o.com) and Reynolds Metals Company Turkey Tips Line® (1 800 745 4000) are but some of the listings offering toll free numbers, along with information and answers to any questions we cooks might have while preparing turkey.

NOVEMBER 25

Barbara's Fabulous Frozen Cranberry Mold
6 to 8 servings

Very much like a rich, homemade ice cream, this luscious cranberry mold will make a great cold and creamy offering to your Holiday Feast. You can serve it un-molded onto a fancy plate, or serve it directly from a glass bowl (that you can put in the freezer and transfer to the table). I would strongly suggest making a second mold to save in the freezer for the day after Thanksgiving—to eat with all those yummy leftovers!

INGREDIENTS
1 can traditional, jellied cranberry sauce
2 tablespoons lemon juice
1 small carton heavy cream for whipping
1/4 cup mayonnaise and
1/4 cup powdered sugar

For the bottom layer, mix the jellied cranberry sauce and the lemon juice until smooth and well incorporated. Pour into mold or dish and set in the freezer, so it begins to set up.

Meanwhile whip the heavy cream with the mayonnaise and powdered sugar, whipping it as stiff as possible. (Because of the mayonnaise it will not whip as stiff as traditional whipping cream.) Pour this cream layer over the cranberry layer (that has begun to set) and return to the freezer. Freeze several hours or overnight, until solid and set. Take out of the freezer just a few minutes before serving, to thaw just slightly, for easier serving. This recipe may be doubled, as I guarantee people will want seconds.

RUSH HOUR WISDOM:
THINGS TO MAKE AND DO
THE DAY OR NIGHT BEFORE THANKSGIVING:

Make ahead any gelatin molds and desserts. Assemble vegetable-casseroles. Store all in the fridge until serving or cooking time the next day.

Even your stuffing can be made ahead and stored, covered, in a non-metal bowl. But remember; do not stuff, I repeat: DO NOT STUFF your turkey until right before cooking. Also remember to pull any giblets, etc. out of the cavity before stuffing and reserve for later use.

For old fashioned cooks, like my mom, these giblets are parboiled and diced, to add texture to the stuffing, or flavor to the gravy. My mom uses them in the gravy and it does make wonderfully rich gravy. She also saves the giblet water and uses that in the gravy as well. These can be parboiled and chopped the day before. (I personally have an aversion to touching anything called a 'giblet'.)

Make sure your special serving dishes are clean and available, that the sterling is polished, and that you have all the necessary ingredients—we don't need a last minute, frantic dash to the market. Pre-set your table and have your kids make appropriate center piece and table decorations.

Thought of the Day
GIVING THANKS NO MATTER WHAT
"How wonderful it is that nobody need wait a single
moment before starting to improve the world."
~Anne Frank

NOVEMBER 26
Our Thanksgiving Feast

To all of my family, friends, readers, and subscribers have a wonderful and blessed Thanksgiving! Here are some extra Rush Hour Tips to keep the cook (or cooks) relaxed and happy in the kitchen on this hectic day.

RUSH HOUR TIPS

Clean as you go…Fill your sink with hot sudsy water and clean all assembly and prep dishes, as you finish using them. Or rinse and put in your dishwasher. Before you sit down to dinner run that first load of dishes.

Have an extra roll of paper towels handy to clean up spills and mishaps as they happen.

Roast your turkey (and make the gravy) in a convenient, disposable aluminum pan.

Prep your casserole dishes with non-stick cooking spray for easy clean up.

If you are using pots and pans on the top of the stove, make sure their handles are tucked to the side. When there are too many cooks in the kitchen, an errant elbow or a traffic jam could easily spill the pot, creating a serious accident and a trip to the emergency room.

To keep your stove top and counter clean, use a small plate, or a paper plate, as a 'spoon rest' for your cooking utensils.

Your turkey should "rest" for 10 to 20 minutes after it's been removed from the oven, for easier carving and slicing.

While the turkey is resting, place your dinner plates in the oven. Warmed dinner plates will keep each person's meal warmer longer at the table.

The smoothest way to make gravy-thickner is to take several tablespoons of flour and mix them in a small amount of water in a separate dish, to form a smooth thickening agent. Or, you can shake the water and flour in a small covered jar until blended, set aside.

While the turkey is resting on your serving platter, remove excess fat from the cooking juices in your roasting pan. Over medium to high heat start to simmer and reduce your cooking juices, being sure to scrape up any browned bits from the bottom of the pan for extra added flavor. Add in the blended flour mixture a little at a time, whisking all the while, until desired consistency is reached. Adjust with additional water, or canned broth, or broth from your cooked giblets. Using the giblets is very old fashioned, but my mom swears by it.. Season with salt and pepper at end of cooking. Add in the finely chopped giblets, if using. Pour the finished gravy into a smaller saucepan to keep warm on low setting on a back burner. Serve the gravy in small portions, keeping the rest warm on the stove.

When everyone has assembled at the table, say grace or give thanks for the bounty set before you.

NOVEMBER 27

Next Day Classic Turkey Club Sandwich
A KID FREINDLY RECIPE

Relax, today is leftover day. This recipe requires no cooking skills, just a bit of assembly know-how. Your kids can help you grab and arrange all the ingredients. Pull that extra cranberry mold out of the freezer and enjoy.

ASSEMBLE IN ORDER GIVEN:
    A plate, followed by...
    Your bottom piece of buttered toast
    A slathering of low-fat mayonnaise
    Crisp (micro-waved) bacon slices (or you could substitute deli ham)
    Leafy lettuce (such as Romaine or Bibb)
    Middle piece of buttered toast
    Sliced tomato or avocado, or none, or both
    Slices of Thanksgiving turkey
    A slice of Swiss-lace Swiss cheese
    Another spread of low fat mayonnaise
    The top piece of buttered toast

Crown your sandwich with festive toothpicks, speared with a black or green olive, and a pearl onion or pickled mushroom. Serve with a *TV Guide* and a Football Game.

NOVEMBER 28
Leftover Turkey Bake

INGREDIENTS
Leftover turkey
Leftover stuffing
Leftover gravy
Leftover mashed potatoes
Butter
Parmesan cheese

In a buttered casserole dish place the leftover stuffing. Layer sliced turkey over stuffing. Pour on gravy, thinned with a little water. (Use jarred gravy if you don't have enough leftover.) Top with a layer of mashed potatoes. Dot with butter. Sprinkle with Parmesan cheese. Cover with foil and bake at 350 degrees for 30 minutes, or until all is heated through and bubbly.

Weekly Challenge

GIFTS FROM THE KITCHEN

It's not too early to start planning your gifts from the kitchen. These homemade favorites are great for hostess gifts, last minute invitations to parties, gift baskets, presents for teachers, the mail man, etc. You will find plenty of recipes throughout this book that are perfect for gift giving and including in theme-gift baskets. Sauces for pasta, salsas for Mexican, jellies along with English muffins, cookies in a tea towel lined basket, drink-mixes included with a decorative coffee mug, vinaigrettes in a decorative bottle ... let your imagination run wild. Decorate the container and include a cute recipe card, along with suggestions for serving. Make a complete basket-presentation, by adding such things as pretty cups, or pretty paper napkins and paper plates, a variety of dried pastas might be included with a pasta sauce, maybe a salad bowl or pretty salad tongs along with a homemade vinaigrette and a jar of toasted nuts for topping. There are so many lovely presentations you can make!

NOVEMBER 29

Lucile's Old Fashioned Skillet Hash
4 servings

INGREDIENTS

2 cups (or more if you have it) of diced (finely chopped) leftover cooked
meat (can be roast beef, turkey, ham, chicken)

2 cups (or more) of finely diced potatoes (precooked or raw)

1 medium onion, diced

Salt and pepper to taste

Minced garlic cloves or garlic powder to taste

A dash of Worcestershire (optional)

2 to 3 tablespoons cooking oil

Ketchup, for children at serving time

In a bowl lightly toss and mix together all ingredients, except cooking oil and
ketchup. Heat oil in a large, non-stick skillet. Spread the beef-hash mixture (or
whatever meat you are using) into the hot oil in the pan, spreading evenly around
the pan. Cook for 10 to 15 minutes, until hash is golden brown and potatoes are
soft and cooked through. Turn the hash frequently to brown thoroughly. (Children usually like ketchup on the side with their hash.)

NOVEMBER 30

Vicki's Portable Macaroni and Cheese
A KID FRIENDLY RECIPE

This versatile recipe comes to us courtesy of Vicki in Madison. Vicki writes, "This recipe has long been a favorite of my co-workers for our monthly potluck lunches. The short assembling time means I can prepare it at home, plug it in when I arrive at work and four hours later it is ready to join the huge spread of other foods. To make it heartier, I have added diced celery, onions, and ham on occasion."

INGREDIENTS
1 (16 ounce) package elbow macaroni, cooked and drained
½ cup butter or margarine
½ cup flour
2 teaspoons salt
4 cups milk
1 (16 ounce) block of processed cheese, cubed
Paprika

Melt butter or margarine in saucepan. Stir in flour. Gradually add milk and stir until thickened. Add cheese and stir until completely melted. Combine macaroni and cheese sauce in deep slow-cooker crockery pot. Sprinkle with paprika. Cover and cook on low setting for 4 hours.

RUSH HOUR WISDOM

Wouldn't this be a great dish to take to any holiday pot-luck party—especially if kids are involved! It always seems like there is never anything "good" for kids to eat, amongst all the fancy holiday fare! Serve this to the kids and you'll be the hit of the party!

A Thought for Today
THIS LAST WONDERFUL, HECTIC MONTH OF THE YEAR

The month of December is perhaps the most exciting, challenging month of the year and though filled with joy and holiday camaraderie, it can also be filled with anxiety and stress. Our expectations run in high gear as we try to orchestrate the perfect holiday, the perfect party, the perfect family gathering, the perfectly cleaned and decorated house. It's December and we are busy shopping, and baking, and planning, and decorating, and entertaining. Whew, I get tired just writing about it!

So my suggestion would be to slow down, take a deep breath and know that you can make the holidays wonderful. Think back about your own holidays, when you were growing up. What favorite things do you remember? Do you recall what gift you got when? No, not really. I bet you remember the treasured gift of "shared time" with your mother, while baking cookies...or the time you sat in your dad's easy chair as he read you a story... or the shared laughter and excitement as you dashed out the door to catch those first falling snow flakes, to let them melt on your tongue. What I'm trying to say is that the gifts of the season are truly found within you, within your own home, within your family and friends, your heritage and history, and the symbolic month of December itself.

As the shorter days and cold, dark nights of the winter solstice fast approach us, let's make time for pause, to light the candles of warmth and caring within our families, our friends, and ourselves. Let's relax into that moment of time when the joy of the season unfolds before us... as if we were children once again...

DECEMBER 1
The Cheesiest Grilled Cheese Ever

Grilled cheese sandwiches and cream of tomato soup (easy, warming, and melt in your mouth comforting) create a quick and simple dinner for this first day in December.

INGREDIENTS
2 slices of good sandwich bread, use white, whole wheat, or even Texas-
    style, per sandwich
Whipped cream cheese, traditional, chive or herb flavor (your choice)
Colby or Cheddar cheese, thinly sliced to fit each sandwich
Mozzarella cheese, thinly sliced to fit each sandwich
Butter or margarine, softened for easy spreading
*Additional options: crisped bacon (my personal favorite), sliced fresh tomato, deli sliced ham
Canned tomato soup at serving time

To build each sandwich, spread a generous layer of cream cheese on one slice of bread. Then layer on the Colby and mozzarella cheese slices. If you wish, top this with one (or all) of your options* bacon, tomato slices, or deli ham. Then place the second piece of bread on the top. Evenly butter both the outer top and the outer bottom of the sandwich. Place your sandwiches in a heated, non-stick sprayed, non-stick pan (or electric skillet, or griddle) and sauté on both sides until golden brown and cheeses have melted. Serve immediately along with a bowl of cream of tomato soup (or my favorite combo chicken noodle).

A Thought for Today
SELF DISCOVERY
"The privilege of a lifetime is being who you are."
~Joseph Campbell

DECEMBER 2
Homemade Cottage-Fried Potatoes
(Cousin of the Hash Browns)
6 servings

Cottage Fried Potatoes make a filling side dish with dinner or when you want to serve "breakfast for dinner" they taste great with eggs! The difference in name is merely in the size of the dice—Cottage Fries being sliced and Hash Browns being finely diced or shredded.

INGREDIENTS
3 to 4 large russet potatoes, peeled (to yield about 2 pounds)
1 tablespoon of salt (for salting boiling water)
½ to 1 teaspoon garlic salt
¼ teaspoon of dried oregano, crushed between your fingers to release flavor
Salt and black pepper to taste

Cut your peeled potatoes in half, lengthwise and then cut those halves into halves again, lengthwise. You should now have 4 elongated wedges for each potato. If the potatoes are really large, you might want to cut the potatoes into 6ths instead of 4ths. Cut these wedges crosswise into about ¼-inch thick slices. Place the potato slices, along with the onion, in a saucepan of cold water to cover and bring them to a boil. Add a tablespoon of salt and par-boil them until just barely knife tender, about 5 minutes. (Don't overcook, better to undercook at this stage.) Drain thoroughly! Preheat your butter or olive oil in a heavy skillet (or your heaviest non-stick frying pan) and then lightly add the pre-cooked potatoes and onion (making sure they are well drained, to avoid spattering). Season with the garlic salt, oregano, salt and black pepper to taste. Sauté for about 5 to 10 minutes, or until crispy brown and golden, gently turning the potatoes over just once or twice. (You don't want to mash the potatoes together.) The potatoes will cook quickly because they have already been *par-boiled. Serve warm as a side dish with dinner, as an accompaniment with eggs and sausage for breakfast, or with a fish entrée for a "shoreline dinner."

RUSH HOUR VARIATIONS
Some people prefer to skip the beginning step of parboiling the potatoes, and move directly on to slicing them and putting them directly into the pan. They will take a little longer to cook this way but the results are the same. Cook them for about 20 to 25 minutes over low to medium heat so you don't burn them. Crumbled sausage or bacon may be added to the Cottage Fries while cooking to make an even heartier dish. And cheese may be melted over the top at end of cooking for another hearty variation, turning them almost into a frittata.

A Thought for Today
THE BIG COUNT DOWN

One of my favorite childhood memories of December and the lead up to Christmas Day was my Advent Calendar. My mom always had one for me and one for my brother and every morning we would dash out to open the little window for the corresponding date and then we would gleefully count down the fact that we were one day closer to the Big Day! It was always so much fun searching for the day and number, hidden in the Christmassy scene on the calendar. I have passed on this tradition to my young daughter, who now enjoys the "count down" as much as I did when I was little.

For those who celebrate Christmas, Advent Calendars may be readily found at card shops, craft stores and Christmas stores. Some even contain little candies, ornaments, or trinkets when you open each window ... however, mine always had cute little pictures and sayings that told a festive story leading up to Christmas Day. I also know that many families design and make their own variations on this theme- (see this week's Kids in the Kitchen Craft Project for December 5th) It's still not too late to enjoy the fun of an Advent Calendar.

DECEMBER 3
Broiled Grapefruit Halves

Today my daughter took part in her school fruit sale, bringing home crates of oranges and grapefruits. As I looked at each case, I remembered how my mom used to make broiled grapefruit.

INGREDIENTS
Fresh grapefruits, cut in half
Brown sugar
Melted butter
Maraschino cherries

Preheat your broiler. While your broiler is preheating, cut your grapefruit in half and then (with a small paring knife) carefully cut around the edges of each grapefruit section to loosen the sections from their fibrous sides. Leave the prepared fruit in their shells (i.e. in their peels). Sprinkle each grapefruit half with brown sugar and drizzle with melted butter. Place under pre-heated broiler and broil just until warm and the brown sugar has melted and glazed the fruit—about 5 to 7 minutes. Garnish with a maraschino cherry in the center and serve warm. Each grapefruit half equals one serving and makes an excellent beginning or side dish to a winter meal.

Weekly Challenge

These wonderful tips are reprinted with permission. Use them to take control of holiday stains this season!

Let them stain, let them stain,
***let them stain...* 'Tis the season for stain tips from the Whirlpool Institute of Fabric Science**

After the halls have been decked and the egg nog has been drunk, the presents under the tree are not all you are left with. These valuable holiday stain removal tips from the **Whirlpool Institute of Fabric Science** are the gifts you can really use this year. Here are 12 tips for dashing through the stains.

Twelve Coffees Spilling

Sponge or rinse stain promptly in cold water. Pretreat with liquid laundry detergent, launder using bleach that is safe for the fabric. Wash in the hottest water safe for the fabric.

Eleven Candy Canes Crumbling

Rinse in warm water to dilute the stain. Wash in warm to hot water and dry as usual.

Ten Egg Nogs Splashing

Rinse in cold water to dilute the stain. Soak up to 30 minutes with detergent, weighted with a towel to keep submerged. Wash in warm to hot water and air dry.

Nine Lipsticks Smudging

Scrape fabric stain with a dull knife. Use a dry-cleaning solvent or pretreat with detergent. Wash in warm water. Air dry.

Eight Greasy Droppings

Gently scrape off excess solids with a dull knife. Apply a small amount of liquid dish detergent to the underside of the soiled area, to break up the grease. Machine wash in the warmest water that the care label permits; if the stain still appears, repeat the process, as the toughest stains may require a little extra persistence

Seven Candles Dripping

Scrape off the excess wax with a dull knife. Place the stain between paper towels and press with a warm iron from the back of the fabric. When all wax has been removed and ironed out, treat stain with a pretreatment solution or soak in detergent with the warmest water possible. Launder as usual.

Six Chocolates Melting

Pretreat with a liquid laundry detergent or soak fabric in warm water and a detergent that contains enzymes. Difficult stains may require using bleach that is safe for the fabric.

Five Fruits a-Flinging

Carefully remove any surface solids with a dull knife. Try to immediately spot treat the affected area by rinsing with cold water to remove excess sugars. Apply a small amount of detergent directly on the stain before washing in the warmest water that is safe for the fabric. Add liquid-chlorine bleach or color-safe bleach to the wash five minutes into the wash cycle, after the detergent has done its job.

Four Salsas Sliding

Scrape off any excess salsa with a spoon or dull knife. Soak fabric in cold water and wash in the warmest water possible for that fabric.

Three Wines Wobbling

Sprinkle salt on the stain as soon as possible to draw wine out of the fibers. Blot fabric with a solution of mild detergent and warm water. Then blot fabric with a mix of one-third cup of white vinegar with two-thirds cup of water. Repeat and sponge with clean water.

Two Sweaty Santas

To remove antiperspirant, place the stain face down on a paper towel. Sponge the back of the stain with a dry cleaning solvent. Let dry and rinse off. Rub on a paste of granular laundry detergent and water. Wash in the hottest water safe for the fabric.

And a sap drip from a pine tree...

Use a dry cleaning solvent and then wash in warm to hot water. Repeat if necessary.

Seasons Eatings...and to all a good night!

DECEMBER 4

Orange Vinaigrette Dressing

Yesterday the grapefruit…today the oranges!

INGREDIENTS
½ cup vegetable oil
½ cup orange juice, use freshly squeezed
1 tablespoon honey or sugar
1 to 2 teaspoons Dijon style mustard, or to taste
A dash of celery salt
* For garnish on the salad greens: chopped pecans and/or thinly sliced onion rings, sliced fresh orange sections or Mandarin orange sections

Shake all dressing ingredients in a tightly covered jar until well mixed. Just before serving time pour over your mixed salad greens and toss lightly to coat. Garnish the top of your salad with * toasted chopped pecans and or/ thinly sliced sweet onion. Or, serve up the salad greens on individual plates and pass the vinaigrette separately, to let each diner drizzle on the amount that they want.

RUSH HOUR TIP

The garnish of pecans greatly benefits from toasting the nuts to gain that extra crispness and nutty taste for your salad. You can toast nuts by stirring them over moderate heat in an un-greased heavy frying pan on the stove top. Stir them constantly until toasted and golden brown, about 5 minutes or so. The addition of freshly cut orange sections, or Mandarin orange slices, would also be nice, mixed in with the greens, contrasting with the crunch of the pecans and the tartness of the onion rings. Use a nice leaf lettuce or spring mix for your salad greens.

A Thought for Today

"Whoever retains the natural curiosity of childhood
is never bored or dull." ~Anonymous

DECEMBER 5

Making an Advent Calendar
A KIDS IN THE KITCHEN CRAFT PROJECT

Now that we are fully involved in the excitement of December and the count-down to Christmas, why don't you and your children make an Advent Calendar, as I suggested earlier in the week? Your children will have great fun partaking in this old-fashioned activity. Here are some ideas for variations if you want to make your own Advent Calendar:

Buy a packet of Holiday Stickers and have your child place one sticker on a regular calendar each December day as it occurs. You could photocopy the page of December and put it on your refrigerator. Put the stickers right next to it and each day the child can choose a special sticker and place it on the correct date.

Make a felt Christmas Tree and 25 numbered-felt ornaments, with the 24th one being the star that tops the tree and the 25th one being a large present for at the base of the tree. Every day have your child decorate the tree by adding 1 of the 25 ornaments, leading up to the star on Christmas Eve and then a mysterious present under the tree. (You can use Velcro on the backs of the ornaments to make them stick.) (This is an easy and festive centerpiece, too!)

With a Styrofoam cone make a Lollipop Tree and every day your child gets to pick one piece of candy (with the appropriate date) off the tree. When the candy is gone...Christmas is here.

On 25 Post-It notes, or similar paper, have your child make 25 little drawings or miniature works of art, symbolizing the Christmas theme (i.e. stars, snowflakes, presents, candy canes, trees, etc.) Scramble and affix the Post-Its onto a large sheet of paper. Then cover the Post-It page with a second sheet of paper (that you have strategically made and cut dotted line windows for) corresponding the windows to the pictures underneath. Number each window from 1 to 25, being sure to scramble the order of the numbers. The top page may also be decorated to make the numbers even harder to find. Each day your child will hunt for the corresponding date on his very own calendar, being able to peek at his artwork underneath and know that he is a day closer to Christmas. And you will have a precious keepsake for the future.

DECEMBER 6

Quick Chicken Quesadillas
4 servings

As you start contemplating all your holiday menus and your festively home-made, "from-scratch" cooking for the season, tonight let's take a breather and let a few "convenience" ingredients help you put together a quick and easy meal. Dinner will be a breeze as you open a couple of cans and jars, add a package of tortillas, assemble and bake... dinner is served.

INGREDIENTS

At least 10 ounces of cooked chicken, cut into bite-sized pieces (or you can use canned, chunk chicken if you like)
1 can of Campbell's ® Cheddar cheese soup, undiluted
½ cup of your favorite salsa (you select the heat)
10 (8-inch) flour tortillas
*Optional garnish: flourished green-onion-sticks (see December 7)

Preheat your oven to 425 degrees. While your oven is preheating mix the first 3 ingredients in a saucepan and heat through to make a warm filling. Divide the warmed filling between 10 tortillas. Spread the filling over half of each tortilla to within 1/2 inch of the edge. Moisten the edges with a little water, fold the tortillas over the filling, and seal around the moistened edges. Place the quesadillas on baking sheets and bake for at least 5 minutes, or until hot. Serve warm with extra salsa to pass and refried beans and/or Spanish rice on the side to round out the meal. Optional garnishes of sour cream and/or guacamole, would add depth to the dish. Add a green onion stick to decorate the plate.

DECEMBER 7
Flourished Green Onion Sticks

The garnish of flourished green-onion-sticks adds excitement to any presentation. To make the frilled sticks, cut both the green end and the white end of each onion, so they are trimmed and clean. Remove any tough or bruised outer layers, so the onion is crispy-white and smooth. With a small paring knife, make approximately 3-inch long slits through each end of the long, narrow onion. Turn the onion and cut again, drawing the knife from the middle down to each end. Repeat once more if you can. Plunge the sliced onions into ice water and the ends will curl and frill—kind of like a fire-cracker or frilled ribbon. Store them in the ice water until ready to use for garnish.

P.S. You might add this little garnish-idea to your holiday repertoire, especially at New Years Eve, as the onions look like festive firecrackers—perfect for the occasion.

DECEMBER 8
Fried Ice Cream
8 Servings

INGREDIENTS
1 quart vanilla ice cream
3 cups crushed cornflake cereal
1 teaspoon ground cinnamon
3 egg whites

Scoop the ice cream into 8 (½ cup size) balls, place on a baking sheet and return to freezer for 1 hour, or until firm. In a shallow dish combine the crushed cornflakes and cinnamon and set aside. In another bowl beat the egg whites until foamy. Roll the ice cream balls in the egg whites and then in the cornflakes to cover the ice cream completely. Return the coated ice cream to the freezer and freeze until firm, at least 3 hours. (This can all be done ahead of time.) Heat oil in a deep fryer or you can use a heavy skillet. Fry the ice cream balls in the pre-heated oil, 1 or 2 at a time, for about 15 seconds. (You are not actually frying the ice cream; you are just frying the outer coating.) Drain on paper towels for a few seconds and serve immediately. (If you are making a bunch, return fried balls back to freezer until all have been made and you are ready to serve them.)

DECEMBER 9

Spices 101

Let's talk spices for a few minutes. Have you checked yours lately? As you put your 'best dishes' forward this holiday season make sure you add the best flavorings possible for maximum taste and effect for all your effort!

It is suggested that spices greatly lose their flavor and freshness after 6 months to 1 year. At time of purchase, it's not a bad idea to sticker and date less commonly used spices, so that when you pull them out of the cabinet you'll know their age and current potency.

Whole spices last longer than ground spices, and are best when ground or crushed just before using. I even like to "crush" already-crushed, dried spices (such as basil, oregano, thyme, and rosemary) between my fingers when adding them to my dish. By crushing them, again, between my fingers I rejuvenate and release extra flavor. And of course, whole peppercorns should be ground right at time of use.

Many spices benefit from being toasted (sesame seeds are a good example). Toasting releases aroma and flavor, and can be done in a dry, heavy frying pan (like we did with the pecans for the December 4th salad recipe).

Roasted fresh garlic cloves take on a smooth, buttery taste all their own…much more flavorful than garlic powder or garlic salt. Roasted, or just freshly minced garlic is a must.

And of course onions and hot peppers turn sweet when cooked, unlike their powdered counterparts.

Fresh parsley (so common and easy to obtain) far outperforms its dried facsimile in a jar.

So add a little spice to your holidays. Buy the real thing and freshly grind, mince, dice, sauté, and toast at time of cooking.

DECEMBER 10
Pleezing, Cheezing Garlic Bread

INGREDIENTS
1 loaf of bakery-fresh French or Italian bread
¾ stick butter (or margarine) softened
1/3 cup grated mozzarella cheese (or more if you like)
5 cloves of garlic, minced (or roasted and mashed)
¼ cup Parmesan cheese (or more if you like)
1 teaspoon dried parley, crushed between finger tips
½ teaspoon dried pepper flakes (optional)

Preheat oven to 350 degrees. Cut the bread loaf in half lengthwise and spread each half liberally with the softened butter. Then sprinkle on the remaining 5 ingredients in the order given (starting with the mozzarella and ending with the pepper flakes). Place the halves on an un-greased baking sheet and bake until cheese has melted and edges are toasty, approximately 12 to 15 minutes. Slice into wedges and serve immediately.

A Thought for Today
"Success is a journey, not a destination. The doing is often more important than the outcome."
~Arthur Ashe, professional tennis player

DECEMBER 11
Oven Barbecued Chicken
1 chicken breast per serving

This recipe takes about an hour in total, from start to finish, but the result yields a taste of summer in what is now becoming winter. So leave the grill in the garage and use your oven instead.

INGREDIENTS
1 bone-in but skinless chicken breast (half) per person (or if you prefer, use cut-up fryer pieces, bone-in but without the skin. Then I would "guesstimate" two pieces per person.)
Non-stick cooking spray or butter
Commercial Barbeque Sauce (your favorite brand and flavor... we use Sweet Baby Rays)
Any spices you might like to add to that sauce, such as minced garlic, minced onion, a dash of Worcestershire, etc—be creative! *This step is totally optional, but gives the custom taste of a homemade sauce. (They'll think you've been slaving over the sauce all day.)

Preheat your oven to 350 degrees. Meanwhile, in a non-stick skillet, sprayed with cooking spray or melted with butter, brown the chicken pieces on both sides over medium heat until golden brown. Transfer the chicken to a non-stick sprayed or buttered baking dish and snuggle them up in a single layer. Pour on your "customized BBQ sauce" and continue to cook the chicken in the oven. Bake for approximately 40 to 45 minutes, or until chicken is thoroughly done and juices run clear. (A safe meat-temperature reading is 170 degrees when the chicken is done.)

RUSH HOUR TIP
For an additional treat, why don't you serve up some (flash frozen) corn on the cob. It's not just for summer anymore! Simmer corn in a pot of boiling water as per package instructions and serve with melted butter and your BBQ'd chicken.

DECEMBER 12

These two apple recipes are quick and easy to make for everyday meals and are just as wonderful for your holiday menus. They require no cooking, just slicing, dicing, and assembling. I know it sounds like an "odd combo" but the Fabulous Apple Salad will make you quite popular. Even my picky-daughter has fallen in love with this recipe. It is another favorite to take to in-store events and demos.

Fabulous Apple Salad

3 to 4 Granny Smith apples, leave skins on for color
3 to 4 red delicious apples, leave skins on for color
6 Snickers® candy bars, standard size (or use a full bag of the Halloween miniature size)
Large container Cool Whip® or similar whipped topping (use low-fat)
1 to 2 cups of miniature marshmallows, or to taste

Coarsely dice the Snickers® bars into small pieces and set aside. Dice the green and red apples (leaving the skins on) and mix into the diced candy bars. Fold in a tub of whipped topping and then lastly fold in mini marshmallows to taste. Refrigerate until serving time. I guarantee everyone will be asking you for this recipe!

Fabulous Taffy Apple Platter

This recipe has no measured ingredients. You just arrange a pretty platter and serve. It is important to arrange the platter as close to serving time as possible to prevent browning of the apples.

INGREDIENTS
Sliced apples, leave the skins on (don't forget to sprinkle with lemon juice to prevent browning)
1 to 2 tubs of commercially prepared taffy apple dip (you'll find this usually next to the apples in the fresh produce section of your market)
Shelled and crushed peanuts
Your prettiest party tray

Slice your apples and arrange decoratively in a single-layer pattern around your platter. Spread, drizzle, or dab your caramel sauce over the apple slices, leaving part of each slice exposed and part covered with dip. (Since this is "finger food" you have to leave part of each slice uncovered for easy handling.) Make sure your caramel dip is at room temperature so it is fairly soft, otherwise it will be very hard to spread. Sprinkle the platter with a generous portion of crushed peanuts.

Apple Tips

When slicing apples, be sure to sprinkle them with fresh lime juice to prevent the slices from browning. (I have been told that pineapple juice works just as well, although I haven't tried it.) To retain crispness and flavor try to wait until as close to serving time as possible to slice and assemble or arrange your apples.

DECEMBER 13
Party Pecans

INGREDIENTS
1½ cups pecans
¼ cup sugar
2 tablespoons water
2 teaspoons instant coffee powder
¼ teaspoon cinnamon

Stir all in an electric skillet at 225 degrees for 5 minutes, to coat and glaze. (Or use a frying pan over low heat on the stove top.) Cool on waxed paper. Store in airtight jar. Great for gift giving.

A Thought for Today
"Do what you can, with what you have, where you are."
~Theodore Roosevelt

DECEMBER 14

Festive Holiday Greeting Card Holders
A KIDS IN THE KITCHEN CRAFT PROJECT

Today's kids in the kitchen project moves us out of the kitchen and into dad's workshop… where we are going to "do what we can with what we have" to make a really easy and festive holiday decoration.

MATERIALS
Childrens wooden, play-building blocks,
   the kind with letters and numbers and little animals painted on them. (Raid your room for no-longer-used blocks or better yet find aged-looking blocks at antique or thrift shops and garage sales. Choose bright colors and the letters that you will need to spell out a word or message.)
A vice and a hand saw (along with an adult's supervision)
Holiday greeting cards, as you receive them
Pencil
Ruler
Safety glasses

Select your blocks with a message in mind. For example you can spell out Ho Ho Ho, or Merry Christmas, or Happy Holidays, or Happy Hanukkah. Or maybe you'd like to spell out a name, such as Johnny or Mom or Dad.

Have an adult help you complete this process and do all the sawing. Put each little block into the vice and secure firmly. Put the letter portion facing you in the vice. With a pencil and a ruler, draw a line across the center of the block's top. Then gently saw across the top and down into the block, following your pencil line. Keep sawing until your slot is about ¾ inch deep, or you have reached about the middle of the block. Saw ever so slightly on the diagonal (this is optional). The saw blade itself will make the perfect width to hold a greeting card, in the slot that you have made. (Remember to wear safety goggles and keep both of your hands on the saw handle. The vice will hold the block steady as you saw. Do not attempt to use a power saw for this project.)

Arrange blocks on the mantel or a hall table or a bookshelf, spelling out the message you would like to say. As your holiday cards arrive, prop your favorites in the card holders and enjoy your display!

A Christmas Story...

SHARE THE MAGIC, BEHOLD THE WONDER

Last night I was sharing with my friends Christmas Stories and memories and traditions from my childhood, when it occurred to me that some of my favorite memories were not of gifts I had received but of gifts that I had given. I especially remember one Christmas when a very good friend's father was stricken too ill to go out and get a tree. He was a very proud man (and up north you went out into the woods and cut down your tree!) but he was now immobilized by MS, and his family's house was filled with sadness and concern.

My Mom (who didn't go out and cut down trees, but had hers delivered right to our door, by an old lumberjack who needed extra money too) ordered two trees that year. As soon as they were delivered we piled the largest one into my brother's truck and dashed over to our friend's house, caroling all the way. That was about 15 years ago and I can still feel the hugs and the tears and see the joy on the Dad's face. He said it was the most beautiful tree he'd ever seen. We stayed for some hot chocolate, helped position and admire the tree. Then we dashed home (caroling all the way) to decorate our own.

I hope each one of you takes the time to spread the joy of the season to someone outside of your family...be it ever so humble or ever so lavish...it will make you (and them) feel wonderful.

DECEMBER 15
Grandpa Jack's Sloppy Joes

Since we are decorating our tree tonight I want to keep my dinner simple. This easy recipe can be expanded or divided to serve the size of your family and no particular timing or gourmet-fussing is involved.

INGREDIENTS
1 pound ground beef (use a lean cut)
1 large onion, diced
½ cup BBQ sauce (your favorite flavor)
2 tablespoons brown sugar
Salt and pepper to taste
Good buns

Sauté the ground beef along with the onion until the beef is cooked thoroughly and the onion is soft. Drain off any excess fat. Add the remaining ingredients, cover with lid and simmer gently to meld flavors. Serve on good buns so your Sloppy Joes won't be too sloppy. Add potato chips and Lucile's Cole Slaw (see recipe index) for a complete meal.

RUSH HOUR WISDOM
Why not triple the batch so you have some ready made sandwiches for lunch or snacks over the busy holidays? Store in the freezer and pull out as needed. Everybody likes Sloppy Joes and they make a great hot lunch after sledding or skating or building that snowman. I also have a quick and easy sloppy joe recipe and chili recipe that can be made in the microwave at the www.rushhourcook.com website.

DECEMBER 16

Toffee Squares
3 dozen dainty cookies

It's time to start thinking about Treats for the Holidays...so today I'd better get started on my Christmas Cookies. I think I'll make some Toffee Squares and some Five Minute Fudge. When my mind gets focused on chocolate, The Rush Hour Cook doesn't mess around! Here are two sinfully rich (easy, but unfortunately caloric) recipes.

INGREDIENTS
1 cup butter, softened
1 cup brown sugar
1 egg yolk
1 teaspoon vanilla
2 cups flour
¼ teaspoon salt
6 standard size Hershey® bars, broken into segments
½ cup finely chopped walnuts (you can chop them in the blender)

Preheat your oven to 350 degrees. Cream together the softened butter, sugar, egg yolk, and vanilla. Blend in the flour and salt until you have a well incorporated dough. Do not over work the dough. Pat the dough into a Teflon® coated jelly roll pan. Bake at 350 degrees for 20 to 25 minutes.

Remove from oven and while still warm, immediately spread the broken Hershey® bars on top of the dough. Use a spatula and spread the melting chocolate all around to completely cover the cookies. Sprinkle on the finely crushed walnuts. Cut into squares while still warm. Make the squares small and dainty, because these cookies are very rich. Let cool before eating. Store in cookie tin between layers of waxed paper.

DECEMBER 17
Darlene's Five Minute Fudge
64 1-inch pieces

This recipe was entered as a favorite in *Frozen Assets Readers' Favorites*, with Deborah Taylor Hough, Champion Press Ltd. (www.championpress.com ISBN 1891400185).

INGREDIENTS
2/3 cup canned Carnation ® milk
1 2/3 cups sugar
½ teaspoon salt
1 ½ cups miniature marshmallows
1 ½ cups semisweet chocolate chips
1 teaspoon vanilla

Over medium heat bring milk, sugar, and salt to a boil. Cook 5 minutes, stirring constantly. Remove from heat. Add in the marshmallows, chocolate chips, and vanilla. Stir until all is melted and fudge is smooth. Pour into a buttered 8-inch square pan. Cool. Cut into -inch squares. Makes 64 candies. Once cooled, store between layers of waxed paper in an airtight container (in the fridge or the freezer).

RUSH HOUR VARIATION
Nuts may be added to this fudge recipe, but I prefer to not use them, keeping the fudge smooth and creamy, and oh so chocolate-y!

Weekly Challenge

THE ART OF THE CHRISTMAS COOKIE

Christmas cookies can seem like a daunting task, but follow a few Rush Hour Tips and your cookie making will be a breeze. Get out the camera and let the whole family join in. You will have plenty of scrapbook memories when you are done!

When making cookies be easy on yourself and don't overwork the dough! Better to under-mix than over-mix; too much handling and the dough will get tough.

When softening butter for creaming (i.e. blending and mixing, usually with sugar) don't let it get too soft, this can be tricky! You need the butter just soft enough to be able to mix it into the sugar to make a creamy, fluffy and smooth mixture. You don't want it melting, or overly softened before you start, because the creaming process won't work then. This is a kind of a bake and learn process and with a little practice you'll have it down perfect.

Also many cookie recipes benefit from chilling the dough after mixing and before rolling out. Follow your directions explicitly.

Let the whole family join in. Put on the aprons and get out the camera and have a ball. Especially when you are making cut-out sugar cookies! Let the sprinkles and Jimmies fly. I have such precious pictures of my daughter immersed from head to toe in cookie dough, flour, and decorations.

And remember, when you turn on the mixer to add the flour or powdered sugar...turn it on low! Or you will have flour and/or sugar all over the kitchen. (I speak from experience.)

Make your cookies and candies dainty and small. Then rather than picking up a huge, ooey gooey treat and feeling "committed" to eating the whole thing, in all its caloric glory, you can enjoy one small morsel instead... and then make the choice to have a second or third, or sample a different flavor. Your recipe (not your waist band) will stretch farther, your cookies will look prettier, and with a little restraint, so will you!

DECEMBER 18
Maple Butter

Today I'm going to hand the cooking over to my Mom, because although I can make this lovely treat it just doesn't taste as good as when she makes it—some things just need a mother's touch. This treat just absolutely has to be made every Christmas in our house.

INGREDIENTS
1 stick unsalted butter, left on the counter to arrive at room temperature and soften just right. (If the butter is too hard or too soft this recipe will not work.)
¼ teaspoon maple flavoring extract
4 teaspoons dark brown sugar
½ cup pure Maple syrup (Use the good stuff!)

With an electric mixer, mix the first 3 ingredients until very creamy and fluffy. Continue to mix while adding in the Maple syrup in a slow drizzle, until all is velvety smooth and perfectly blended. Store in a covered container in the refrigerator. This recipe works best made one batch at a time—do not double recipe. This butter is best served on warmed English muffins, crumpets, popovers, warm home baked bread or toast … letting it melt into all the nooks and crannies. It is too delicate for pancakes, waffles, or French toast.

RUSH HOUR VARIATION
This recipe also works well with fine quality fruit syrups such as Knott's Berry Farm ® Boysenberry Syrup or Blueberry Syrup. If using a fruit syrup change the sugar to light brown or white, the extract to vanilla, and follow the amounts and directions as above.

RUSH HOUR GIFT IDEA
Make up a pretty basket with a jar (or two) of the flavored butters, a package of good English Muffins, and some decorative napkins. Your recipient will be thrilled.

DECEMBER 19
Bernie's Bacon Bites

So far we have been talking a lot about sweets so today and tomorrow I want to switch to a couple of appetizers. Serve these to your guests and you'll be the hit of the party. Or make your own special occasion—serve pre-dinner (in the living room or den) with a relaxing drink of your choice and get caught up on the day. Then move to the table for the rest of your dinner. You will feel so pampered with your "aperitif-break" from your every day dinner routine. Here are two different recipes for two different nights. Again, each is so easy, but oh so good!

INGREDIENTS
Soft white bread slices, crusts removed
1 can of Cream of Mushroom Soup, left undiluted
Bacon slices (use standard, not extra thick)

Preheat your oven to 350 degrees. Spread each bread slice with cream of mushroom soup and roll up jelly roll fashion. Diagonally wrap a slice of bacon around each bread roll. With a sharp knife cut each roll into three bite-size pieces. Arrange on a non stick cookie sheet and bake at 350 degrees for 30 minutes. Drain and pat with paper towels. Serve warm.

RUSH HOUR TIP
You may want to secure each roll with 3 toothpicks before slicing into threes, but this is not necessary. Don't forget to remove the toothpicks after baking and before serving.

DECEMBER 20
Lucile's Beau Monde Stuffed Celery Sticks

INGREDIENTS
1 (6 ounce) block of cream cheese, softened
A scant bit of milk
2 ½ teaspoons Beau Monde ® Seasoning (You'll find this in the Spice Islands ®
  Seasonings Rack)
¼ teaspoon each: Thyme, Marjoram, and Savory
1 teaspoon crushed Parsley
1 bunch of fresh, crisp celery, or celery hearts

Mix the cream cheese and spices with just enough milk to make a spreadable filling. Wash and *de-vein the celery and cut each stalk into about 3 -inch pieces. Pipe or fill the celery with the cream cheese filling. Store in refrigerator until serving time. Serve cold.

RUSH HOUR TIP
Note: Celery stalks have tough, stringy veins running down their curved backs. With a knife, carefully pare off the veins—they will pull off like string. Discard. This process is especially important on the larger stalks. Once you get into the hearts (the tender, center stalks) this is not important.

RUSH HOUR TRIVIA
Did you know that you spend more calories chewing celery than you consume while eating it?

A Christmas Story...

THE LOAF OF BREAD

My mother has told me this story (more than once) about a darling woman for whom she had gotten a last-minute holiday-airfare, so that the woman could afford to travel to be with her elderly mother. The next day it began to snow, those real heavy, Christmassy snow flakes and the view outside the Travel Agency's window was getting prettier and prettier and blusterier and blusterier as well. In walked the woman all bundled from head to toe and covered with snow, with a brown bag wrapped in a scarf and cradled in her arm. She had just come from her home with a gift of freshly baked bread, still warm from the oven in spite of her 3 or 4 block walk. The bread smelled so good and as soon as she entered, its holiday aroma filled the office. She literally made my mother's day! My mother also received many other gifts from clients, but it was the simple loaf of bread and the woman's walk through the snow that she remembers best.

DECEMBER 21

An Audubon Tree
A KIDS IN THE KITCHEN CRAFT PROJECT

Now that it's getting blustery and snowy outside, let's make a festive tree for our outdoor friends. See how many different birds you can identify as they come to enjoy your buffet of offerings. For your Audubon Tree you will need some (or as many) as you wish of the following:

INGREDIENTS
Peanut butter
Congealed bacon grease (you can save this in a can in the refrigerator—
    have your mom do that whenever she cooks bacon)
Nuts
Raisins
Bird seed
Bread crumbs
Popcorn and cranberries
Bagels
Pinecones
Halved apples and oranges
Indian corn
String
Wire coat hangers
A tree in your back yard

Smear bagels and pinecones with peanut butter or bacon grease and roll to coat with a variety of birdseed, crushed nuts, breadcrumbs and/or chopped raisins. Tie the pinecones or bagels with string and hang like ornaments from the branches of a tree in your yard. Watch the chickadees and cardinals flutter among the edible ornaments. Make a garland with the popcorn and cranberries, string and hang that on the tree as well. The apples and oranges should be cut in half and skewered through the middle with a wire hanger (you can even bend a perch on the bottom of the hanger). Add these to the tree and watch the wood peckers and nuthatches peck away at the fruit. Put out any Indian corn that you have leftover from fall for the squirrels and blue jays. Be sure to pick a strategic tree so that you can watch all the action from a convenient window. And hang the edible ornaments high out of reach of any stray cat that might come cruising through! This gift is "for the birds."

RUSH HOUR BONUS PROJECT

Make a journal about all the wildlife that you see. You might even be able to make a report or school project for extra credit. Repeat next Christmas and see which birds come back or which new ones find your treats; remember to compare notes in your journal. Which birds do you like best? Which are the funniest? Which are the meanest? Which are the shyest? This would also be a good 4-H or scouting project.

Weekly Challenge

A CAROLING PARTY

Why not have a Caroling Party and spread the Christmas Spirit throughout your neighborhood? Round up a bunch of your friends and make the rounds of your neighborhood. You'll be amazed at how many people will come to their door to hear your song and if you're lucky some will even offer refreshments along the way. You don't have to be a trained singer to belt out a song or two and people are so appreciative of the 'old fashioned' entertainment you've provided them. When you are cold and your voices have given out, return to your house for a buffet of Cheese Strata or a big pot of Chili, followed by Rosette Christmas Cookies, Five Minute Fudge, and Warm Cranberry Tea (all recipes found in this book).

DECEMBER 22
Cheese Strata
4 to 6 servings

This is an easy, cheesy, and tasty recipe that can be made in advance and served for either a light dinner, or for a Holiday brunch, or Christmas morning breakfast.

INGREDIENTS
6 slices of bread, buttered and cubed, divided in half
1½ cups shredded Cheddar cheese, divided in half
3 to 4 eggs
1½ to 2 cups milk
½ to 1 teaspoon dry mustard (optional)
Dash of cayenne
½ teaspoon salt
1 tablespoon Worcestershire

Place one half of the buttered bread cubes in a buttered casserole or baking dish. Sprinkle on one half of the shredded Cheddar cheese. Repeat these two layers with remaining bread and cheese. In a separate bowl beat the eggs, milk and spices until well blended; then pour over the layers in the casserole dish. Cover and let stand all day or overnight in the refrigerator. This recipe works very well for assemble-ahead convenience. At time of cooking remove from refrigerator while oven is preheating and let sit at room temperature, just to take the chill out of the dish (This is important especially if you have doubled the recipe—as larger and colder amounts take longer to cook through.) Bake in a pre-heated 325-degree oven for 50 to 55 minutes, or until strata is set. Let stand 10 minutes before cutting into wedges and serving.

RUSH HOUR VARIATIONS
There are many options that you could add to this recipe to change the taste and please all palates. Try sprinkling in some sun dried tomatoes and/or black and green olives. Sautéed mushrooms and/or onions are good too. Crumbled cooked sausage or bacon or cubed ham can turn your strata into even a heartier dish. Or you could make one of each!

Try topping the casserole with grated Parmesan or crushed chips or crushed cornflakes and a drizzle of melted butter for a yummy, crunchy topping.

DECEMBER 23

Christmas Rosettes

There are some Christmas Cookies that do not store well and are best if eaten the day they are made. Christmas Rosettes are one of these cookies. Freshly made these delicate snowflake shapes, sprinkled with powdered sugar, literally melt in your mouth. They are a challenge, and require some practice, but are well worth the effort (however I have to admit I do let my mother tackle these).

BEFORE YOU BEGIN
For this recipe you will need 2 to 3 specific pieces of equipment before you start.

1. A Rosette Iron (this specialty item may be found in most culinary departments or cooking stores and even at old fashioned hardware stores, such as Ace Hardware®)
2. Something in which to deep fry or heat up at least an inch of cooking oil (a sturdy deep pot, Dutch oven, deep fryer, or electric skillet)
3. A cooking thermometer would be handy but not absolutely necessary

INGREDIENTS
2 eggs, slightly beaten (do not over-beat)
1 tablespoon powdered sugar
¼ teaspoon salt
1 cup sifted flour
1 cup milk (add both the flour and milk alternately in small amounts, blending well each addition)
¼ teaspoon vanilla
Additional powdered sugar when cookies are done

PROCEDURE
Blend ingredients (except for additional powdered sugar) to make a smooth, rich batter. (Your batter should be similar to popover batter when correctly mixed.) Heat cooking oil to 365 degrees and place the rosette iron in the hot fat till well heated. Dip the heated iron into the batter (being careful to not overlap the top of the iron) and then immerse completely in the hot oil. Brown for 25 to 30 seconds and slip off the iron onto paper towels to drain. Repeat process with each cookie (i.e. heat iron, carefully dip in batter, cook quickly to golden brown and drain on paper towel). You might have to make a "test cookie" or two (that flop) before everything reaches the right temperature and you arrive at success. Once cooled dust the Rosettes with powdered sugar to look like snow flakes.

RUSH HOUR NOTES

These cookies are very fragile and are best if eaten the day they are made, but they can be stored in an airtight tin for 2 to 3 days if necessary.

Cook's note* If batter drops from iron, the fat is too hot. If rosettes are soft, they've cooked too quickly. If the batter "blisters," the eggs have been over-beaten. Don't forget to preheat the iron in the oil before dipping into batter, each time. These cookies are a little tricky but with a little practice you will be able to gauge the procedure very quickly and every one will absolutely love the results!

A Thought for Today
INSTANT CHRISTMAS CARDS

Take the time to keep in touch with all your valued friends. It's too late to mail out cards through the postal system, but the internet provides many greeting card sites to find everything from clever and entertaining to thoughtful and sentimental electronic cards. So get yourself a cup of tea and a couple Christmas cookies, kick back and peruse the web. You will find that many of these sites offer a selection of free cards, outside of their membership collection. You can type the words 'greeting cards' into your search engine and many sites will list automatically.

A few that I have used are:
www.flowgo.com
www.americangreetings.com
www.bluemountain.com
www.123greetings.com

DECEMBER 24
The Rush Hour Cook's Christmas Eve Chili
served with Caleb's Beer Bread

Well here it is, Christmas Eve. The presents are wrapped, the stockings are hung, the groceries have been bought and the family is gathering. For Christians, tonight becomes one of our holiest of nights as the snow begins to fall and the world becomes blanketed with peace and reflection. Homes and hearths all over the world take pause to rejoice in their religious beliefs, unity of family and time-long traditions, passed down from generation to generation. For a few moments we enjoy a balance of beauty and grace, humility and peace, brotherhood and compassion. As my family gathers around me, let me remember to carry on the qualities of Christmas far beyond the date of December 25.

My mom started this Christmas Eve recipe when Caleb and I went off to college. Our holiday visits home were so short and so concentrated that none of us wanted to spend our time being a slave to the kitchen and a full turkey dinner...so we started our great chili contest and arrived at the following recipe. We all loved chili, we all threw in our "two cents worth" and the rest of the time was spent relaxing and laughing and visiting. Add a loaf of freshly baked (from your grocery) French Bread and a nice salad.

I am married now and have a family of my own. My brother passed away 8 years ago and my mom now comes to my house for Christmas. We still carry on our family's tradition of making chili, and always at least a double batch. Tucked away in her recipe box, Mom found a recipe for a hunting-camp style bread that Caleb used to make, so this year we are going to add his hearty Beer Bread to our menu (see bonus recipe).

This recipe may be doubled or tripled as necessary.

INGREDIENTS
For the base:
1 pound lean ground beef, browned
1 medium onion, chopped and browned with meat
2 cloves garlic, mashed or minced, sautéed with meat
1 (14.5 ounce) can of Mexican-style stewed tomatoes
1 small can tomato paste
½ teaspoon cumin
¼ teaspoon salt

Add as many and as much as you like:
1 (14 ounce) can sweet corn
1 (14.5 ounce) can kidney beans
1 tablespoon red pepper flakes
1/8 cup jarred jalapenos (juice included if you like it hot)
   or 1 to 2 fresh jalapenos, seeded and diced (wear gloves when
   handling peppers and wash hands immediately when done)
1 red bell pepper, seeded and chopped
1 green bell pepper, seeded and chopped
3 tablespoons chili powder
1 tablespoon oregano
1 tablespoon crushed basil
1 tablespoon Cajun spice mix or Chili mix

Choose one or two:
1 cup red wine
1 bottle beer
1 cup coffee
1 cup beef broth

Choose one or two "Secret Ingredients:"
1 tablespoon brown sugar
1 tablespoon granulated sugar
3 Hershey Kisses® or 2 tablespoons chocolate chips or 1 tablespoon
   cocoa
1 teaspoon instant coffee
1/4 teaspoon cinnamon

Remember you are choosing all your add-ons in relation to the original base recipe. If you triple the base, you must triple or at least double your add-ons. Each year your chili will taste a little different as each cook adds their favorites to the pot.

RUSH HOUR WISDOM
We like to serve our chili quite spicy over hot white rice (use instant) and/or cooked elbow macaroni. The bland pasta and/or rice offer a nice contrast to the hot spicyness of the chili itself. The true key to the whole thing is the addition of some chocolate and/or coffee and/or cinnamon, for a truly south of the border taste. And people love trying to guess the secret ingredient!

Caleb's Beer Bread

I loaf of rustic, peasant-style bread.

INGREDIENTS
3 cups self rising flour* (this recipe will only work with self-rising flour)
3 tablespoons sugar
I can of standard beer

Mix thoroughly. Spread into a greased loaf pan. Bake at 350 degrees for I hour. Serve with your favorite chili.

RUSH HOUR WISDOM

When is bread done? Before taking your bread out of the oven and out of the pan, tap on the top of the loaf. You should get a sort of hollow sound and the top crust should be sturdy feeling.

Kitchen Potpurri

Kitchen Potpourri is easy to make and a delight to have filtering throughout the house. Make a simmering pot on your back burner of your stove with some water and oranges studded with cloves and cinnamon sticks. Slowly let the pot simmer on a cold winter day to infuse your house with spicy aromas and a little extra humidity. Your slow cooker can also be utilized in this fashion. Just keep an eye on either pot and add more water when necessary. If using a crockery-pot slow cooker I would perhaps keep one just for this purpose ... as you don't want your food tasting like potpourri. Whether it's the Christmas Season, or just a rainy, damp day during May Showers, you can fill your house with the enticing aromas of kitchen potpourri.

A Thought for Today
"A wise man makes more opportunities than he finds."
~Francis Bacon, Philosopher

DECEMBER 25

This year make your Christmas Breakfast special (and leave the dinner to someone else!) There is nothing more luxurious than nibbling away on a wonderful Christmas Brunch while opening presents and visiting around the tree with family and friends. So this year why not try a special Christmas Breakfast and leave the Christmas Dinner to Aunt Sally or your favorite restaurant? Even the grocery stores have Christmas "dinners-to-go" from the deli. The following menu offers holiday elegance with the greatest of ease and very tasty results. If you are in charge of hosting the holiday dinner meal, stop by www.rushhourcook.com to find my complete dinner menu with shopping list.

The Rush Hour Cook's Menu for Christmas Breakfast

MENU
Champagne Mimosas and/or Homemade Eggnog (see recipes that follow)
Pitchers of orange juice, apple juice and/or cranberry juice
Broiled Grapefruit (see recipe index)
And/or
Fruit Cup Ambrosia (see recipe index)
Cheese Strata(see recipe index)
And/or
Brunch-Style Eggs in Canadian Bacon Cups (see recipe index)
And/or
Mother's Scalloped Potatoes (see recipe that follows)
Assorted Sweet Rolls and Bakery Items from your Local Bakery
Cranberry Tea (See recipe that follows)
Coffee
Assorted Christmas Cookies
Candy Canes and Old Fashioned Ribbon Candy

Champagne Mimosas

INGREDIENTS
Simply pour equal amounts of champagne and orange juice into long stemmed glasses. (Or pour champagne over scoops of frozen orange juice concentrate.) Can add a dash of Kirsch if you have it.

Homemade Eggnog

INGREDIENTS
6 eggs, separated (Beat yolks till creamy. Beat whites till stiff.)
Beat ½ cup sugar into the yolks.
Beat ¼ cup sugar into the stiff whites.

Fold both together to form the basis of the drink. Then fold in the remaining ingredients in order given:

1 cup heavy cream (such as whipping cream)
3 ½ cups milk
1 cup Bourbon
2 tablespoons rum

Serve chilled in little cups. (*Note the eggs in this recipe are not cooked.)

Fruit Cup Ambrosia

Arrange fresh orange and grapefruit slices in your fanciest stemware. Sprinkle with freshly grated coconut. Garnish with a stemmed maraschino cherry.

Mother's Scalloped Potatoes
8 servings

INGREDIENTS
4 large potatoes, peeled, thinly sliced and boiled in water for 5 minutes. Drain.
1 onion, thinly sliced (optional)
½ pound Gruyere or Swiss cheese, thinly sliced from the deli
Salt and pepper
Dijon mustard, to taste
1 cup dry white wine, milk, water, or chicken broth
½ cup dried bread crumbs
½ cup Parmesan cheese.
Butter

Preheat oven to 350 degrees and butter a shallow glass baking dish. Place 1/3 of the potatoes on the bottom of the casserole. Top with a layer of sliced Gruyere or Swiss cheese. Lightly add some mustard, a sprinkle of onions and salt and pepper to taste. Repeat the layers, ending with final 1/3 of potatoes on top. Sprinkle on the wine, water, milk, or broth. Top with bread crumbs and Parmesan cheese. Dot with butter and bake covered for 40 minutes, then uncovered for 15 minutes more.

Cranberry Tea

INGREDIENTS
8 cups water
4 tea bags
1½ cups sugar
1 cup orange juice
½ cup lemon juice
1 quart cranberry juice

Boil 8 cups of water. Remove from heat and steep with 4 standard tea bags to make tea. When tea has steeped, remove tea bags, and add remaining ingredients. Tea may be served warm or cold.

Candy Canes

Purchase Red and White Peppermint Candy Canes and display on the table in a lovely crystal compote by the coffee and tea. People who use sugar in their coffee or tea can use the candy canes for stirrers, rather than sugar and a spoon, if they so wish.

Old Fashioned Ribbon Candy

Also display an arrangement of delicately swirled Ribbon Candy in a clear glass container. Not only will this make a beautiful decoration, but will add to your menu of sweets as well.

Assorted Christmas Cookies

Pull out all the stops! Make a decorative arrangement with all those delicate confections you've been making, or have been given. Get out a silver platter and line it with doilies or a tea napkin. The cookies, along with the candy canes and ribbon candy will make an impressive ending to your wonderful meal.

A Thought for Today

"I will honor Christmas in my heart, and try to keep it all the year."
~Charles Dickens

As we move from the enjoyment of Christmas to the ushering-in of a brand new year, let us remember all that we are thankful for, all that we have enjoyed, and all that is yet to come. Allow yourself time to relax today and to take stock of how full and wonderful this last year has been. Think about the positives and how they've outweighed the negatives.

Start thinking about what you want to accomplish in the upcoming year. What short-term goals and what longer-term goals do you see for your family?

DECEMBER 26

A KIDS IN THE KITCHEN DAY
PIZZA AND THANK YOU NIGHT

Today "all the cooks" are on vacation! Call out for Pizza! Have your children write thank you notes for gifts received from distant friends or relatives that couldn't join you for the holidays. Take the time to touch base with those you love and thank them for their thoughtfulness. Be creative. Design the cards with crayon drawings or stamping or cut outs. Grandparents especially love a hand-made note, along with an updated picture or two. Take your time and use your best penmanship. For those of you for which it is appropriate, write Santa a thank you letter. Every year we make sure he gets our "wish list," but how many of us remember to thank him afterward? I know you left cookies and milk, but I bet he'd really appreciate a thank you note too. Have your mom or dad mail it for you and won't Mr. Claus be surprised that you took the time and made the effort to write to him personally.

Weekly Challenge

"What three things do you want to accomplish this coming year? Write them down and place them on your refrigerator for inspiration all year long." ~Brook Noel

Think about three opportunities you can "make" to enhance the lives and goals of your family for this coming New Year. They don't have to be monumental ideas, but just something that can change your life or a situation for the better.

A simple idea might be rearranging the mudroom closet (with a lower shelf and some lower hooks) so "little people" can hang up their coats with ease (rather than dropping them on the floor or hitching them over the back of a dining room chair for you to hang up). An afternoon spent remodeling the mudroom, or an entry hall closet, will lead to a year's worth of order and neatness, less frustration for you, and time saved in the years to come.

What about starting today to save for a child's future, a college education, or some major item on your wish list (like, say a new car)? A complex goal, but one that can be tackled simply by every night placing your pocket's worth of change in a jar. If you spend paper money (rather than credit card money) during the day save all of that changefor the jar.

Another simple act? Reaching for that candy bar while waiting in the checkout line, or the bag of chips, or the can of soda? Put it back. You don't really need it. Right there you've saved yourself a couple of bucks and more than a couple of calories!

Starting a diet for the New Year? Don't treat it as a mad-dash-marathon to exclude everything from your culinary habits, lose 10 pounds in a week, and melt cellulite away in two. only to experience some short-lived program of denial, deprivation, and delusion. Another unsuccessful diet down the tubes. Instead, why don't you try eating half of what's on your plate, saving the rest for lunch the next day? Dressing a salad? Put on half the usual amount of dressing. Topping a sundae? Put on half the syrup and nuts that you usually would. In other words, eat what you normally like to eat, but only eat half. Also eat more slowly, enjoying each bite. Take twice as long to eat half as much. You'll be less likely to cheat or abandon your plan because you are still partaking in the pleasures of eating what you like. Add a brisk walk to your daily routine (the dog will like this too) and pretty soon you'll notice you've begun to lose weight, tone muscle, and well, "you'll just feel lighter…and better." By springtime you will be well on your way to a healthy lifestyle of eating and a trimmer you without the strict deprivation and calorie counting of a diet that takes a rocket scientist to calculate and an army sargeant to administer.

DECEMBER 28

Wendy Louise's Bistro Pound Cake
6 servings

Rich and elegant, this dessert approaches the level of sinful. Can be enjoyed any time of day along with a strong coffee. (Just remember your half-sizes rule!)

6 (¾ -inch) slices of store bought pound cake
2 eggs
4 tablespoons whole milk or cream (such as half-and-half)
Butter to coat bottom of skillet
Strawberry sauce or preserves, or fruit preserves of choice (such as apricot or cherry conserves) at room temperature
Sour cream, whipped cream, or crème fraiche

Beat egg and milk, or cream, together to blend. As if you were making "French toast," dip pound cake slices in egg mixture to coat. Gently sauté in heated butter till golden brown, turning once. Serve warm, topped with strawberry sauce or your favorite fruit preserves. Garnish with whipped cream, sour cream, or crème fraiche. Accompany with full-bodied, after-dinner coffee or espresso.

DECEMBER 29
Turkey-Veggie Meatloaf
6 servings

This recipe is a great way to get the fiber and vitamins you need from vegetables and oats. It is also packed with protein. You can pour ketchup on top before baking.

INGREDIENTS
1 ½ pounds ground turkey breast
1 (10 ounce) package frozen chopped spinach, thawed and all water squeezed out
1 cup rolled oats
½ cup onions, chopped
1 clove garlic, chopped
½ cup carrots or red bell pepper, chopped
2 egg whites
1/3 cup skim milk
1½ teaspoons Italian seasoning
½ teaspoon salt
¼ teaspoon black pepper

Preheat oven to 350 degrees. In a large bowl, mix all ingredients. Gently press meat loaf mixture into a 9 x 5-inch greased loaf pan. Bake for 45 to 50 minutes or until juices run clear.

The Winter Sun
Planning any outdoor activities over the holidays? Maybe you're going to try out those new skis, or that new snowboard...or perhaps you are sailing, or hiking, or sky diving, or fishing...or maybe you are just outside shoveling the driveway. Don't forget your sunblock, lotion, and sunglasses. The winter sun still casts its harmful rays. The winter winds still dry your skin. And the winter reflection of sun off of snow (or water) makes eye protection a necessity. Be sure to continue your use of a sunscreen with a full spectrum block of at least 15 followed by a good quality lotion. Throw a lip balm in your pocket or backpack, and invest in a good pair of UV protection sunglasses to lesson winter's glare.

DECEMBER 30

Mikey's Really Good German Pot Roast
8 servings

This recipe requires some overnight preparation and all-day cooking the next day.

INGREDIENTS
1 (4 pound) beef brisket, trim off the fat and reserve
2 teaspoons McCormick's Season-All®
1 teaspoon ground ginger
1 garlic clove, smashed
1/2 teaspoon dry mustard
2 cups red wine vinegar
1 cup water
2 onions, quartered
2 bay leaves
2 teaspoons mixed pickling spices
1 teaspoon whole black peppercorns
8 whole cloves
1/2 cup sugar
2 teaspoons vegetable oil
6 ginger snaps, crushed

Rub meat with Season-All®, ginger, and garlic clove. Place in large bowl. In a saucepan combine remaining ingredients, except trimmed fat and ginger snaps. Bring to a boil and pour over meat. Cool, cover tightly, and place in refrigerator overnight to marinate. Remove meat and save the marinade. Pat the roast dry with a paper towel. Heat the fat in a heavy skillet until it is sizzling. Carefully sear the roast on all sides. Place in slow cooker. Pour the reserved marinade over the roast. Cover with lid and cook on low setting for 8-10 hours, or until meat is fork tender. Remove roast to serving platter and slice. Serve with spatzle or buttered noodles and gravy made from the cooking juices.

A Thought for Today
"Do not wait for extraordinary circumstances to do good; try to use ordinary situations" ~Jean Paul Richter

DECEMBER 31

Fancy Bourbon Steaks
4 servings

This recipe is fancy, yet easy, elegant, and perfect for New Year's Eve. The recipe is written to make 4 servings. Add a salad and freshly baked stuffed crescent rolls (see recipe index) and you have an elegant meal. Follow with a luscious dessert of remaining Christmas cookies and Champagne while you watch the ball drop in Times Square at midnight.

INGREDIENTS
4 slices of beef tenderloin
Butter
Salt and pepper to taste
2 teaspoons Worcestershire
½ cup warm bourbon* (see Rush Hour Wisdom)
1 cup brown sauce
4 teaspoons Dijon-style mustard
4 teaspoons sour cream
Cooked egg noodles at serving time

In a skillet, sauté the slices of beef tenderloin quickly in the butter. Season with salt and freshly cracked black pepper and Worcestershire sauce to taste. Warm the bourbon in a ladle and pour* (see tip) over the steaks, ignite to burn off the alcohol. Transfer the steaks to a warm platter and hold in a 200-degree oven while you finish the sauce. To the pan juices add the brown sauce, mustard, and sour cream mixing well and carefully bring just to a boil* (see tip). Pour the sauce over the steaks and serve with hot, buttered egg noodles on the side.

RUSH HOUR WISDOM
*When pouring an alcohol or wine into a sauté pan, never, never pour the liquor directly from the bottle into the pan! You risk explosion of the bottle and major burns from the flames. You are literally holding a bottle rocket over the stove! Always pour the measured amount needed from a small cup or ladle. Another good idea is to flambé the alcohol in a long handled ladle and gently pour it into the cooking dish while flaming. When finishing sauces with sour cream, heavy cream and/or dairy products you want to be careful to not boil the sauce, causing the cream to curdle. The curdling isn't harmful but it does jeopardize the aesthetic quality of the sauce. If it is your preference the bourbon can be replaced with a substitution of tea or broth or water.

A Thought for Today
PAUSE TO REFLECT

"Enjoy the little things,
for one day you may look back
and realize they were the big things."

Rush Hour Index

ENTREES (CHICKEN):

ENTREES (PASTA):

Entrees (Fish /Seafood):

Beer-Batter for Fried Fish 185
Colorful Shrimp and Scallop Kabobs
Sindi's Salmon 150
Shrimp de Jonghe 36
Super-Fast Salmon 26
Tuna Melt Sandwiches 62

Entrees (Pork/Ham):

Brown Sugar Chops 302
Casual-Night-Sandwich-Dinner 334
Cal-Zoned Out 170
Cranberry Crock Pork Roast 308
Crocks Chops and Potatoes 301
Home Made Corn Dogs 42
Ham Slice Dinner 72
Hammy Noodles in a Flash 181
Mambone's Pork Chops 32
Mom's Easy as 1-2-3 Pork Roast 305
Mom's Ham and Broccoli Roll-Ups 200
Pork Chop Casserole 306
Pork Chop and Sweet Potato Casserole 37
Rustic Pork Chop Casserole 38
The Monte Cristo Sandwich 64
The Bachelor's Perfect Pork Roast 147

Entrees (Turkey/Poultry):

B-L-Turkey Roll-Ups 255
Cozumel Turkey or Chicken Quesadillas 257
Leftover Turkey Bake 352
Next Day Classic Turkey Club Sandwich 351
Oven Roasted Cornish Hens 258
The Whitehall Sandwich Served with Mornay Sauce 65
Turkey Meat Loaves 256
Turkey-Veggie Meatloaf 395

Entrees (Cheese):

Green and Gold Cornbread Casserole 238
Rush Hour Quick Quesadilla Bites 168
Tomato Provolone Casserole 279
The Cheesiest Grilled Cheese Ever 356
Vickie's Cheesy Hashbrown Casserole 107

SIDE DISHES: SALADS

SIDE DISHES: FRUIT

SIDE DISHES: VEGETABLES

SIDE DISHES: MOLDS

APPETIZERS:

BREADS:

SOUPS:

WEEKLY CHALLENGES: (IN CHRONOLOGICAL ORDER)

COOL ONLINE FINDS:

INDEX, CHARTS & REFERENCES

WEIGHTS AND MEASURES

A dash = less than ⅛ teaspoon
4 tablespoons = 1/4 cup
1/2 cup = 8 tablespoons
1/2 pint = 1 cup
4 quarts = 1 gallon
8 ounces = 1/2 pound
16 ounces = 1 pound
64 ounces = 1/2 gallon
1 quart = .95 liter

3 teaspoons = 1 tablespoon
1/3 cup = 5 tablespoons + 1 teaspoon
2/3 cup = 10 tablespoons + 2 teaspoons
1 quart = 4 cups
8 ounces = 1 cup liquid
16 ounces = 2 pints or ½ quart liquid
32 ounces = 1 quart
1 liter = 1.06 quarts

TEMPERATURE
FAHRENHEIT/CELSIUS(IN DEGREES)

Fahrenheit	Celsius
32	0
212	100
250	120
275	140
300	150
325	160
350	180
375	190
400	200
425	220
450	230
475	240
500	260

BAKING PAN SIZES

American	Metric
8x1 ½-inch round	20x4cm cake tin
9x1 ½-inch round	23x3.5cm cake tin
11x7x1 ½ inch baking pan	28x18x4cm baking tin
13x9x2-inch baking pan	30x20x3cm baking tin
2 quart rectangular dish	30x20x3cm baking tin
15x10x2-inch baking pan	30x25x2cm baking tin
9-inch pie plate	22x4 or 23x4cm pie plate
7 or 8-inch spring form pan	9x5x3-inch loaf pan
1 ½ quart casserole	1.5 liter casserole
2 quart casserole	2 liter casserole

YIELDS AND EQUIVALENTS

Apple	1 medium, chopped=about 1 cup
	3 medium=1 pound or 2 and 3/4 cups, sliced
Bacon	½ cup crumbled=8 slices crisply cooked
Bananas	3 large or 4 small=2 cups sliced or 1 1/3 cups mashed
Beans, dried	1 cup =2and 1/4 to 2 and 1/2 cups cooked
Beef, cooked	1 cup 1/2 inch pieces=5 ounces
Butter	1 ounce butter=2 tablespoons
	1 stick butter=1/4 pound or 8 ounces
	1 cup butter=2 sticks or 1/2 pound
Celery	2 medium stalks=2/3 to 3/4 cup
Cheese	1 pound=4 cups shredded
	1 cup shredded=1/4 pound
	2 cups cottage cheese=16 ounces
	6 tablespoons cream cheese=3 ounces
Cherries	1/2 pound=1 cup pitted
Chocolate	1 ounce=1 square
	1 cup chips=6 ounces
Cranberries	1 cup fresh makes 1 cup sauce
	1 pound=4 cups
Crumbs	1 cup cracker crumbs=28 saltine crackers
	1 cup graham cracker crumbs=14 square graham crackers
	1 cup cracker crumbs=24 rich round crackers
	1 cup bread crumbs=soft 1 and 1/2 slices or dry 4 slices
	1 cup vanilla wafer crumbs=22 wafers
	1 cup chocolate wafer crumbs=19 wafers
Eggs	1 cup=4 large eggs
	1/2 cup liquid egg substitute=1 egg
	1 cup egg yolks=10 to 12 egg yolks
	1 cup egg whites=8 to 10 egg whites
Garlic	1 clove fresh=1/2 teaspoon chopped or ⅛ teaspoon garlic powder
Grapes	1 pound=2 cups halved
Green Pepper	1 large=1 cup diced
Herbs	1 tablespoon fresh, snipped=1 teaspoon dried or ½ teaspoon ground
Lemon	Juice of 1 lemon=3 tablespoons
	grated peel of 1 lemon=about 1 teaspoon
Lettuce	6 cups bite-size pieces=1-pound head
Macaroni	1 to 1 and 1/4 cups=4 ounces or 2 to 2 and 1/2 cups
	Cooked --16 ounces=about 8 cups cooked
Marshmallows	10 miniature=1 large
	1 cup=11 large
Mushrooms (Fresh)	8 ounces= 2 and 1/2 cups sliced or 1 cup cooked
	1 cup sliced and cooked=4 ounce can, drained
Mustard	1 teaspoon dry=1 tablespoon prepared
Nuts	1 cup chopped=1/4 pound or 4 ounces
	1 cup whole or halved= 4 to 5 ounces
Oats	1 and 3/4 cups cooked=1 cup raw
Olives	24 small=2 ounces=about ½ cup sliced
Onions	1 medium, chopped= ½ cup
	1 medium=1 teaspoon onion powder or 1 tablespoon dried minced
Orange	Juice of one orange=1/3 to 1/2 cup
	Grated peel of 1 orange=2 tablespoons

Peaches/Pears	1 medium=1/2 cup sliced
Potatoes	3 medium=2 cups sliced or cubed
	3 medium=1 and 3/4 mashed
Rice	1 cup white rice(long grain)=about 7 ounces=3 to 4 cups cooked
	1 cup white rice(instant)=2 cups cooked
	1 cup brown rice=3 cups cooked
	1 cup wild rice=3 to 4 cups cooked
	1 pound cooked wild rice=2 2/3 cup dry
Sour cream	1 cup=8 ounces
Spaghetti and Noodles	
	8 ounces=4 cups cooked
	1 pound=8 cups cooked
Strawberries	1 quart=2 cups sliced
Sugar	Powdered / 4 cups=1 pound
	Brown / 2 and 1/4 cups, packed=1 pound
	Granulated / 2 cups=1 pound
Tomatoes	1 cup canned=1 1/3 cups fresh, cut up
Whipping Cream	1 cup=2 cups whipped
Yeast	1 package=2 and 1/4 teaspoons regular or quick active dry

EMERGENCY SUBSTITUTIONS

Baking Powder:	1 teaspoon=1/2 teaspoon cream of tartar plus 1/4 teaspoon baking soda
Balsamic Vinegar:	Sherry or cider vinegar
Beer:	Apple juice or beef broth
Broth:	1 teaspoon granulated or 1 cube bouillon dissolved in one cup water
Brown Sugar, Packed:	Equal amount of granulated sugar
Buttermilk:	1 teaspoon lemon juice or vinegar plus milk to make 1 cup; let stand 5 minutes
Cajun Seasoning:	Equal parts white pepper, black pepper, ground red pepper, onion powder, garlic powder and paprika
Chocolate:	1 square, unsweetened:3 tablespoons cocoa plus 1 tablespoon butter. For 1 square semisweet: 1 square unsweetened+1 tablespoon sugar For 2 squares, semisweet: 1/3 cup semisweet chips
Corn Syrup:	For light or dark: 1 cup + 1/4 cup water For dark:1 cup light corn syrup or 1 cup maple syrup or 3/4 light corn syrup + 1/4 cup molasses
Cornstarch:	For 1 tablespoon: 2 tablespoons all-purpose flour
Cream of Mushroom	For one can: 1 cup thick white sauce + 4 ounce can mushrooms, drained and chopped
Eggs:	For 1 egg: 2 egg whites or 2 egg yolks or 1/4 cup liquid egg substitute
Flour: Cake flour:	1 cup minus 2 tablespoons all-purpose flour. Self-rising: 1 cup all-purpose flour + 1 teaspoon baking powder and 1/2 teaspoon salt.
Honey:	1 and 1/4 cup sugar +1/4 cup water
Leeks:	Equal amounts green onions or shallots
Lemon Juice:	For 1 teaspoon: 1 teaspoon cider vinegar or white vinegar
Milk:	½ cup evaporated(not condensed) milk plus 1/2 cup water
Molasses:	Equal amount honey
Mushrooms:	For 1 cup cooked: 4 ounce can, drained
Poultry Seasoning:	For 1 teaspoon: 3/4 teaspoon sage + 1/4 teaspoon thyme
Pumpkin Pie Spice:	For 1 teaspoon:1/2 teaspoon cinnamon + 1/4 t teaspoon ground ginger + ⅛ teaspoon ground allspice + ⅛ teaspoon ground nutmeg
Red Pepper Sauce:	4 drops=⅛ teaspoon ground cayenne(red) pepper
Sour Cream:	equal amount of plain yogurt
Tomato sauce:	For 2 cups sauce: 3/4 cups paste + 1and 1/4 cup water
Wine: For white:	apple juice, apple cider, white grape juice, chicken or vegetable broth, water.
For red:	apple cider, chicken, beef or vegetable broth, water.
Yogurt:	equal amounts of sour cream

FREEZER STORAGE

Breads, Baked	2 to 3 months
Cakes	3 to 4 months
Cookies	3 to 4 months
Dairy Products:	
Butter or Margarine	9 to 12 months
Cottage Cheese	3 months
Cream	1 to 4 months
Hard Natural Cheese	6 months
Processed Cheese	months
Soft cheese	6 months
Yogurt	1 to 2 months
Eggs:	
Whole eggs	Do not freeze
Egg yolks (cover in water)	1 year
Egg whites	1 year
Egg substitute	1 year
Fruits/Juices	8 to 12 months
Meats:	
Beef, roasts or steaks	6 to 12 months
Beef, ground	3 months
Beef, stew meat	3 to 6 months
Lamb	6 to 9 months
Pork, roast or chops	3 to 6 months
Pork, ground	2 months
Veal	6 to 9 months
Cured meat, ham or bacon	1 to 2 months
Hot dogs	1 to 2 months
Sausages	2 to 3 months
Poultry, pieces	6 months
Poultry, whole	1 year
Fish-fatty(salmon, mackerel, trout)	2 months
Fish-lean(cod,haddock,pike)	6 months
Fish-breaded, cooked	2 to 3 months
Shellfish	2 to 4 months
Pies, Baked or Pie shells	4 months
Pies, unbaked	2 months
Nuts, shelled	3 months
Vegetables	8 months
Cooked Foods:	
Casseroles	3 months
Meat	1 to 3 months
Soups	4 months

REFRIGERATOR STORAGE

(Always check dates on package before purchasing)

Breads	5 to 7 days
Condiments	12 months

Dairy:

Buttermilk	2 weeks
Sour cream	2 weeks
Yogurt	2 weeks
Cottage Cheese	10 to 30 days
Cream Cheese	2 weeks
Hard Cheese	3 to 4 weeks
Sliced Cheese	2 weeks
Spread Cheese	1 to 2 weeks
Cream, heavy	3 to 5 days
Cream, half-and-half	3 to 5 days
Milk	5 days

Eggs, whole	1 week
Eggs, yolks or whites	2 to 4 days

Butter	2 weeks
Margarine	1 month
Mayonnaise	6 months
Salad Dressings (purchased)	6 months
Salad Dressings (homemade)	3-7 days

Fruit:

Apples	1 month
Apricots	3 to 5 days
Avocados	3 to 5 days
Berries	2 to 3 days
Cranberries	1 week
Citrus	2 weeks
Dried fruits	6 months
Grapes	3 to 5 days
Melons	3 to 5 days
Peaches	3 to 5 days

Pears	3 to 5 days
Pineapple	2 to 3 days
Plums	3 to 5 days

Meat, Poultry, Seafood:
Fresh:

Chops	3 to 5 days
Ground	1 to 2 days
Roasts	3 to 5 days
Steaks	3 to 5 days

Processed:

Cold cuts(unopened)	2 weeks
Cold cuts(opened)	3 to 5 days
Cured bacon	1 week
Hot dogs	1 week
Ham-sliced	3 to 5 days

Ham-whole	1 week
Poultry/Seafood	1 to 2 days
Vegetables:	
Asparagus	2 to 3 days
Broccoli	3 to 5 days
Cabbage	2 weeks
Carrots	2 weeks
Cauliflower	1 week
Celery	1 week
Corn, sweet	1 day
Cucumbers	1 week
Green Beans	1 week
Green Onions	3 to 5 days
Green Peas	3 to 5 days
Green Peppers	1 weeks
Lettuce	3 to 5 days
Radishes	2 weeks
Tomatoes	1 week
Squash	3 to 5 days

Brook Noel
(a.k.a. The Rush Hour Cook)

Brook Noel was born without a domestic gene in her body. However, with the help of her mother, she has learned to cook, and she has learned a few other things along the way.

She is the author of over 15 books, the C.E.O. of Champion Press, Ltd., and she has appeared on *CNN Headline News, ABC World News, Fox & Friends* and hundreds of other shows and stations.

Noel has earned the title of one of the most successful business people under age 40 by the *Business Journal.*

Learn more at www.brooknoel.com
Contact the author at:
brook@changeyourlifechallenge.com

BROOK NOEL … PHOTO CREDIT SARA PATTOW

Wendy Louise
(a.k.a. Brook's Mother)

Wendy Louise is content to let her daughter have the spotlight. Known for her fabulous slow-cooking style, it is all she can do to keep up with her Rush-Hour-Cook of a daughter. While Brook roams the country, Wendy is roaming around the test-kitchen, trying to find where Brook mysteriously stored the measuring spoons.

Wendy is the author of two other cookbooks, *The Complete Crockery Cookbook* and *The Sensational Skillet Cookbook (*both published by Champion Press, Ltd*.)*. In addition to cooking up fabulous fare, she is the Editorial Director of *The Daily Rush* Column.

A 70-Day Life Makeover Program for Women

- Unclutter your life and get organized for good
- Create a cleaning system that works for you!
- Improve relationships, self-esteem and uncover core values
- Take control of your finances
- Conquer meal management with weekly menus
- Stop dieting and discover a nutritional plan that works for you
- much more!

The Change Your Life Challenge is a 70 Day Program created by lifestyle expert and best-selling author Brook Noel. The Challenge is designed to help women makeover virtually every area of their life.

Thousands of women have come to this Challenge as skeptics--wondering if this program could work for them. These women are now enjoying the positive, unparalled benefits offered by this well-researched, comprehensive, step-by-step, proven Program.

If you think you have "tried everything" and there "isn't any hope left," think again. That is what hundred of "challengers" thought prior to completing this 70 Day Step-by-Step Challenge.

Unlike other programs, this Challenge takes a fresh approach, incorporating internal and external exercises to foster lasting lifestyle change. Each day is carefully outlined leaving no room for "guessing" how to make the program work. Organize your life, control clutter, prioritize and more with this innovative program.

Log on to www.changeyourlifechallenge.com
to read what women are saying about the program
and to get started with your own Challenge today!

Join the Daily Rush....

WWW.RUSHHOURCOOK.COM

* Quick recipes
* Fun trivia
* Kitchen tips for the crazed cook
* Join the free "Daily Rush" cooking club
* **NEW!** Rush Hour recipes for your microwave and micro-oven
* Have your recipe included in the next Rush Hour cookbook
* Recipe swap

THE FIVE RULES OF RUSH HOUR RECIPES:

1. All ingredients may be pronounced accurately through the phonetic use of the English Language.

2. Each ingredient can be located in the market without engaging on a full-scale scavenger hunt.

3. No list of ingredients shall be longer than the instructions.

4. Each recipe is durable enough to survive the Queen-of-Incapable Cooking and elicit a compliment.

5. The Rush Hour Cook's finicky child will eat it—or some portion of it.

Also available from Champion Press, Ltd.